Born This Day

Dear Jean —
Even if he's a
guy and doesn't
want to be tickled
pink, at least he'll
know who shares his
special day.

Love,

Degen

Also by Ed Morrow
The Grim Reaper's Book of Days

Born This Day

A Daily Celebration of Famous Beginnings

Ed Morrow

A Citadel Press Book
Published by Carol Publishing Group

A Citadel Press Book
Published by Carol Publishing Group
A Citadel Press Book is a registered trademark of Carol
Communications, Inc.
Editorial Offices: 600 Madison Avenue, New York N.Y. 10022
Sales and Distribution Offices: 120 Enterprise Avenue, Secaucus,
    N.J. 07094
In Canada: Canadian Manda Group, One Atlantic Avenue,
    Suite 105, Tornoto, Ontario M6K 3E7
Queries regarding rights and permissions should be addressed to
Carol Publishing Group, 600 Madison Avenue, New York, N.Y.
10022

Carol Publishing Group books are available at special discounts
for bulk purchases, sales promotion, fund-raising, or educational
purposes. Special editions can be created to specifications. For
details, contact: Special Sales Department, Carol Publishing
Group, 120 Enterprise Avenue, Secaucus, N.J. 07094

Manufactured in the United States of America
10 9 8 7 6 5 4 3 2 1

Library of Congress Cataloging-in-Publication Data

Morrow, Ed.
    Born this day : a daily celebration of famous beginnings / by
Ed Morrow.
        p. cm.
    "A Citadel Press book."
    ISBN 0-8065-1648-8 (paperback)
    1. Birthdays—Chronology. I. Title.
CT105.M63   1995
920.02—dc20
    [B]   94-46377
                                                  CIP

Introduction

Each of us has a day that belongs to us—our birthday. It is an odd occasion when you think about it. There you are: the center of attention, naked, unable to explain yourself, and amidst those to whom you have not been formally introduced. It's no wonder that we start howling. Then, strangely, we memorialize this embarassing event every year for the rest of our lives. Would we treat any other social disaster the same way? For example, if we started snoring in the middle of our boss's daughter's piano recital, would we eat ice cream and cake on that date year after year? Or, if we, in our dotage, had the mischance to laugh and launch our dentures across the dinner table while entertaining the mayor, would we expect our friends and family to annually send us cards recalling the incident? I think not. And of what use are birthdays? All they do is remind us that we are aging—that on our drive down the highway of life our gas gauge needle is slumping nearer and nearer the big red "E" marking empty. I say abolish them. Then we could be whatever age we wanted. Three-year-olds could choose to be 18 and vote. Eighty-year-olds could be 20 and join the Marine Corps. I would choose to skip the even years and remain forever odd. But no, we are slaves to custom, and so, to the 1/365.25 (adjusted for leap years) of you reading this who were born on today: Happy Birthday!

If today isn't yours, check inside and see whose it is. Mine was August 16, 1952. My parents were Edward and Emma Morrow of Lunenberg, Vermont. The day after I was born, my delivering doctor dropped dead. Which brings to mind my last book, *The Grim Reaper's Book of Days*, a day-by-day record of the deaths of the famous and infamous. If you really hate birthdays, maybe you'll like the opposite.

Acknowledgments

Once again, I must thank my wife, Laura Morrow, for her kind help in compiling this book. Every day she gives me good reason to celebrate her birthday.

I also want to thank my agent, Sheree Bykofsky. Her advocacy, advice, and support were essential in completing this book. Anyone embarking on a journey through the tangled jungle of publishing would do well to find such an expert guide.

References

In compiling this work, I have consulted hundreds of books. I have attempted to be as accurate as possible, but, somehow, especially in the case of theatrical people, birthdays become amorphous things and sometimes vary from source to source. When I've come across situations like this, I have chosen to use the newer, improved dates.

Some of the more valuable sources used in compiling this book were the Contemporary Biography series, *People* magazine, Liz Smith's *The Mother Book, Star Mothers* by Georgia Holt and Phyllis Quinn with Sue Russell, the *New York Times,* Earl Blackwell's *Celebrity Register*, the *Newsmakers* series, Doris Faber's *The Presidents' Mothers, The Intimate Sex Lives of Famous People* by the Wallaces and D. Wallechinsky, Paul Harvey's numerous books, Oxford University Press's *Dictionary of National Biography*, and *The New York Public Library Desk Refrence* (Paul Fargis and Sheree Bykofsky, Editorial Directors).

"When I was born, I was so surprised I couldn't talk for a year and a half."—Gracie Allen (1906–1964)

***

"No man is responsible for his father. That is entirely his mother's affair."—Margaret Turnbull (?–1942)

***

Lady Louise Moncrieff had sixteen children. Upon the birth of the sixteenth, Lady Elizabeth Arthur, who was in attendance, cried, "It's all right, Louise, and you have got another little boy!" Lady Louise tiredly replied: "My dear, I really don't care if it is a parrot."

January 1

1735 Boston.

As a child, Huguenot refugee Appollos De Revoire had fled to America to escape French religious wars. He became a silversmith and anglicized his name to Revere. On this date, Revere had a son. He named him Paul.

Paul Revere followed his father into silversmithing, becoming an expert at the craft—which was fortunate, because he married young and had many children. Revere explored many schemes to support his family. In addition to crafting silverware, he produced surgical instruments and spectacles, engraved plates for printing, and even fashioned replacements for missing teeth. A clever, hard-working man, Revere was successful, becoming a prominent member of Boston's artisan class.

In the 1760s, American businessmen were being stifled under British laws that limited the development of American industry. The British wished to keep their colonies unindustrialized sources of cheap raw materials that British industries could transform into expensive finished goods. Restrictive trade laws and new taxes produced a growing rebelliousness in the colonies. The entrepreneurial Revere sided with anti-British groups. In 1765, he joined the Sons of Liberty, becoming a link between rebel intellectuals and Boston's craftsmen. In 1770, he produced the famed engraving of the Boston Massacre, which became one of history's most successful pieces of propaganda. Depicting brutal Redcoats firing on defenseless citizens, it neglected to relate that the citizens were actually a mob and the soldiers were acting in self-defense.

Revere also participated in the Boston Tea Party of 1773, but his most important contribution was as the principal courier of Boston's Committee of Safety. He carried messages from the Massachusetts provincial assembly to the Continental Congress and to the bands of militiamen who styled themselves Minutemen, after their vow to turn out for duty at a minute's notice. It was arduous, dangerous work and Revere had much to lose if the British arrested him. On April 18, 1775, Revere was sent to warn the Minutemen that the British Army was marching on Lexington and Concord to confiscate rebel munitions and arrest rebel leaders John Hancock and Samuel Adams. Revere slipped past British sentries to give warning. When the British were confronted at Lexington by the Minutemen, fighting erupted and the American Revolution began.

In 1779, Revere commanded a military expedition to Penobscot, which failed badly. To counter reports of his cowardice, Revere demanded a court martial. He was cleared, but his military skills had been shown to be poor and he returned to munitions work.

After the war, Revere's foundry cast bells and manufactured marine fittings for the U.S. Navy. Revere also helped build Robert Fulton's steamboats. Living to 1818, the hero of the Revolution was also one of the important players in America's industrial development.

Other Birthdays

1745	"Mad" Anthony Wayne	1909	Dana Andrews
1752	Betsy Ross	1909	Barry Goldwater
1895	J. Edgar Hoover	1919	J. D. Salinger
1900	Xavier Cugat	1940	Frank Langella

January 2

1904   Elkton, Missouri.

Helen Gould Beck was born. Her father was a retired army colonel and her mother was a schoolteacher who wrote for several newspapers. Teenaged Helen got a job as a chorus girl in a Kansas City nightclub. She was a good dancer and, after a critic gave her a glowing review, was signed by a prestigious vaudeville company. They trained her in voice, acting, and dance. Soon she was in Hollywood, where she became a bit player in silent movies. Cecil B. DeMille, inspired by a copy of the Rand McNally Atlas, renamed her Sally Rand, but her movie career failed to take off. She became an acrobat with the Ringling Brothers Circus then formed her own vaudeville troupe.

In the early 1930s, Rand was on tour when the play she was in folded unexpectedly, stranding her in Chicago. She was forced to take a job dancing in a South Side speakeasy. One day, looking in a used costume shop and hoping to save money, she spotted a pair of worn ostrich plume fans. She later said, "I remembered my days as a youngster in Missouri when I watched the ducks and geese and the herons flying south, their wings graceful against the sky. I had wanted to fly like a heron and I then thought of a dance that would incorporate their movements." Using just the fans for a costume, Rand both saved money and delighted her audience. She was still performing at the speakeasy a year later, however, when the 1933 Chicago World's Fair was about to open.

Perhaps recalling "Little Egypt," the dancer who made herself an international star at an earlier world's fair, Rand wanted to perform at the Chicago Fair's risqué "Streets of Paris" concession, but they wouldn't hire her. To snare a job, Rand used a week's pay to rent a white horse and a horse trailer on the date of the fair's preview for a select group of celebrities and the press. She startled the assembly by riding in as "Lady Godiva." The resulting headlines got her the job and she did, indeed, become a national sensation.

Rand, who never lost her figure, performed her fan dance till she was well into her seventies. She married three times and adopted a son. She was also active in civic affairs, including the Parent-Teacher Association of her son's Glendora, California, school.

According to film historian Peter Hay, in Rand's Hollywood days, while playing a slave girl in DeMille's epic *The King of Kings* (1927), Rand became the constant companion of H. B. Warner, who played Christ in that film. Their romantic activities complicated the making of the movie. One day, when they showed up late for shooting, DeMille angrily barked through his megaphone, "Miss Rand, leave my Jesus Christ alone! If you must screw someone, screw Pontius Pilate!"

Other Birthdays
1863   Lucia Zarate, record lightest adult (5.7 pounds at age 17)
1920   Isaac Asimov
1936   Roger Miller

January 3

1956   Peekskill, New York.

Mel Gibson was born the sixth of his railroad worker father's eleven children. When Mel was 12, his family moved to Australia. Because his new friends thought of America in terms of the movies they'd seen, Gibson had trouble living up to their expectations. Perhaps having to fashion an artificial self to win their acceptance turned Gibson into an instinctive actor. He appears to have been unaware of this skill and originally thought he might become a journalist or a chef. His sister, however, recognized his talent. She jokingly got him to fill out an application to the National Institute of Dramatic Arts, but he didn't take it seriously. Where the form asked for the reason he wanted to become an actor, he entered: "I've been goofing off all my life. I thought I might as well get paid for it." Gibson's sister sent in the application and, perhaps amused by his cheek, the Institute admitted him.

In 1977, after appearing in a forgettable teen flick, Gibson secured an audition for a bigger-budget movie. Unfortunately, the night before the audition, he got into a brawl. Gibson was afraid that his bruised face would cost him the part, but the bruises turned out to be in character. The film was *Mad Max*, a violent, postnuclear highway patrol movie. Gibson got the role, which led to a series of successful parts.

Gibson now says of the fortune he has earned as a star, "My sister wants 10 percent."

Other Birthdays

1898	Zasu Pitts	1939	Bobby Hull
1903	Ray Milland	1945	Stephen Stills
1909	Victor Borge	1950	Victoria Principal
1932	Dabney Coleman		

January 4

1896 Pekin, Illinois.

Republican statesman Everett McKinley Dirksen was born. After attending the University of Minnesota, he served in the U.S. Army during World War I. Upon his discharge, he became a washing machine manufacturer, then the manager of a dredging company, and, finally, a bakery operator. In the course of these varied occupations, Dirksen became a financial success. In 1930, he left business for politics. His first bid for Congress failed, but in 1932, he won a seat.

In order to better serve his constituency, Dirksen earned a law degree while in office and while weathering a variety of physical ailments. In 1948, an eye ailment forced him to leave the House. After recovering in 1950, he sought and won a Senate seat. In 1959, he became the Republican leader in the Senate.

Dirksen was known for his flowery oratory, which earned him the nickname The Wizard of Ooze. Despite this reputation, he was a thoughtful, erudite man. Of civil rights legislation, which he supported, Dirksen said, "There is no force so powerful as an idea whose time has come." Dirksen said of his oratory, "I must use beautiful words, I never know when I might have to eat them."

Other Birthdays
1643   Isaac Newton
1930   Don Shula
1935   Floyd Patterson
1939   Dyan Cannon

January 5

1946   Los Angeles, California.

Jack and Dorothy Hall had a daughter, Diane Hall. She grew up in Santa Ana. In high school, she impressed her drama teacher so much that he suggested she go to Manhattan to study acting. Hall did just that at 19, using her mother's maiden name, Keaton.

After some minor roles, Diane Keaton auditioned for a part in the first production of *Hair*. She was turned down and was leaving the theater when the director called her back and gave her a job as an understudy to the female lead. When the star left the play, Keaton got her part, despite refusing to appear nude. Following this role, she auditioned for the stage comedy *Play It Again, Sam*. She got the part and the attention of the play's creator, Woody Allen. Keaton starred in a number of his films, including *Annie Hall* (1977), which Allen named for her after discarding the original title, *Anhedonia*, a psychological term for the incapacity to feel pleasure. Keaton won a Best Actress Academy Award for that film. After her relationship with Allen ended, Keaton went on to several other film roles.

One typical Keaton-Allen movie exchange was the following from *Sleeper* (1973), in which Allen plays a man frozen for two centuries. She: "It's hard to believe you haven't had sex in 200 years." He: "204, if you count my marriage."

Other Birthdays
1855   King Camp Gillette, safety razor inventor
1918   Jeane Dixon
1928   Walter F. Mondale
1931   Robert Duvall
1942   Charlie Rose

January 6

1878   Galesburg, Illinois.

Carl Sandburg was born. An adventurous boy, he left school at 13 to travel west as a hobo. After serving in the U.S. Army during the Spanish-American War, he worked his way through Knox College. Upon graduation, Sandburg wrote ad copy, then became a foreign correspondent in Scandinavia. After returning to the United States to work for the Chicago *Daily News* as an editorial writer, he began writing poetry in his spare time. *Chicago Poems*, published in 1916, marked his emergence as a poet of note. He also pursued interests in children's literature, folk songs, and biography. In the last, he achieved his most popular successes with his study of Abraham Lincoln, winning a Pulitzer Prize for *Abraham Lincoln: The War Years* (1939). He won another Pulitzer for his *Complete Poems* (1950).

Sandburg was both a kindly and an acute man. He kept a flock of goats and, on one cold night, brought them into his house to stay warm, then soothed them by playing his guitar. On another occasion, a playwright sought out Sandburg's opinion of his play. Sandburg obligingly attended a rehearsal but fell asleep halfway through. Afterwards, the playwright angrily snapped, "Don't you know how much I want your opinion?" Sandburg answered, "Sleep *is* an opinion."

Other Birthdays
1412   Joan of Arc
1880   Tom Mix
1883   Kahlil Gibran
1913   Loretta Young
1914   Danny Thomas

January 7

1800   Near the village of Summerhill, New York.

Thirteenth U.S. President Millard Fillmore was born. Fillmore was Zachary Taylor's vice president and, when Taylor died in 1850, became the thirteenth President. He is noted for being un-notable. His party refused to nominate him for the next election, and Fillmore was later the unsuccessful presidential candidate of the anti-Catholic, anti-immigrant Know-Nothing Party.

In 1917, H. L. Mencken pulled one of the most successful hoaxes in history, when, in a newspaper article about bathtubs, he stated that Fillmore was the first president to put a bathtub in the White House. It was a complete fabrication. Bathtubs had been in common use for centuries. The public swallowed the story, however, and many still believe it is true.

Other Birthdays
1844   Saint Bernadette of Lourdes
1912   Charles Addams
1948   Kenny Loggins
1957   Katie Couric

January 8

1935 Tupelo, Mississippi.

Rock's first multimillionaire, Elvis Aaron Presley, was born to Gladys and Vernon Presley in a small farmhouse that lacked electricity, an indoor toilet, and running water. He was one of a set of twins, but his brother, Jesse Garon Presley, was born dead. The Presleys had no other children.

Presley's laborer father was considered a low-class layabout by his neighbors. He was sentenced to a three-year stretch in prison in 1938 for forging a $4 check. He served just eight months, but his reputation made it hard for him to find work. The Presley household barely scraped by. Despite this, they managed to put together $12.95 to buy Elvis a guitar at the Tupelo Hardware Store for his 12th birthday. They couldn't afford the bicycle that he had asked for (some biographers say he wanted a shotgun). Presley soon started strumming out tunes with his mother's encouragement. Both dreamed that he might escape poverty by becoming a singing star.

By the time Presley turned 18, the family had moved to Memphis, Tennessee. Presley worked in a machine shop, then as a trucker. He'd grown his sideburns long, mastered his guitar, and learned dozens of songs, but he wasn't any closer to stardom than were thousands of other young singers. One day, Presley decided to make a recording for his mother's birthday. He went to Sun Records and paid $4 to record two sides. After hearing Presley, an office assistant passed on his name and a copy of the recording to her boss, Sam Philips.

Philips set up a recording session to test Presley's abilities. Presley sang country western standards that failed to impress Philips. Presley could feel his chance slipping away. During a break, while standing in a studio corridor, Presley angrily slammed out a version of the rhythm-and-blues song "That's All Right." Philips overheard him from the control room, jumped out, and yelled, "That's it!" In a week, Elvis's recording was number four on Memphis's country western charts.

This success didn't lead to immediate riches for Presley. He went on tour throughout the South, performing for as little as $10 a night. The first time he appeared, he was startled by his audience's reaction. He later said, "I didn't know what the yelling was about. I didn't realize how my body was moving—it was just a natural thing for me. When I got backstage I said to the manager, 'What'd I do?' and he said, 'I don't know, but get out there and do it again!'" Soon, Presley was noted for his wild, hip-twisting delivery. He modestly said, "I'm not kidding myself. My voice is ordinary. If I stand still while I'm singing, I might as well go back to driving a truck."

In 1955, Presley signed a management contract with former carnival barker "Colonel" Tom Parker. Parker was neither a colonel nor even an American: he was an illegal alien from Holland. In return for 25 percent (later 50 percent) of Presley's earnings, Parker pushed Presley into every money-making scheme he could concoct. Presley earned hundreds of millions of dollars; however, Parker's demands and neglect also fueled Presley's fall into drug abuse, which eventually killed him at 42.

Presley retained a rural gentility throughout his life. He helped his relatives, friends, and employees, was generous and polite to fans, and, in 1958, when he was drafted into the U.S. Army, he willingly served his country. His business associates wanted to use backdoor pressure to keep him out, fearing he would be a has-been by the time he was discharged in two years. Elvis insisted that it wouldn't be right for him to weasel out. He lost considerable income but didn't lose his fans.

Other Birthdays
1911   Butterfly McQueen
1912   Jose Ferrer
1923   Larry Storch
1930   Soupy Sales
1939   Yvette Mimieux
1942   Stephen W. Hawking
1947   David Bowie

January 9

1913   Yorba Linda, California.

Richard Nixon was born. His mother, Hannah Milhous Nixon, was of an Indiana Quaker family who had been part of the Underground Railroad. The Milhouses moved to the Quaker community of Whittier, California, in 1897. In 1903, Hannah married Frank Anthony Nixon. They moved to Yorba Linda and bought a lemon farm where Richard was born (Hannah named him after Richard the Lionhearted). Richard had a difficult youth. At three, he was nearly killed when he fell from a carriage and split open his skull. At four, he nearly died again when he contracted pneumonia. Perhaps this added to his reserve. A relative later said, "He wasn't a little boy that you wanted to pick up and hug. It didn't strike me that he wanted to be hugged."

The Nixons had three other sons. The family alternately froze and roasted in their tiny farmhouse, while barely earning a living. In 1922, they sold the farm and moved back to Whittier to open a gas station. When they were offered two properties for their business, Frank chose one and Hannah chose the other. Frank got his choice and oil was discovered on the other property.

Despite this error and the rigors of the Depression, the Nixon family did well with their gas station, expanding it to sell groceries. Unfortunately, two of Richard's brothers contracted tubercular diseases and died. Hannah later said, "I think that Richard may have felt a kind of guilt that Harold and Arthur were dead and he was alive."

Richard Nixon was studious, attending Whittier College, where he was elected student body president and was a member of the football team. He was admitted to Duke University Law School, where he was once again elected student body president and was active in student theater. After obtaining his law degree, he returned to Whittier and went into practice. He had applied for a position with the FBI but his application was misplaced and was never answered, so he remained in California. One day, Nixon met a hopeful young actress, Thelma Catherine Patricia Ryan, who went by the name Pat, while both were auditioning for roles at a local community theater. Nixon immediately asked her to marry him. "I thought he was nuts," she later said. She wouldn't date him, but he persisted, even offering to drive when other boys took her out. Eventually she relented. Two years later, they married.

During World War II, Nixon worked as an attorney for the Office of Price Administration in Washington, D.C. Since he was a member of a Quaker family, he could have stayed out of the war. Instead, he secured a commission in the U.S. Navy in 1942. He served in the Pacific, where he built airstrips and became notorious for his poker skill. It is said that the $10,000 bankroll he put together with this talent financed his winning run for a seat in Congress following the war. That victory ultimately brought him to the White House.

In 1990, Nixon was asked to summarize his contentious and controversial career. He dryly answered, "Won some. Lost some. All interesting."

Other Birthdays
1914   Un-clothes horse Gypsy Rose Lee
1928   Judith Krantz
1935   Bob "Gilligan" Denver
1941   Joan Baez
1951   Crystal Gayle

January 10

1945   Glasgow, Scotland.

Rock star Rod Stewart was born. Raised in Highgate, a working-class section of London, Stewart planned to escape poverty through soccer. He played professionally after finishing school, but soccer proved less remunerative than he had hoped. Stewart had to moonlight as a grave digger. During the early 1960s, Stewart joined a rock group despite his rather strained, high-pitched voice and his inability to play any instrument save the harmonica. Not unexpectedly, Stewart was dumped from a series of groups. Eventually, he formed his own band, which began scoring hit after hit in the 1970s, including "Maggie Mae," "Tonight's the Night," "Hot Legs," "Do You Think I'm Sexy?" and "Some Guys Have All the Luck." Stewart's raw-edged voice was perfect for pounding, sex-charged rock.

Stewart has mitigated his wild living. He once said, "I'll be dead by the time I'm 40." Considering his marriage to model Rachael Hunter, he seems quite alive indeed.

Other Birthdays
1737   Ethan Allen
1883   Francis X. Bushman
1904   Ray Bolger
1943   Jim Croce
1949   George Foreman
1953   Pat Benatar

January 11

1755   Charles Town, The Island of Nevis, British West Indies.
American statesman and patriot Alexander Hamilton was born to Rachael Fawcett. The identity of his father is problematic. Fawcett, a beautiful and spirited woman, was married to a West Indian merchant but found him unsatisfying. After she took several lovers, her husband had her arrested for adultery. She avoided serious punishment and took up with a less-than-respectable Scot named James Hamilton. He soon decamped, but Fawcett gave his name to her son, Alexander. Fawcett ran a grocery, where her son kept books until she suddenly died when he was 12. Hamilton became a clerk in St. Croix, then, in 1773, left to study law in New York City.

When Hamilton arrived in New York, the American colonies were percolating with independence sentiments. Hamilton wrote pamphlets supporting rebellion, and, when the Revolution broke out, he organized a company of artillery. He attracted the notice of General George Washington and became a lieutenant colonel and aide to the general. After the war, Washington appointed Hamilton the first secretary of the treasury. Hamilton instituted strong fiscal policies. If not for him, the United States might easily have gone down in financial ruin.

Hamilton had fierce enemies, some of whom attacked his parentage. A few even attributed his success to Washington's paternal favor, citing the fact that George Washington had been in the West Indies at the time of Hamilton's conception.

Other Birthdays
1821   Fedor Dostoevski
1930   Rod Taylor
1946   Naomi Judd

January 12

1876   San Francisco.

Jack London was born. The circumstances were scandalous. His mother, Flora Wellman, was a psychic who cohabitated with spiritualist W. H. Chaney. When Wellman informed Chaney that she was pregnant and demanded he marry her, he threw her out on the street. Wellman went straight to the newspapers, claiming that Chaney had insisted she have an abortion and that he had refused to acknowledge his paternal duties despite her two suicide attempts. Chaney said the unborn child wasn't his because he had been impotent at the time it was conceived. The whole story was luridly detailed in the newspapers. Chaney never married Wellman.

London was raised in poverty on San Francisco's tough waterfront. Wellman married a farmer named John London, whose name the young London took. At 10, he peddled newspapers. As a teenager, he worked as a cannery laborer, as an oyster pirate, a member of the police organization that chased oyster pirates, and a sailor on a sealing schooner. At 18, he was traveling America by boxcar. A job in a sweltering steam laundry convinced London that there must be better ways to earn a living. He decided to become a writer.

Since London had little education, a writing career seemed a remote dream. He set out to educate himself, reading voraciously and writing as much as he could. He sometimes spent twenty hours a day in self-schooling. At 21, London was lured by tales of riches into joining the Klondike gold rush. Though he found little gold, he did find inspiration for his writing and, at 23, he sold a magazine his first story, "To the Man on the Trail," for $5. He sold more stories and, within a year, published a collection. In two years, he published his first novel, *A Daughter of the Snows.* His second novel, *The Call of the Wild*, became an international success. At 29, after publishing *The Sea Wolf* and *White Fang*, London became the most popular and best-paid writer in America.

1954   New York City.

Howard Stern was born to Ben and Ray Stern. He grew up on Long Island. Stern's father says of his son, "He was a very creative kid. He did puppet shows all the time." His mother says, "Howard was a very sensitive child." Stern says his father's "favorite sport was yelling," and that his mother "ran her household with the intensity of Hitler." Stern attended Boston University, where he got himself fired from the college radio station after airing a skit called "Godzilla Goes to Harlem." Stern went on to be fired again and again but wound up with one of the most successful radio shows.

Stern told *Rolling Stone*, "I'd watch my dad commute, and when he was stuck in the car, he'd just sit and listen to CBS news. And I thought, 'Wouldn't it be great if he was laughing? If he heard a deejay say something funny, something that made him glad he was there?' Whenever I ran into bosses who tried to tell me my kind of show wouldn't work, I always thought of that one miserable bastard on the parkway in his car. And I just *knew* if I could make him happy, I'd be all the rage."

Stern *has* become all the rage with 3 million listeners. His show is number one in New York, Los Angeles, and Boston. He earns $2 million a year.

Other Birthdays
1737   John Hancock
1905   Tex Ritter
1906   Henny Youngman
1951   Kirstie Alley
1951   Rush Limbaugh

January 13

1884   Russia.

Sophia Kalish was born to Jennie Kalish, a Russian Jew, who was on her way to join her husband in Boston. Sophia's husband took the name Charles Abuza and raised Sophia and her three siblings in Hartford, Connecticut. The family ran a restaurant. Sophia helped out but hated the work. Despite weighing 145 pounds at the age of 13, she began playing piano for her sister in amateur vaudeville contests. Sophia sang along. She later recalled, "Gradually, at the concerts, I began to hear calls for 'the fat girl'.... Then I would jump up from the piano stool, forgetting all about my size, and work to get all the laughs I could get." Sophia was sold on entertaining, but didn't immediately enter the profession. Instead, she married. Her husband, Louis Tuck, drove a beer wagon. They had a son, but Tuck couldn't support his family. Sophia left him, settled her son with her parents, changed her name to Tucker, and went to New York to break into show business.

Tucker entered amateur contests. Contest managers thought so little of her appearance—she now weighed 165 pounds— that they insisted she hide herself behind blackface makeup. She still went over well. In 1908, she became a blackface singer in a burlesque show. She hated the makeup, but couldn't escape it until, one day, by chance, she lost her kit. Tucker appeared without the makeup and the audience loved her. By 1909, Tucker won a spot in Ziegfeld's *Follies*. She became "The Last of the Red Hot Mamas," spending the next sixty years performing around the world using the signature song "Some of These Days."

Sophie Tucker once cracked, "I have been poor and I have been rich. Rich is better."

Other Birthdays
1832　Horatio Alger
1919　Robert Stack
1943　Richard Moll
1961　Julia Louis-Dreyfus
1964　Penelope Ann Miller

January 14

1941　Bascom, Florida.

Faye Dunaway was born. An army brat, she grew up on military bases around the world. She attended the University of Florida, then studied theater at Boston University's School of Fine and Applied Arts. Her studies helped her obtain roles in *A Man for All Seasons* and *After the Fall*. Her film debut was in the 1967 movie *The Happening*. The film was poorly received, but Warren Beatty, impressed by Dunaway's performance, cast her as Bonnie to his Clyde in *Bonnie and Clyde* (1967). The violent film made Dunaway a star. The finale, in which Beatty and Dunaway were riddled with truckloads of bullets, became a classic cult-movie moment.

Dunaway went on to star in many important films, including *Network* (1976), in which she played a corrupt television executive, and *Mommie Dearest* (1981), portraying child-abusing Joan Crawford. Ironically, before her death in 1977, Crawford had observed, "Of all actresses, to me only Faye Dunaway has the talent and courage to be a real star."

Other Birthdays
1791 Calvin Phillips, at 26½ inches, the shortest man on record
1875 Albert Schweitzer
1892 Hal Roach
1896 John Dos Passos
1920 Andy Rooney

January 15

1929   Atlanta, Georgia.

The Reverend Martin Luther King, a Baptist minister, and Alberta Williams King had the second of their three children, Martin Luther King Jr. The birth had been difficult and, when the infant didn't cry, it was at first thought he was stillborn. He would later speak very loudly indeed.

In 1965, King recalled the first moment in which he became aware of racial hatred. "When I was 14, I had traveled from Atlanta to Dublin, Georgia, with a dear teacher of mine, Mrs. Bradley; she's dead now. I had participated there in an oratorical contest sponsored by the Negro Elks. It turned out to be a memorable day, for I had succeeded in winning the contest. My subject, I recall, ironically enough, was 'The Negro and the Constitution.' Anyway, that night, Mrs. Bradley and I were on a bus returning to Atlanta, and at a small town along the way, some white passengers boarded the bus, and the white driver ordered us to get up and give the whites our seats. We didn't move quickly enough to suit him, so he began cursing us, calling us 'black sons of bitches.' I intended to stay right in that seat, but Mrs. Bradley finally urged me up, saying we had to obey the law. And so we stood up in the aisle for the ninety miles to Atlanta. That night will never leave my memory. It was the angriest I have ever been in my life."

King became the principal leader of the civil rights movement of the 1960s.

Other Birthdays
1823   Matthew B. Brady
1915   Lloyd Bridges
1918   Gamal Abdel Nasser
1951   Charo

January 16

1909   New York City.
Song-belter Ethel Merman was born. Merman's most famous role was as Rose, the ultimate stage mom in *Gypsy*. Merman was known for her lack of stage fright. On the opening night of *Annie Get Your Gun*, she stood in the wings calmly chewing gum. A nervous showgirl, who was quivering in her dance shoes, asked her in amazement, "Miss Merman! Aren't you nervous?" Merman coolly deposited her gum in a trash can and answered, "Why should I be nervous? I know my lines."

Other Birthdays
1911   Dizzy Dean
1935   A. J. Foyt
1946   Ronnie Milsap
1950   Debbie Allen

January 17

1806   Washington, D.C.
James Madison Randolph, grandson of President Thomas Jefferson, became the first child born in the White House.

1942   Louisville, Kentucky.
Cassius Marcellus Clay Jr. was born to Cassius Marcellus Clay and Odetta Lee Grady Clay. Clay Jr. changed his name to Muhammad Ali after becoming heavyweight boxing champ.

Clay Senior was a prosperous sign painter and the grandson of a freed slave. Odetta, too, was the descendant of slaves, and she was also part Irish. Her grandfather, a Mr. O'Grady of County Clare, Ireland, emigrated to America in 1870. Ali revealed a talent for boxing at 18 months: while Odetta held him in her arms, he playfully socked her in the teeth, knocking one loose.

Ali traces his career to a childhood incident. On his 12th birthday, he received a bicycle, which he rode to a fair at a gymnasium. After enjoying the festivities, Ali discovered that his bike had been stolen. Policeman Joe Martin saw the crying Ali and, while he couldn't return the bike, he comforted the boy. Ali told the policeman that he would beat up the thieves. Seeking to divert the boy, Martin suggested that boxing lessons might help Ali accomplish this. Ali undertook the lessons, winning his first boxing match just six weeks later. Martin was a spectator at that contest. Ali was eager to become a professional boxer, but Martin advised him to avoid small-time preliminary matches that could turn into a dead end. He suggested Ali train for the Olympics. Ali again followed Martin's advice and became the 1960 Olympic Gold Medal winner. Afterwards, through a carefully crafted campaign of taunts, he got a shot at Sonny Liston's heavyweight title. Psychological game-playing, such as confronting Liston at the airport and demanding to fight him on the spot, helped Ali beat Liston and secure his standing as one of history's first-rank boxers.

Reportedly, in the hospital, just after Ali's birth, a nurse put the wrong infant in his mother's bed. Odetta immediately informed the nurse of the mistake. She said she knew it wasn't Ali, "because the other baby was a quiet, nice baby."

Other Birthdays
1706   Benjamin Franklin
1924   Betty White
1928   Vidal Sassoon
1931   James Earl Jones
1934   Shari Lewis

1944   Joe Frazier
1949   Andy Kaufman
1956   David Caruso
1962   Jim Carrey

January 18

1904   Bristol, England.

Tailor's presser Elias Leach and his wife, Elsie, had a son, Archibald, whom they called Archie for short. He wasn't their first child. They had had a son in 1899, but he had died in his mother's arms just before his first birthday. Consequently, Elsie was painfully attached to her second son. She trundled him about in his baby carriage until she couldn't cram him in it anymore. She let his hair grow into long ringlets, dressed him in girls' clothing until he was four, and sometimes called him "Alexandra." She also grew distant from her husband, demanding he make more money and insisting they move to a more expensive house. Elias worked long hours to please her, but he didn't have the skills to earn enough. In 1912, telling his wife and friends that he was going to work in different factory, Elias left town to live with another woman. His new job, however, couldn't support two households. He was forced to return and plead for reconciliation.

Elsie accepted him back, but began to act peculiarly. She compulsively washed her hands. She sat motionless, staring into the fire for hours. She hoarded food. She locked every lock in the house. She asked strangers to tell her where her dancing shoes were. Elias consulted medical authorities and, on their advice, Elsie was committed to an institution in 1914 while Archie was at school. He would not see her again for twenty years.

Archie was suddenly left to his own devices. Elias had to work and had little time for the boy. Archie restlessly sought purpose. When a teacher took him to see the Bristol Hippodrome's electrical system, Archie became enthralled by theater life. He left school to join The Pender's Knockabout Comedians, who were young, acrobatic mimes. The group spent 1921 touring America. Archie so enjoyed the United States that he decided to remain.

Archie performed in vaudeville in a variety of acts. For a time, he used his acrobatic skills to work on stilts at Coney Island. He was knocked down several times a day by hooligans. A single broken kneecap could have ended his career, but he persisted because he made good money. However, Archie decided he wanted to be more than a stunt performer. He carefully copied Noel Coward's mannerisms and, despite his poverty, tried always to dress well. He started to win roles in legitimate theater, then a screen test led to a movie contract at Paramount.

One of Paramount's big stars was Gary Cooper. Cooper wanted more control of his career so, as a bargaining tactic, he went to Africa for an extended holiday. Paramount decided to scare Cooper by hiring Archie, whom they considered a "Gary Cooper type." To increase the pressure, they chose a stage name for Archie that they thought was similar to Gary Cooper's. Archie was renamed Cary Grant.

Other Birthdays
1782   Daniel Webster
1882   A. A. Milne
1892   Oliver Hardy
1913   Danny Kaye
1955   Kevin Costner

January 19

1946   Locust Ridge, Tennessee.

Country star Dolly Parton was born. Her father was a farm laborer and her grandfather a preacher. Parton grew up in poverty, sharing a two-room shanty with eleven siblings. She says, "We had runnin' water when we'd run and git it."

Parton wanted a more glamorous life: "I always wore too much makeup 'cause I really did pattern myself after the town tramp. When I was little, I thought she was the prettiest thing I'd ever seen. She always wore bright red nails and toenail polish and makeup. So I just couldn't wait to get my hands on it. From the time I could scrape up enough money, I would buy a bottle of bleach. I did it 'cause it made me feel prettier. And Grandpa would have a fit. He would say, 'The devil has got into that young' un.'... My granddaddy believed that wearin' makeup was a sin." Parton also says, "I just didn't want to stay back there, get married, have a house full of kids, let my teeth rot out, and have no clothes and nothin'. But it wasn't about what I *didn't* want—it was about what I *did* want. And what I *needed*. I needed the attention. Momma and Daddy loved us, but they didn't have time for us unless we were sick or in trouble. The only time we really got picked up was when we were being nursed or when we were gonna get our butts popped."

Parton, who cobbled together a guitar out of an old mandolin, was singing in her grandfather's church when she was six. Although she never learned to read music, she wrote numerous songs, which, by the time she was 10, she performed on local radio and television. After high school, she moved to Nashville. Just one day after arriving, she met Carl Dean, her first and only husband. In 1967, after three years in Nashville, Porter Waggoner selected Parton to replace his departing costar on his country western show. Parton soon became a star with her own solo career. Her recordings include such hits as "My Tennessee Mountain Home" and "Coat of Many Colors."

Parton has been admired for her beauty, amiability, and intelligence. She says, "It's a nice compliment, but I ain't all that smart, to be honest. I'm just smart about what I know. I'm a very professional Dolly Parton." Parton is currently worth over $100 million and owns a theme park, a production company, and a cosmetics line.

Other Birthdays
1807   Robert E. Lee
1809   Edgar Allan Poe
1839   Paul Cézanne
1922   Guy Madison
1923   Jean Stapleton
1931   Robert MacNeil
1935   Tippi Hedren
1943   Janis Joplin
1944   Shelley Fabares
1953   Desi Arnaz Jr.

January 20

1896   New York City.

Pants presser Louis Phillip Birnbaum and his wife, Dorothy, had a son, Nathan. The couple were from Europe, and their marriage had been arranged by their parents. They had never seen each other before their wedding, which took place when Louis was 16 and Dorothy was 14. They had twelve children, so the match must have been well devised.

The Birnbaums led a hard life. Nathan would one day joke that he used to steal garbage from a rich neighbor to put in his family's trashcan: "I wanted people to think we were doing well." Still, all the children turned out fine. Nathan credited his parents: "I never remember my mother slapping me, and I'm sure that went for my brothers and sisters. We may have deserved a good wallop once in a while, but that wasn't the way my mother operated. She was a very practical lady, and she dealt with our problems with patience and understanding." Of his dreamy, impractical father, who earned a tiny living and died when Nathan was seven, Nathan wrote, "There was an aura about my father. I don't know how to describe it, but there was something so impressive about him that with no particular effort he commanded love and respect.... It's true that my father may not have provided me with too many material things, but he did give me a sense of responsibility, and he taught me the difference between right and wrong. For that I will always be grateful to him."

Nathan loved to sing. With three friends, he formed the Peewee Quartet when he was seven. When they earned 42¢ in tossed pennies, Nathan was hooked on show business. He spent many years in vaudeville doing everything from singing to roller-skating to working with a seal. Then, he met an Irish girl with a talent for playing the daffy wit. Together, as George Burns and Gracie Allen, they became stars.

Burns says, "What made us a good combination was that I could think of stuff and she could do it. Before I met her, I thought of stuff, but I couldn't do it." He also said, "She married me for laughs. I got more laughs in bed with Gracie than I did when I played Las Vegas."

Other Birthdays
1906   Aristotle Onassis
1920   Federico Fellini
1920   DeForest Kelley
1926   Patricia Neal
1934   Arte Johnson
1946   David Lynch

January 21

1925   Southhampton, England.

Alfred Hill was born. His father had been a circus performer and Hill enjoyed his father's stories of show business. However, after Hill left school at 16, he became a milkman. When this employment grew tiresome, he got a job as a props manager for a London theatrical company. One night, a straight man got drunk and Hill replaced him. He began performing regularly, but World War II interrupted his budding career. Following service with the British Army in France, Hill paired up with comic Reg Varney to appear in English clubs. In the 1950s, he began performing on television. He soon had his own program, which relied on broad, often-corny humor and lots of pretty girls, and ran from 1968 to 1988. By then he had changed his first name to honor his favorite comic, Jack Benny. Alfred Hill became Benny Hill.

Other Birthdays
1824   Thomas J. "Stonewall" Jackson
1905   Christian Dior
1924   Telly Savalas
1926   Steve Reeves
1939   Wolfman Jack
1940   Jack Nicklaus
1947   Jill Eikenberry
1956   Robby Benson
1957   Geena Davis

January 22

1788   London.

George Gordon was born to Captain John Byron and Catherine Gordon of Gight, Scotland. Captain John probably married Catherine for her large fortune. Short, chubby, vulgar, unpleasant, and possessed with a propensity for hurling nearby objects when angry, Catherine had little other than her money to recommend her as a bride. Captain John had few virtues himself. He drank too much, and by 1791 he had spent all of Catherine's fortune, run off to France, and dropped dead, leaving his family broke. Fortunately for the Gordon family, a relative died, and George inherited a peerage in 1798.

Little money came with the title, and the new peer seemed to have all the vices of both of his parents along with the sex drive of a small city; the title did, however, give the boy entrance into society. His poetry was published and his fame assured as the hell-raising poet Lord Byron, the flashiest of the great Romantics and the model for the Byronic hero.

Other Birthdays
1875   D. W. Griffith

1931   Sam Cooke
1932   Piper Laurie
1934   Bill Bixby
1940   John Hurt
1959   Linda Blair

January 23

1899   New York City.

Humphrey DeForest Bogart was born. His father, Dr. Belmont DeForest Bogart, was one of the city's foremost internists, and his mother, Maud Humphrey, was a successful portrait artist who once used her son as a model for a baby food ad. Bogart's father enrolled his son in Phillips Academy in Andover, Massachusetts, hoping that Bogart would attend Yale Medical School. Bogart, however, wasn't the studious type. He left school and enlisted in the U.S. Navy during World War I.

Although Bogart saw little action, he did acquire both a love for the sea and a scarred lip. Some say he received the scar during maneuvers aboard the U.S.S. *Leviathan.* Others say he got it from a prisoner who resisted while Bogart was conducting him to prison. Some even suggest that Bogart deliberately avoided having his lip sewn up after a barroom brawl to acquire a tough-guy appearance. Whatever the source, the scar gave Bogart his trademark lisp and subtle sneer.

After Bogart left the navy in 1919, a friend helped him obtain a job as a stage manager for a Broadway production office. Bogart got to see show business from the inside and decided that the money was in front of the audience, not behind a desk. In 1922, he appeared in the play *Swifty* as an immature rich boy who seduces, then pesters, the leading lady. Alexander Woollcott reviewed his performance as "what is usually and mercifully described as inadequate." Bogart later claimed it was his favorite review.

Bogart continued to collect bad reviews, perhaps because he

continued to be cast in similar callow juvenile roles. In 1925, he got a break when he appeared with Mary Boland in *Cradle Snatchers*. It was a success, and Bogart was offered a film contract. However, none of his films were remarkable, and he bounced from stage to film and back to stage until he was cast as an escaped convict in Robert E. Sherwood's play *The Petrified Forest*.

Bogart was shockingly good in the criminal role, costarring with Leslie Howard. When Warner Brothers decided to film the story with Howard and Bette Davis, Howard insisted that Bogart be signed, too. The film was a success but the studio ignored Bogart's talents. He usually played the second-string crook who winds up shot by Jimmy Cagney or Edward G. Robinson. He was even cast as a vampire in *The Return of Dr. X* (1939). Finally, in 1940, after Jimmy Cagney, Paul Muni, and George Raft turned the role down, Bogart was given the lead in *High Sierra*. Again playing a gangster running from the law, Bogart got great reviews. He went on to a succession of starring roles.

Bogart's career might easily have turned out differently. The 1925 play with Mary Boland, which got him his first positive notice, was almost a missed opportunity. He had been in a play years earlier with Boland and, while offstage, had forgotten he was supposed to come back on-stage. Boland and the rest of the cast had been left to improvise an ending to the play. She banned Bogart from her productions and reluctantly relented in 1925 only after trying nearly every other actor in New York City.

Other Birthdays
1832   Edouard Manet
1898   Randolph Scott
1919   Ernie Kovacs
1957   Princess Caroline
1963   Akeem Olajuwan

January 24

1941   Coney Island section of Brooklyn.

Singer-songwriter Neil Diamond was born. Originally, he planned to be a doctor, but he dropped out of New York University to try songwriting. Because he had difficulty selling his songs, he performed them himself. In 1966, he scored his first hit with "Solitary Man." He went on to write dozens more, including "Song Sung Blue," "I'm a Believer," "Another Pleasant Valley Sunday," and "You Don't Bring Me Flowers." The last of these he performed as a duet with Barbra Streisand. It wasn't the first time they had sung together. They had both attended the same high school and had sung in the same choral group. At the time, however, neither noticed the other's musical talent.

Other Birthdays
1705   Farinelli (Carlo Broschi), famed Italian castrato soprano who had few groupies
1917   Ernest Borgnine
1918   Oral Roberts
1922   Ava Gardner
1939   Ray Stevens
1943   Sharon Tate
1949   John Belushi
1960   Nastassja Kinsi
1968   Mary Lou Retton

January 25

1759   Alloway, Scotland.

Poet Robert Burns was born. He was one of seven children of Agnes Broun Burns and William Burns, the head gardener for a wealthy doctor. In 1765, William decided to become a farmer. The children all helped, but the work was endless drudgery that ended in 1784 with bankrupcty and William's death. The children would have been responsible for their father's debts but for a bit of cleverness. Anticipating failure, they had themselves legally recognized as their father's employees. His creditors couldn't touch their small funds nor make them spend the rest of their lives paying off their father's bills. But for this device, Robert Burns might not have had the opportunity to write his poetry. His poems, featuring rural Scots life and written in Scots vernacular, made Burns one of the foremost poets of his time. Before his early death in 1796, Burns composed such works as "Sweet Afton," "A Red, Red Rose," and the famous "Auld Lang Syne."

Other Birthdays
1874   W. Somerset Maugham
1882   Virginia Woolf
1919   Edwin Newman
1935   Dean Jones

January 26

1925   Cleveland, Ohio.
    Paul Newman was born. His German-Jewish father and Hungarian-Catholic mother gave him a middle-class upbring- ing, provided by the proceeds of the family's successful sporting goods business. When Newman attended Kenyon College, he balanced his interest in the arts and his parents' more pragmatic concerns by majoring in both dramatics and economics. Following college, Newman served as a radio man in navy torpedo planes during World War II (ironically, he couldn't become a pilot because his trademark blue eyes are partially colorblind). Upon his discharge, he attended the Yale School of Drama, hoping to earn a master's degree and become a film director or to return to Kenyon as a drama instructor. Both were sensible goals, and, in the summer, he decided to seek work in New York to gain some experience. He couldn't get any stage work, but he did find employment in the

then-new medium of television, a role on *The Aldrich Family,* earning $50 a week. This success was intoxicating, and Newman abandoned academics.

Newman retained enough pragmatism to realize that his acting skills needed more training. The Actors' Studio in New York was the premiere avenue for such improvement. Entrance to the Studio was highly competitive and required auditioning. Newman later observed, "I just got very lucky. . . . I guess they must have misunderstood sheer terror for honest emotion. When I did my first scene for them later, there must have been some agonizing reappraisal."

Newman was cast in William Inge's *Picnic* in 1953. This led to a Warner Brothers contract and his film debut in *The Silver Chalice* (1954). The film was such a disaster that years later, when it was scheduled to appear on television, Newman took out a full-page newspaper ad to apologize to the public. Still, it got him better roles and he became one of Hollywood's major leading men.

Newman says of his success, "I figure that on my tombstone, it's going to say, 'He was a terrific actor until one day his eyes turned brown.'"

Other Birthdays
1880   Douglas MacArthur
1905   Maria Von Trapp
1928   Eartha Kitt
1929   Jules Feiffer
1946   Gene Siskel
1957   Eddie Van Halen
1961   Wayne Gretsky

January 27

1756   Salzburg, Germany.
Anna Maria Pertl Mozart and her husband, Leopold Mozart, were considered the most attractive couple in Salzburg. Anna, the daughter of a government official, was

poorly educated but cheerful and kind. Although Leopold's family had wanted him to be a clergyman, he became a composer and violinist for the Archbishop of Salzburg. Anna and Leopold's marriage produced seven children, but only two survived childhood—Maria Anna, nicknamed Nannerl, and Wolfgang Amadeus, who was born on this date.

Wolfgang Amadeus Mozart soon evinced signs of musical genius. He was composing minuets before he turned five. His older sister Nannerl was also a prodigy, having mastered the clavier by nine. They toured Europe giving concerts. Although Mozart's mother usually stayed home, she and her husband routinely exchanged letters, and the family remained close. Mozart was an affectionate child, and although strict, Mozart's parents seldom punished him.

As Mozart's fame increased, tours grew longer and more difficult. Anna died during one of them. The children began losing their novelty as they got older. Mozart grew into a short, pale, ordinary-looking young man with ordinary appetites. It was difficult for him to find a patron. Although he married happily, he had trouble supporting his wife and was reduced to cranking out hack pieces and teaching untalented students. At 35, he died of kidney disease stemming from overwork and malnutrition. Fortunately, Mozart finished his masterpiece, the *Requiem*, before he died.

The happily married Mozart once said, "A bachelor, in my opinion, is only half alive."

Other Birthdays
1832   Lewis Carroll
1921   Donna Reed
1936   Troy Donahue
1948   Mikhail Baryshnikov
1964   Bridget Fonda

January 28

1873   Saint Sauveur-en-Puisaye, France.

Captain Jules Joseph Colette and his wife, Adèle-Eugénie-Sidonie, had their second child, Sidonie Gabrielle. The captain and his wife were happy. Indeed, Sidonie's mother later said that her husband was so devoted to her that he neglected his career. He lost the family fortune, and they were forced to move in with their son, who had become a doctor. Their attractive daughter, Sidonie Gabrielle, had been a tomboy and was known to her friends by just her surname, Colette. She married at 20.

Colette's husband, Henry Gauthier-Villars, was a 35-year-old writer and friend of Colette's father. He had numerous mistresses and a collection of naughty French postcards. He encouraged his wife to write a saucy novel. It featured a schoolgirl named Claudine and became a sensation. Colette wrote three more such novels, and all were successful. Colette's husband, however, insisted on putting his name on his wife's books. Colette grew angry at this and finally divorced him. She began publishing under her own name. Colette's lifestyle became as famous as her fiction. Her escapades included a stint as an erotic mime and several lesbian liaisons.

Colette, who was 72 when she wrote *Gigi*, her best-known novel, once observed, "There is no need to waste pity on young girls who are having their moments of disillusionment, for in another moment they will recover their illusion."

Other Birthdays
1912   Jackson Pollock
1936   Alan Alda
1950   Barbi Benton

January 29

1945   Detroit, Michigan.

Tom Selleck was born. His parents, Martha and Bob Selleck, were high school sweethearts. Selleck was the second of their four children. Following wartime service in the army air corps, Bob moved his family to Sherman Oaks, California, and entered the real estate business. He had an office in Los

Angeles on Hollywood Boulevard and Martha occasionally brought the children to visit their father at work and see the footprints of movie stars in the cement at Graumann's Chinese Theatre.

Selleck was a quiet boy who helped his mother with his younger siblings. He was bashful as a teenager. Once, when he was struck in the groin by a baseball just before a date, Selleck was too shy to explain to the girl why he couldn't go out. His mother had to make his excuses. He was a good athlete, winning a basketball scholarship to USC, where he studied business administration. While a student, Selleck made extra money by appearing in television commercials. His good looks helped sell products such as Pepsi, Salem cigarettes and Close-Up mouthwash. He appeared twice on television's *The Dating Game*, where he failed to be picked both times. Selleck enjoyed these forays into "show biz" and decided to be an actor. Selleck's family was supportive, which was helpful, because it took Selleck years to achieve stardom.

This interval included roles as male window dressing for Mae West in the film fiasco *Myra Breckinridge* (1970), as a husband whose wife turns out to be a witch in the horror flick *Daughters of Satan* (1972), as a brain-dead source for spare parts in *Coma* (1978), as a soap opera hunk, and as an irritatingly perfect detective on *The Rockford Files*. The *Rockford* part proved a turning point and helped Selleck land his *Magnum, P.I.* role, which, in turn, led to a star on Hollywood Boulevard near his father's old office.

Of his films, Selleck is most embarrassed by *Daughters of Satan*. When his mother saw it, she managed to be positive. Selleck later observed, "To see her come out with a big smile and say, 'You were great!'—that's where I got my acting ability."

Other Birthdays
1843   William McKinley
1860   Anton Chekhov
1880   W. C. Fields (sometimes given as 2/10/1879)

1916 Victor Mature
1918 John Forsythe
1939 Germaine Greer
1954 Oprah Winfrey
1975 Sara Gilbert

January 30

1882 Hyde Park, New York.

Thirty-second U.S. President Franklin D. Roosevelt was born. His family was rich and influential, with many connections. In fact, he was related to eleven other presidents through blood or marriage. These presidents were Washington, both Adamses, Madison (a second cousin), Van Buren, both Harrisons, Taylor (a second cousin), Grant, Teddy Roosevelt (a fifth cousin), and Taft.

Other Birthdays
1866 Gelett "I Never Saw a Purple Cow" Burgess
1925 Dorothy Malone
1930 Gene Hackman
1933 Louis Rukeyser
1937 Vanessa Redgrave
1937 Boris Spassky
1950 Phil Collins

January 31

1882 St. Petersburg, Russia.

Ballet star Anna Pavlova was born. Her mother was Lyubov Fedorovna Pavlova, the wife of Matvey Pavlovitch Pavlov, a peasant turned soldier. In later life, Anna didn't speak of her father, and it has been speculated that her real father was Lazar Jacovlevitch Poliakoff, a Jewish banker. When Matvey died in 1884, Pavlova's mother was working in a laundry. Despite this humble employment, she could afford some luxuries, such as stays at a summer *dacha*, which suggests that someone was helping her financially.

Lyubov, who was illiterate, liked listening to her daughter read aloud her favorite fairy tales in which virtue was rewarded. When Pavlova turned eight, her mother took her to a performance of Tchaikovsky's ballet *Sleeping Beauty*. Like many girls who see this ballet, Pavlova decided she simply must become a ballerina. Unlike the majority of these girls, however, Pavlova's talent and work earned her a spot in the Imperial Ballet school. She became Russia's most famous ballerina.

Other Birthdays
1903   Tallulah Bankhead
1919   Jackie Robinson
1923   Carol Channing
1923   Norman Mailer
1929   Jean Simmons
1937   Suzanne Pleshette
1947   Nolan Ryan

ΞΛ

February 1

1901   Cadiz, Ohio.

William and Adeline Gable had their only child, Clark Gable. He was a large baby, weighing nine and a half pounds. Adeline died when Clark was 7 months old. William, an oil wildcatter, passed the boy on to relatives while he worked, but in 1906, he remarried and reclaimed his son. His new wife, Jennie, was a good mother to Clark, who called her one of the "kindest, most loving, tender persons" he'd ever met.

The family took up residence in Hopedale, Ohio. When Gable turned 15, they moved to a farm. Gable hated the drudgery of farm life, and, as soon as he could, left home. He and a friend dropped out of high school to work in Akron's Firestone Tire factory. Because Gable was six feet tall and weighed 155 pounds, he had little trouble passing for 18. By chance, he met two actors at an Akron hamburger joint. They invited him to see their play. Gable loved it and begged himself an unpaid job as a callboy. He spent his days at the factory and his nights running errands at the theater. Eventually, he was given a few walk-ons.

Gable went to New York City to become an actor, but the only theater work he could find was again as a callboy. He became friends with Lionel and John Barrymore, but, when the play ended, Gable was out of work. He spent the next two years working in the Oklahoma oil fields with his father. This delighted his dad but depressed Gable. When he turned 21, Gable joined a small Kansas City repertory company, but it disbanded within two months, stranding Gable in Butte, Montana, with just $3. To support himself, he worked in a mine, as a surveyor, as a lumberjack, and, finally, as a tie salesman.

Gable's coworker behind the tie counter was also a would-be actor. When his friend went to a tryout for a theater company, Gable joined him. At the tryouts, Gable met and fell in love with actress Franz Doerfler. She returned his admiration, and they became a couple touring together. She was the first in a string of women—two of whom he married—who sponsored the handsome actor. They were usually older than Gable, who professed an admiration for older women. The romances had their pragmatic side. Through them Gable received financial support, training, help in securing roles, and entry into society. Gable probably would never have become Hollywood's greatest ladies' man if he hadn't *been* a ladies' man.

Other Birthdays
1902 Langston Hughes
1931 Boris Yeltsin
1938 Sherman Hemsley
1947 Garrett Morris
1954 Billy Mumy
1965 Princess Stephanie
1968 Lisa Marie Presley-Jackson

February 2

1954   Pacific Palisades, California.

Christie Brinkley was born. Her stepfather was a television producer, and the family lived in expensive digs in Malibu. Christie wasn't interested in show business, however. She dropped out of UCLA at 17 to become an artist. She worked at odd jobs, including selling ice cream and working as a salesgirl in a clothing store, in order to put together enough money to travel to Paris. There, like the stereotypical art student, she rented a garret in Montparnasse, the traditional artists' quarter. Also like the traditional American in Paris, she found romance. Christie met and married Jean François Allaux, a French illustrator. One day, Christie's life in Paris took a less expected twist. While taking the family dog for a walk, she was spotted by a photographer who recognized her as model material. Soon, she was gracing fashion magazines and achieved supermodel status after she appeared on the cover of the swimsuit edition of *Sports Illustrated* in 1979.

Brinkley is also noted for her work for Cover Girl makeup. She got the job by telling a fib. Cover Girl planned a photo spread including a girl riding a horse. Brinkley said she could ride, though she couldn't. When her horse was spooked by a light, it ran off with her vainly trying to stop it. Two male models on horseback rode after her, but the horse seemed to think it was in a race and only ran faster. Some anxious moments ensued before Brinkley was rescued. She took the incident in stride and is now a champion cutting horse rider.

Brinkley says of herself, "I was a very self-conscious teenager—chubby, 140 pounds, chipmunk cheeks. I still harbor some of those hangups."

Other Birthdays
1650   Nell Gwyn
1882   James Joyce
1905   Ayn "Who is John Galt?" Rand

1923   Liz Smith
1937   Tommy "Mom liked you best!" Smothers
1947   Farrah Fawcett

February 3

1874   Allegheny, Pennsylvania.

Gertrude Stein was born. Her prosperous parents were restless people. They spent long stretches in Vienna and Paris before settling in Oakland, California, by which time Stein was fluent in German and French. Of Oakland, Stein said, "The thing about Oakland is that when you get there, there's no there there."

When Stein's mother died in 1888, her domineering father took charge of her upbringing. He insisted she study medicine. He died when Stein was 17 but left her a lasting unfavorable opinion of men. Nevertheless, she attempted to fulfill his ambitions, entering Johns Hopkins School of Medicine. Unfortunately, she flunked out after four years when an unhappy lesbian love affair disrupted her studies. She set off for Paris to live with her brother Leo, an art critic.

Stein and her brother set up a salon. Notables such as Ernest Hemingway, F. Scott Fitzgerald, Picasso, and Matisse become their friends despite Stein's much-noted egoism. Stein also began writing, using a unique style that often drove critics nuts. Her most successful work, *The Autobiography of Alice B. Toklas*, was an autobiography of Stein told from the viewpoint of her companion, Toklas.

Hemingway, whose friendship with the brusque Stein was sometimes strained, once said, "Gertrude Stein and me are just like brothers..."

Other Birthdays
1894   Norman Rockwell
1907   James Michener
1918   Joey Bishop

1940   Fran Tarkenton
1943   Blythe Danner
1960   Morgan Fairchild

February 4

1902   Detroit, Michigan.

Charles Lindbergh Jr. was born to Charles and Evangeline Lindbergh. His mother was a teacher; his father, an attorney and bank manager, had been a U.S. congressman, before destroying his political career by opposing American entry into World War I. He died before his son made his historic flight. Years later, his son nearly destroyed his own reputation by opposing American entry into World War II. Lindbergh's parents had an unhappy marriage. Although they never divorced, they led separate lives.

Evangeline raised her son to be studious and stout-hearted. Lindbergh was devoted to her. She was pleased when he entered the University of Wisconsin but was worried when he left to study aviation. She later said, "It almost broke my heart." Nonetheless, she didn't hold him back from doing what he wanted. Lindbergh bought himself a $500 army surplus biplane and became a U.S. Airmail pilot. It was an extremely dangerous occupation, but it taught Lindbergh the skills he used to make the first transatlantic solo flight in 1927.

The newspapers sent reporters and photographers to witness Lindbergh's takeoff. One photographer asked Evangeline to pose kissing her son goodbye. She refused, but this didn't indicate a lack of affection. When Lindbergh landed in Paris, the first person he telephoned was his mother.

Many years later, when Lindbergh was gray-haired, he was a passenger on a Boeing 747 crossing the Atlantic. The pilot introduced him to the passengers. Lindbergh took a bow, then sat. He had trouble refastening his seat belt. A flight attendant helped him buckle it and kindly burbled, "Is this your first crossing, Mr. Lindbergh?"

1948   Detroit, Michigan.

Vincent Damon Furnier was born. A preacher's son, he was a sickly child who was plagued by asthma and eczema. At 23, Furnier changed his name to Alice Cooper and became a shock-rock phenomenon. He once said, "The best things in life—don't make sense."

Other Birthdays
1913   Rosa Lee Parks
1918   Ida Lupino
1921   Betty Friedan
1931   Isabel Perón
1945   David Brenner
1947   Dan Quayle

February 5

1943   Ogden, Utah.

Nolan Kay Bushnell was born. The son of a cement contractor, he was repairing radios, televisions, and washing machines while still a child. In 1968, he earned a bachelor's degree in electrical engineering at the University of Utah. After working for a games arcade at an amusement park, Bushnell decided to devise an electronic game. In 1971, he produced "Computer Space," a game that delighted his engineer friends but, when he tried to market it, didn't sell. Bushnell devised a much simpler game in 1972. He called it "Pong." He scrapped together $500 and set up Atari Inc. to manufacture the game (*atari* is Japanese for "prepare to be attacked"). "Pong" became a sensation, selling 100,000 units by 1974 and launching the video game industry.

Other Birthdays
1848   Belle Starr
1919   Red Buttons
1934   Hank Aaron
1942   Roger Staubach

1945   Bob Marley
1948   Barbara Hershey
1962   Jennifer Jason Leigh

February 6

1895   Baltimore, Maryland.

George Herman "Babe" Ruth was born. His father owned a working-class bar. Ruth's family lived over the establishment. The rough-and-tumble business wasn't a wholesome environment for Ruth, who became wild and troublesome. Concerned that he would turn out badly, his parents sent him to a Catholic orphanage when he was seven. The priests controlled the boy well and, while they trained him in music and tailoring, they also encouraged his skill at baseball. In the winter of 1914, he signed up on a minor league team. His teammates nicknamed the young player Dunn's Baby, after their manager Dunn and Ruth's rookie status. This was quickly shortened to "Babe" and, nearly as quickly, Ruth's contract was bought by the Boston Red Sox. In the big leagues, Ruth became the "Sultan of Swat," hitting 714 home runs, a record that lasted forty years. He became so famous that during World War II, Japanese soldiers, seeking a vile insult to scream across the lines at American soldiers, would yell, "To hell with Babe Ruth!"

Ruth was known for his prodigious appetite. Before a game, he often had triple servings of his dinner with a quart of orange juice. He commonly topped this off with a fifth of gin. After games, Ruth would eat six or seven sandwiches, each washed down with a bottle of pop or beer. At his prime, Ruth had a 17-inch neck, a 42-inch waist, and 60-inch hips.

1911   Tampico, Illinois.

President Ronald Reagan was born. His father, Jack Reagan, was a shoe salesman with an alcohol problem. His mother was

Nelle Reagan, whose optimism dispelled her husband's cynicism and kept the family going. Reagan, nicknamed Dutch, was raised in Dixon, Illinois, where he played football for his high school team. He was a powerful swimmer who rescued seventy-seven people while serving as a lifeguard. After graduating from Eureka College in Illinois, Reagan got a job as a radio announcer for the Chicago Cubs. While covering the team's spring training on Catalina Island, he was spotted by a film scout. Aptly, his first film role was playing a radio announcer in *Love Is on the Air* (1937). He went on to make over fifty films, including *Knute Rockne, All American* (1940), *Santa Fe Trail* (1940), and *Kings Row* (1942). He also had a career on television in the 1950s and 1960s, with the *General Electric Theater* and *Death Valley Days*.

Reagan became prominent in the Screen Actors Guild, serving as its president for six years. In 1964, he gave a strong speech supporting Barry Goldwater at the Republican National Convention. In 1966, he ran for the governorship of California against Pat Brown. Brown mockingly joked that "an actor killed Lincoln," but wasn't laughing when Reagan won by a million votes. In 1980, Reagan beat Walter Mondale to become president.

One of the central themes of Reagan's political life has been his criticism of large government. In 1973, he said, "In our nation today, government has grown too big, too complex—and possessed of what Cicero called the 'arrogance of officialdom.' Remote from the wishes of the people, it forgets that ours is a system of government by the consent of the governed—not the other way around."

Other Birthdays
1918 or 1920 or 1923 or ?   Zsa Zsa Gabor
1922   Patrick Macnee
1931   Rip Torn
1940   Tom Brokaw
1943   Fabian
1950   Natalie Cole

February 7

1812   Portsea, England.

Elizabeth Barrow Dickens and clerk John Dickens had Charles, the second of their five children. The couple were ill-equipped to raise a family. Elizabeth was selfish and impractical. John earned a good living but spent more than he earned and soon wound up in debtor's prison. Charles, just 12 years old, was forced to leave school and go to work in a blacking factory laboriously scraping carbon from soot-darkened lamp chimneys. His father eventually rescued the boy from this dirty drudgery, but Elizabeth thought he should continue working. Charles never forgave her for valuing his meager wages more than his happiness. Nevertheless, after Charles became a famous and successful writer, he took better care of his parents than they had of him.

Other Birthdays
1804   John Deere
1817   Frederick Douglass
1867   Laura Ingalls Wilder
1883   Eubie Blake

February 8

1920   Wallace, Idaho.

Julia Jean Mildred Frances Turner was born in a tough mining town. Her father was killed when she was a child and her mother told her that he had died a war hero. Actually, after winning big in a crap game, his head had been smashed by a robber with a blackjack. Some years later, Turner was living in Los Angeles. One day, she played hooky from high school. She was sipping a soda in a Hollywood drugstore called the Top Hat Malt Shop (not Schwab's) when she was discovered by the publisher of the *Hollywood Reporter*, who had been admiring her figure. The publisher took her to talent agent Zeppo Marx, who told her she needed a new name. She suggested Lana Turner. Marx got her a small job in *They Won't Forget* (1937) as a sweatered schoolgirl who gets murdered. The sweater was very tight and the men in the audience certainly didn't forget her. She became a national sensation. Turner made many movies, the best of which was *The Postman Always Rings Twice* (1946).

Turner once remarked, "A successful man is one who makes more money than his wife can spend. A successful woman is one who can find such a man."

Other Birthdays
1820   William Tecumseh Sherman
1828   Jules Verne
1925   Jack Lemmon
1931   James Dean
1940   Ted Koppel
1940   Nick Nolte
1968   Gary Coleman

February 9

1945   Los Angles, California.

Movie director John Farrow and actress Maureen O'Sullivan had a daughter they named Mia. When Mia decided to try acting, she could have used family connections to start her career, but instead got her first acting job through an open casting call. She was selected from a group of fifty girls for a role in a production of *The Importance of Being Earnest*. Her success there led to a movie contract and a starring role in the television soap series "Peyton Place." At 19, Mia was known across the nation. When she turned 20, her fame was increased when she married 50-year-old Frank Sinatra. Since then, Mia's life has been a series of critically well-received roles interspersed with lurid tabloid headlines. Perhaps because of this, seven of her eleven children had their own psychologists by 1992.

Other Birthdays
1773 William Henry Harrison
1909 Carmen Miranda
1928 Roger Mudd
1941 Carole King
1943 Joe Pesci

February 10

1940 Black Mountain, North Carolina.

Singer Roberta Flack was born. Flack studied music assiduously as a child, learning to sing and play the piano. By the time she was 13, she could play the entire score of Handel's *Messiah*. She hoped to become an opera star but contented herself with singing with her church choir. After attending Howard University, she became a teacher in Washington, D.C., supplementing her income by playing piano in a Georgetown restaurant. In 1972, she recorded "The First Time Ever I Saw Your Face." It was a hit. Flack proved this wasn't a fluke by recording another hit, "Killing Me Softly With His Song," the next year.

Other Birthdays
1879 W.C. Fields (sometimes given as 1/29/1880)
1890 Boris Pasternak
1893 Jimmy Durante
1907 Lon Chaney Jr.
1930 Robert Wagner

February 11

1925? Budapest.

Eva Gabor was born. She is the youngest of the famed Gabor sisters. Their mother, Jolie, was proud of them and, when they were girls, lined them up like dolls in the family's chauffeured Mercedes convertible. Zsa Zsa Gabor, Eva's sister, observed, "If we had not been pretty, I think we would have been drowned like little dogs. That's my mother." The girl's father was Major Vilmos Gabor, an aristocratic gentleman who lost his fortune when World War II broke out. The girls, educated in exclusive Austrian and Swiss boarding schools, seemed hardly prepared to earn a living, especially since their parents had raised them to accept only the best. The solution came when Jolie took her girls to Hollywood, where the exotic beauties soon piled up cash and ex-husbands.

The girls' maternal grandmother, Francesca Tilleman, and their Uncle Alexander remained behind in Hungary during the war. They survived the Nazis but were killed by the "liberating" Russians. Zsa Zsa said, "My mother said my grandmother would not be comfortable anywhere but the Hotel Ritz. And the Russians shot and killed her right there in the Ritz. She was a very rich lady and they would have shot you for a gold bracelet or a coat."

1926   Canada.

Leslie Nielsen was born. His father was a Royal Canadian Mountie, and Nielsen spent his boyhood in a tiny settlement near the Arctic Circle. Nielsen says, "I grew up in a Mountie family, I played with Mountie kids, and I ran around in the North eating snow." It was a tough life and one of his early memories was watching his father stitch up his brother's badly cut lip without any anesthetic because the nearest doctor was hundreds of miles away. Nielsen says, "You can hardly see the scar today."

Nielsen's uncle was involved in a completely different business—the movie industry. When Nielsen told his friends about this Hollywood connection, they didn't believe him until he showed them pictures of his uncle with movie stars. "I could see a distinct change in their attitudes. Right then I said, 'There must be something to this acting business.'"

Nielsen took his first step into show business when he got a job as a radio engineer and announcer in Calgary in Canada.

He won a scholarship to study acting at New York's Neighborhood Playhouse. Nielsen made his stage debut in summer stock in Boston, then went into television, where he appeared in forty-six shows in 1950 alone. Unfortunately for Nielsen, these were all small parts, and he made under $5000 for the entire year. Nielsen's fortunes changed when he went to Hollywood and made the science fiction classic *Forbidden Planet* (1956). He went on to a series of leading roles.

In 1980, Nielsen experienced a major career shift when he exhibited a wonderful talent for comedy in the disaster movie spoof *Airplane!* This led to a starring role as boneheaded Detective Frank Drebin in the comedy television program "Police Squad," and a series of movies.

In 1993, Nielsen published an "autobiography" called *The Naked Truth*. Of this book, he said, "It is absolutely true—except the facts." In it, Nielsen claimed to have co-starred with Peter O'Toole in *Lawrence of Arabia*, and to have won the coveted "Nobel Prize for Good Acting."

Other Birthdays
1847   Thomas Alva Edison
1934   Tina Louise
1936   Burt Reynolds

February 12

1809   Near Nolin Creek, Kentucky.

Thomas and Nancy Hanks Lincoln had a second child, a boy, whom they named Abraham after his grandfather, Abraham Lincoln. The elder Abraham had been an associate of Daniel Boone and had come from Pennsylvania to settle in Kentucky in 1782. He was ambushed and shot dead by Indians while working in the fields with his 10-year-old son, Thomas. An Indian warrior grabbed up Thomas, but was felled by a shot fired by Thomas's older brother, Mordecai. Had their father not been killed, the Lincolns might have become prosperous landowners. Instead, the fatherless boys grew up without direction and drifted apart.

Nancy Hanks was born out of wedlock to Lucy Hanks. Abe Lincoln later thought Nancy's father was a Virginia gentleman. If so, the gentleman's reluctance to marry Nancy's mother might have been related to her mode of life. In 1789, Lucy was charged with fornication. She avoided prosecution by marrying Henry Sparrow. Sparrow's parents virtually adopted Nancy and saved her from a life similar to her mother's.

Thomas Lincoln married Nancy Hanks in 1806 and built a home in Elizabethtown, where he worked as a carpenter. After they had a daughter, Sarah, they moved to a farm on Nolin Creek, where the younger Abraham was born. In 1818, a disease called "milk-sick" killed Nancy Lincoln. Abraham helped his father build her coffin. He later said, "God bless my mother, all that I am or ever hope to be I owe to her."

With children to raise, Thomas Lincoln quickly found a new wife, Sarah Bush Johnson. Even though she had a son and two daughters of her own to take care of, Sarah was a good mother to Abraham and Sarah. Thomas was nearly completely illiterate. Nancy is thought to have been able to read and write a little. Sarah, who was better educated, encouraged Abraham to study. His father seems to have thought it a waste of time, but he didn't stop Abraham, who, after a few months of schooling, taught himself enough to become first a successful lawyer and then president.

After Abraham Lincoln became president, there was much interest in the circumstances of his birth. By then, most witnesses were dead. The nearest surviving relative was Abraham's cousin, Dennis Hanks, who had been nine when Abraham was born. He remarked how, when he picked up baby Abraham, the infant screamed loudly. Dennis gave the child back to its mother, saying, "Aunt, take him! He'll never come to much!"

Other Birthdays
1809   Charles Darwin

1895   R. Buckminster Fuller
1915   Lorne Greene
1919   Forrest Tucker
1926   Joe Garagiola
1936   Joe Don Baker
1945   Maud Adams
1958   Arsenio Hall

February 13

1919   Bristol, Tennessee.

Ernest Jennings Ford, better known as Tennessee Ernie Ford, was born. He first sang in public with his Methodist church choir. After college, Ford went to work in his hometown as a $10-a-week disc jockey. Ford spent part of his pay on voice lessons at the Cincinnati Conservatory of Music. His studies were interrupted by World War II. Ford served in the army air corps as a bomber-navigator.

After the war, Ford wound up in Pasadena, California, where he began singing on Cliffie Stone's "Hometown Jamboree" radio show. Stone was impressed with Ford's mellow voice. He persuaded Capitol records to give him a contract in 1948. Ford recorded a number of hits for them, including "Mule Train," "The Cry of the Wild Goose," and "Shotgun Boogie." He also began making appearances on television programs. The most important appearance was a recurring role on *I Love Lucy* as Lucy's country cousin. After recording his biggest hit, "Sixteen Tons," which sold 20 million copies, Ford got his own television show, which ran from 1956 to 1961.

Ford's TV sign-off line, "Bless your pea-pickin' hearts," was corny but heartfelt. He never lost his religious beliefs. Even when he performed in Las Vegas, he always finished with a gospel song.

Other Birthdays
1933   Kim Novak

1938   Oliver Reed
1944   Stockard Channing

February 14

1894   Chicago, Illinois.

Benjamin Kubelsky was born. His father, Meyer Kubelsky, had escaped anti-Semitic pogroms in Lithuania by crossing the border hidden in a wagonload of empty bottles. After fleeing to America and working as a traveling peddler, Meyer opened a saloon in Waukegan, Illinois. When he decided to marry, a matchmaker offered him the choice of an introduction to a wealthy girl or to a pretty girl. Meyer asked to meet the pretty one, Emma Sachs, first. He never asked to meet the rich one. Meyer and Emma soon married, and on this date they had a son, Benjamin.

The Meyers bought Benjamin a violin when he was six. Benjamin learned to play so well that the city of Waukegan offered to pay for him to study in the best European schools. Benjamin refused: He didn't like school. After flunking out of high school and a business school and being fired by his own father, who had become a haberdasher, Benjamin began playing violin at a vaudeville hall. Minnie Marx, the mother and manager of the Marx Brothers, offered him a job as their music director, but Benjamin's mother wouldn't let him go on tour with them. Benjamin kept pursuing show business, and eventually his parents relented. He became a vaudevillian and, after years of struggle, one of the most successful men in show business, under his stage name—Jack Benny.

Other Birthdays
1913   Jimmy Hoffa, cornerstone of the Teamsters Union
1921   Hugh Downs
1934   Florence Henderson
1946   Gregory Hines

February 15

1882   Philadelphia.

John Barrymore was born. His elder brother was famed actor Lionel Barrymore, and his elder sister was actress Ethel Barrymore. John Barrymore started out as an editorial cartoonist for a New York City newspaper, but unfortunately, he was extremely lazy. He had also begun drinking at 14. These qualities made it difficult for him to meet his deadlines, and he was fired. Barrymore took the first job he could find—membership in an acting troupe bound for Australia by way of San Francisco. Barrymore arrived in San Francisco just in time for the 1906 earthquake, which he slept through, having gone on a bender the night before. When he eventually stumbled out of bed, the Army was assembling work gangs at bayonet point to clear rubble. Barrymore's uncle remarked, "It took a calamity of nature to get him out of bed and the U.S. Army to make him go to work."

After his tour of Australia, Barrymore became a successful stage actor, noted for his Shakespearean roles. He went to Hollywood and became a matinee idol, starring in many classic films, including *Grand Hotel* (1932) and *Dinner at Eight* (1933). However, he also starred in what is undoubtedly one of the most absurd movies ever made—the 1930 version of *Moby Dick*. The story got the full Hollywood treatment. Not only is Ahab recast as a merry jackanapes given to acrobatic swinging from his ship's mast, but there is also a love interest, which sours after Ahab's leg is bitten off by the title character.

Other Birthdays
1820   Susan B. Anthony
1907   Cesar Romero
1927   Harvey Korman
1951   Melissa Manchester
1951   Jane Seymour
1954   Matt Groening

February 16

1935   Detroit, Michigan.

Sonny Bono was born to Sicilian immigrants Santo and Jean Bono, who moved to Los Angeles when he was an infant. Their troubled marriage ended when Sonny was seven. Sonny did poorly in school. He dropped out at 16 to work as a delivery boy, a waiter, a butcher's assistant, a construction worker, and a truck driver. He married, had a child, and divorced. Bono filled his idle moments with songwriting. He had no success till 1957, when he sold "High School Dance." While it made it to only number ninety on the charts, it helped him get a job with a record company. Bono worked with Sam Cooke and Little Richard. He wrote more tunes, including "Needles and Pins" for the Searchers and "Koko Joe" for the Righteous Brothers. In 1963, Bono met Cherilyn La Piere (see 5/20/1946). She was a runaway, looking for a singing career. Bono promised to make her a star and they married in 1964.

Bono left his record company job to write songs for himself and Cher. Under the name Caesar and Cleo, their recordings didn't garner much attention. They returned to their own names and, in 1965, scored a hit with "I Got You, Babe." They became an instant success. In 1964, they had earned $3,000, but, in 1965, they pulled in $3 million. They sold 40 million records with such tunes as "Bang Bang," "All I Really Want to Do," and "The Beat Goes On." However, the passing of interest in flower child rock sent their careers into a tailspin. *Chastity* (1969), an ill-advised film starring Cher, was an embarrassing flop, costing them over half a million dollars.

Bono changed their hippie image to appeal to older fans. He arranged a nightclub act in which he wore a tuxedo and Cher almost wore an evening gown. They traded jokes, with Bono playing the goof to Cher's disdainful beauty, then sang. The act went over well. It led to the television show *The Sonny and Cher Comedy Hour.* This was also a success, but, in 1974, Cher abruptly divorced Bono. He observed, "I thought we loved each other. I guess what was going on in her head and what was going on in mine were two totally different things. I was thinking, 'All right! I've delivered. I've made Cher a star.' That's why our breakup was such a surprise. It literally came overnight. I never saw it coming."

Cher went on to a successful recording and acting career. Bono floundered. His recording career disappeared, a television series flopped, his acting roles were minor, and, when he remarried, the marriage failed. He had better luck with his fourth wife. Bono opened a successful restaurant in Palm Springs. A problem with the local planning board got him interested in politics. Palm Springs was having problems with a huge deficit. Under the slogan "Growth through glitz," Bono successfully ran for mayor. In 1994, he became a U.S. congressman.

Other Birthdays
1903   Edgar Bergen
1957   LeVar Burton
1959   John McEnroe

February 17

1908   Columbus, Mississippi.

Red Barber was born. When he was 10, his family moved to Florida where, while still in school, Barber worked as a truck driver, was a celery picker, and carried hot tar up ladders to roofers. At 21, he went to Gainesville, hoping to enter the University of Florida. He worked as a woodsplitter, waiter, tennis court attendant, and janitor. He was cleaning at WRUF when a guest failed to show up. Barber was hastily stuck in front of the microphone. He did so well he was hired and eventually became director of the radio station.

In 1934, Barber was hired by the Cincinnati Reds to broadcast their games. The first major league game he saw was also the first game he broadcast. He went on to the

Brooklyn Dodgers in 1939. His chatty style larded with Southernisms, such as describing a fight as a "rhubarb" and good fortune as "walking in tall cotton," made Barber very popular. Ball club owners had avoided broadcasting games in the past for fear of undermining attendance. Barber's efforts proved that broadcasting actually made more fans and increased attendance. Women, in particular, learned to follow baseball by listening to Barber. It was said that on a summer game day you could walk from one end of Brooklyn to the other and hear him describe the complete game from radios in the open-windowed homes you passed.

Other Birthdays
1925   Hal Holbrook
1936   Jim Brown
1962   Lou Diamond Philips
1963   Michael Jordan

February 18

1933   Tokyo.

Yoko Ono, the person most often blamed for breaking up the Beatles, was born. "Yoko" means "ocean child" in Japanese. Ono's father was a Japanese banker and her mother was an heiress who taught her daughter not to smile in public. The family moved to San Francisco in 1936, but, when World War II began, they went back to Japan. The family survived the war and returned to America to live in the prosperous community of Scarsdale, New York. Ono enrolled in elite Sarah Lawrence College, where she studied art.

In the 1950s, Ono dropped out of school to join the arty crowd in Greenwich Village. She became a conceptual artist, marrying avant-garde composer Toshi Ichiyanagi. Ono's art included such projects as a hole for moonlight to fill. In 1964, Ono divorced Ichiyanagi, then married filmmaker Tony Cox. Ono and Cox collaborated on artwork and films. One of their efforts was the filming of 365 naked backsides, one for each day of a non–leap year. When John Lennon wandered into one of their London exhibits, he and Ono struck up a friendship.

Ono and Lennon tape-recorded their first romantic encounter and used the tape in their first album, *Two Virgins*. Its cover featured a photo of the couple, nude. The pair divorced their spouses and married in 1969. Ono became a fixture at the Beatles' recording sessions and fed Lennon's artistic pretensions. "Revolution 9," which features the repetition of the word *nine*, was recorded because of her influence on John Lennon. Other Beatle members didn't want the tune included on the group's *White Album*. Although Ono cranked up the tension in the group, they had already developed differing interests. This was more of a factor in the Beatles' 1970 dissolution than Ono. Nevertheless, Ono has been reviled by Beatles fans. Comic Judy Tenuta cracked, "If that guy had aimed a little to the left, he would have been a hero."

Other Birthdays
1895   George "Win one for the Gipper" Gipp
1920   Jack Palance
1922   Helen Gurley Brown
1925   George Kennedy
1950   Cybill Shepherd
1952   Juice Newton
1954   John Travolta
1957   Vanna White
1964   Matt Dillon
1968   Molly Ringwald

February 19

1924   New York City.

Actor Lee Marvin was born. Though Marvin became known for playing tough guys with lowly origins, Marvin's father was a prosperous Madison Avenue executive and his mother was a fashion editor. A troublesome boy, Marvin was kicked out of several private schools. During World War II, he served with the Marines in the Pacific, where he was wounded in the spine. He recovered and, after his discharge, set out to become an actor. He played in numerous films, winning Best Supporting Actor in 1965 for his performance as a washed-up, drunken gunfighter in *Cat Ballou*.

Marvin said of his acting, "Stimulation? Thursdays. Motivation? Thursdays. Pay-days. That's it. It's important not to think too much about what you do. . . . You see, with my way of thinking there are always Thursdays—no matter how the picture works out."

In 1970, Marvin made legal history when his former live-in companion successfully sued him for "palimony." The ruling was eventually overturned.

Other Birthdays
1911   Merle Oberon
1940   Smokey Robinson
1955   Jeff Daniels
1959   Sarah Ferguson, wife, then ex-wife, of Prince Andrew
1960   Prince Andrew
1966   Justin Bateman

February 20

1927   Miami, Florida.

Actor Sidney Poitier was born. He was raised in the Bahamas on a Cat Island tomato farm. Poitier received only a year and a half of grammar school education. After a hitch in the army, he decided to try acting. He failed his first audition for Harlem's American Negro Theater because of his strong Island accent. Poitier was reduced to living in public restrooms and doing menial odd jobs. He didn't give up, however, but diligently studied the accents of those around him and, when he reauditioned for the same casting director, was signed.

Poitier filled several small roles before getting a lead in 1948 on Broadway in *Anna Lucasta*. His performance was a success and, in 1950, he got a film contract. His films include *Blackboard Jungle* (1955), *Porgy and Bess* (1959), *A Raisin in the Sun* (1961), *Lilies of the Field* (1963), *In the Heat of the Night* (1967), and *Guess Who's Coming to Dinner?* (1967). He received the Academy Award for Best Actor for *Lilies*, becoming the first black to receive this honor.

Other Birthdays
1908   Edward Albert
1924   Gloria Vanderbilt
1929   Amanda Blake
1934   Bobby Unser
1939   Dick Smothers
1946   Sandy Duncan
1949   Jennifer O'Neill
1955   Kelsey Grammer
1963   Charles Barkley
1966   Cindy Crawford

February 21

1927   Dayton, Ohio.

Housewife-humor columnist Erma Bombeck was born. Bombeck earned a degree in English from the University of Dayton, then married William Bombeck. She wrote features for the women's page of the Dayton *Journal-Herald* until she became pregnant and left writing for ten years to raise her two children. She returned in 1963 with a column that became a national favorite. Bombeck gives this reason for going back to writing: "I was too old for a paper route, too young for social security and too tired for an affair." The column led to a series of bestsellers that include *If Life Is a Bowl of Cherries, What Am I Doing in the Pits?* and *Motherhood, the World's Second Oldest Profession*.

Bombeck wrote, "In general, my children refused to eat anything that hadn't danced on TV."

Other Birthdays
1915   Ann Sheridan
1925   Sam Peckinpah
1934   Rue McClanahan
1946   Tyne Daly

February 22

1732   By Pope's Creek, Westmoreland County, Virginia.

George Washington was born. His father, Augustine Washington, was an obscure man who went by the name Gus. His mother was Mary Ball Washington, a demanding and dependent women who constantly and unreasonably complained about her son's neglect. George tried hard to please her but never succeeded.

According to legend, George's parents met in England. Mary, a Virginia plantation heiress, was visiting relatives when Augustine, a prosperous Virginia planter, rode past. Augustine lost control of his horse and was thrown and injured. The householders hospitably cared for him. Mary served as his principal nurse, then became his bride. Augustine had three children from a previous marriage; with Mary, he had George and three other children. Augustine died suddenly when George was 11.

George's older half brothers had been educated in England, but his mother saw no reason for George to enjoy that privilege. At 14, he tried to enlist in the British Navy, but she kept him home. He escaped her to work as a frontier surveyor. Later, when the French and Indian War broke out, George distinguished himself. When the American Revolution began, he became the logical choice for commander. In the meantime, his mother greedily kept a large part of his inheritance for herself and demanded additional money from him at every opportunity. When George was serving as commander for the Continental Army, his mother petitioned the Virginia Legislature for a pension, claiming she was starving. George was forced to explain that any of her children would happily sacrifice "to relieve her from *real* distress."

One story about Washington's mother relates how a young officer was sent out into the Virginia countryside to confiscate horses for the use of the Continental Army. He saw two horses standing by a large house. When he told the woman of the house that the U.S. Army needed them, the woman told him that she must keep the horses for the spring plowing. The officer insisted, saying that General George Washington had ordered him to fetch horses. The woman replied, "Tell George his mother says he can't have her horses." George didn't get the horses.

Other Birthdays
1908   John Mills
1918   Robert Pershing Wadlow, who grew to become the tallest man on record at eight feet eleven inches.
1932   Edward M. Kennedy
1934   Sparky Anderson
1950   Julius "Dr. J" Erving
1975   Drew Barrymore

February 23

1939   Los Angeles, California.

Henry Fonda and his wife, Frances Brokaw, had their second child, Peter Fonda. When Frances committed suicide in a mental hospital, the elder Fonda told his children that she had died of a heart attack. When Peter later discovered the truth, he was so upset that he shot himself. He survived and followed his father into acting, after attending the University of Omaha.

Fonda made his Broadway debut in 1961 in *Blood, Sweat and Stanley Poole*. He played a young doctor in his first film, *The Interns* (1962). He seemed destined to play wholesome, clean-cut types until he tried LSD. Fonda quickly immersed himself in the drug culture. Drugs were featured in his most successful role in *Easy Rider* (1969). Unfortunately, Fonda has also suffered from drug problems that have limited his success.

Other Birthdays
1395   Johannes Gutenberg (also given as 1400)
1633   Samuel Pepys
1685   George Frederick Handel

February 24

1938   Portland, Oregon.

Philip H. Knight was born. While earning an MBA at Stanford University in 1960, Knight wrote a research paper on the sneaker industry. After receiving his degree, he went to Japan and secured the sole U.S. distributorship for the sneaker company Onitsuka. For the next eight years, he and, Bill Bowerman sold the sneakers out of their car trunks at track meets. They called their company Nike.

In 1972, Nike scored its first coup when Knight persuaded a number of Olympic marathoners to wear his shoe. This allowed Nike to later claim that four of the top seven marathoners had worn their shoe. They neglected to mention that the first three finishers had worn another brand. Knight gave Nike its second big push when he decided that he could design a lighter, more cushioned shoe. Using his family's waffle iron and urethane rubber, he concocted a new kind of sole that made Nike one of the largest shoe companies in the world.

1947   Boyle Heights, California.

Actor Edward James Olmos was born. His father, Pedro Olmos, had left Mexico for Los Angeles at 21 with just a sixth-grade education. Through hard work he became a successful businessman. His wife, Eleanor, was also poorly educated.

Both earned high school diplomas as adults. Unfortunately, their marriage failed when Edward was eight.

Olmos became obsessed with a portion of his life that he felt was under his control. He says, "I was lucky. It could have been drugs. It could have been drinking. But it was baseball." Olmos didn't become a professional ballplayer, but he did learn self-discipline, which helped him develop his other talents. One of these talents was dancing. By the time Olmos was 13, he was performing with a group called the Pacific Ocean. Olmos says, "I sang terrible, but I could scream real good and I could dance." The group helped Olmos pay his way through college.

Olmos took theater courses to improve his singing and theater became his major. After graduation, he got small parts in television while supporting himself and his wife moving furniture. Olmos's break came in 1978 with the Tony Award–nominated play *Zoot Suit*. He went on to starring roles, most notably in television's *Miami Vice*, and in the film *Stand and Deliver* (1987).

Olmos's early television roles were usually nasty villains. He says of an appearance on *Hawaii Five-O*, "I was the only person Jack Lord shot in the back, ever.... That's how bad I was."

Other Birthdays
1874   Honus Wagner
1921   Abe Vigoda
1945   Barry Bostwick
1956   Paula Zahn

February 25

1943   Liverpool, England.

Beatle George "the serious one" Harrison was born. His father was a schoolbus driver. Harrison was the youngest of four children and the family favorite. He was a solitary boy, who, when he got a guitar in 1956, decided to become a pop musician. He found learning to play more difficult than he had anticipated. It took many weeks. His mother stayed up late into the night with him while he practiced chords.

Harrison was inspired by his school pal Paul McCartney, who had hooked up with John Lennon and Lennon's band, the Quarrymen (see 10/9/1940). Harrison desperately wanted to join, but Lennon considered the three-years-younger Harrison a child. He relented when Harrison's mother allowed the Quarrymen to use her house for the band's noisy rehearsals, but Harrison didn't expect quick stardom. He hedged his future by becoming an electrician's assistant. When he discovered he had little talent for that occupation, he committed himself to music. It proved a much better trade than house wiring when the Quarrymen, under the name the Beatles, became the most successful rock group in history.

Other Birthdays
1840   Auguste Rodin
1873   Enrico Caruso
1901   Zeppo Marx (see 3/22/1887)
1913   Jim Backus
1918   Bobby Riggs
1943   Sally Jessy Raphael

February 26

1916   Brooklyn, New York.

Herbert John Gleason, second son of Mae Kelly and Herb Gleason, was born. Mae Kelly was 15 when she married 25-year-old insurance company clerk Herb Gleason. Five years later, their first son, Clemence, was born. A sickly child, he spent all day indoors, never playing outside. Mae called her second son Jackie, and it was as Jackie Gleason that he became a television superstar. Clemence didn't have as bright a future. He died at 14 in 1919.

Clemence's death had a bad effect on Herb. He frittered away his paycheck on booze. Mae became overprotective of Jackie, keeping him out of school until he was eight. When he finally enrolled, he didn't fit in and hated it. His homelife worsened when, shortly before Christmas in 1925, Herb disappeared. Mae and Jackie never heard from him again.

Left in poverty, Mae and Jackie moved to cheaper lodgings. Mae got a job as a subway change-maker. Jackie joined a gang, hung out in pool halls, smoked, and tippled bathtub gin. Mae struggled to keep her chubby boy fed. He later said, "The surroundings were dismal, just a round table and an icebox and a bureau that everything went into. The light bulbs were never very bright and the rooms were always bare." This clearly inspired the set of *The Honeymooners.* Jackie also said, "But she was a good mother and things were very pleasant, with a lot of affection."

Jackie's first show business success was in an eighth-grade graduation show. Intoxicated by the experience of getting a laugh, he dropped out of the ninth grade. He did odd jobs to help his mother but spent most of his energy trying to get into vaudeville. Then, Mae became ill with a septic skin disease. She had a superstitious dread of doctors, so the illness went untreated, and she died in 1935. After her funeral, Jackie had just 39¢ left in the world. Fortunately, he ran into a friend who got him a job as an amateur contest emcee. He became a comic, then went to Hollywood. He had little success in films, but his nightclub act was a hit. When the DuMont television network needed a host for their variety show, *Cavalcade of Stars,* they hired Gleason. At 34, he became a success. He went on to star in the classic television comedy *The Honeymooners.*

1932   Kingsland, Arkansas.

Country singer Johnny Cash was born. He had five siblings and the family barely fed themselves by raising cotton on a tiny farm. Cash earned extra money selling appliances in Memphis but had musical hopes. Cash says, "I got the idea of singin' for a livin' because I was starvin' to death. You don't have to have lived in poverty to be a successful country singer, but it helps."

Cash won a recording contract in 1955, but it wasn't until the 1960s that Cash scored hits with "Ring of Fire" and "I Walk the Line." His other hits include "A Boy Named Sue" and "Folsom Prison Blues." Cash's resonant voice reflects his hard-scrabble background, which many believe included a stretch in prison. Actually, Cash wasn't a convict. He said, "Only been in jail twice, and just overnight, but you don't need much to see what it's like."

Other Birthdays
1887   William Frawley
1914   Robert Alda
1920   Tony Randall
1928   Fats Domino
1953   Michael Bolton

February 27

1932   Heatherwood House, Wildwood Road, Golders Green, London.

Illinois-born art dealer Francis Taylor and Kansas-born actress Sara Viola Taylor had their second child, a girl. Their first child, Howard, had been a beautiful infant. This was not surprising, since his parents were an attractive couple. Sara also credited the child's good looks to her own positive, prenatal thinking. However, positive thinking didn't seem to have helped the second child's appearance. Her mother later called her "the *funniest*-looking little baby I have ever seen!" The baby had dark hair across her ears, shoulders, and arms and wouldn't open her eyes. When the doctor gently pulled back their lids, all that was visible were their whites.

Sara didn't give up. She prayed and continued thinking positive thoughts. On the tenth day, she was rewarded. The infant girl's eyes opened, and they were a lovely violet. Sara swore that her daughter smiled at her. By the age of sixteen months, the child's extra hair disappeared, and the ugly baby had become a strikingly beautiful toddler. When World War II came, the family returned to America. They settled in Los Angeles, where Sara had little trouble getting the movie studios to take notice of her little girl. Soon, Elizabeth Taylor's violet eyes were known around the world.

Taylor, who has been married seven times, once said, "I've only slept with the men I've been married to. How many women can make that claim?"

Other Birthdays
1902   John Steinbeck
1930   Joanne Woodward
1934   Ralph Nader
1962   Adam Baldwin
1980   Chelsea Clinton

February 28

1533   The château of Montaigne, near Bordeaux, France.

Michel Eyquem de Montaigne was born. His father, Pierre Eyquem, was a wealthy merchant and a firm believer in education. Latin was essential to the educated mind of his day. To teach his son Latin, Montaigne's father hired a German tutor who knew no French. Tutor and student could communicate only in Latin, which guaranteed no laxity.

Montaigne was a good student, mastering the law while a teenager. Later, he turned to writing. He is credited with inventing the personal essay. His work emphasized the importance of a questioning attitude, an open mind, and tolerance. Montaigne's own family provided plenty of room for tolerance. His mother was of a distinguished Spanish-Jewish family, his brothers were Protestants, and his sister became a Catholic prioress so noted for her piety that, in 1949, she was canonized.

Montaigne once wrote, "One should always have one's boots on, and be ready to leave."

Other Birthdays
1901   Linus Pauling
1906   Bugsy Siegel
1915   Zero Mostel
1931   Gavin MacLeod
1933   Charles Durning
1939   Tommy Tune
1940   Mario Andretti
1948   Bernadette Peters

February 29

1896   Brookline, Massachusetts.

Film director William A. Wellman was born. Wellman was a fighter pilot during World War I. After the war, Wellman went to work as a laborer at Sam Goldwyn's studio. When General "Black Jack" Pershing, the commander of American forces in France during the war, was due to visit the studio, all ex-military employees were ordered to show up in their old uniforms to welcome him. As the general passed Wellman he stopped and said, "Where have I seen you before?" Wellman said he'd rather not say, but Pershing suddenly smiled, exclaiming, "That's it. What can I do for you?" Wellman replied in a whisper, "Take me over behind that fig tree and talk to me for a few minutes and make me important." The general obliged, and the two had a pleasant conversation away from the assembled studio employees, movie executives, and Pershing's entourage. The next day, Goldwyn summoned Wellman into his office. Wellman later said, "I was told I was the kind of man they wanted on that lot, and they made me an assistant director. I didn't tell them Black Jack and I had got together when we were both on a toot in Paris."

Wellman's films included *Wings* (1929), *The Public Enemy* (1931), *Call of the Wild* (1935), *A Star Is Born* (1937), *Beau Geste* (1939), and *The Ox-Bow Incident* (1943).

Other Birthdays
1860   Herman Hollerith, who introduced the punched card

March 1

1910   Kirriemuir, Scotland.

Actor David Niven was born. His parents were William Edward Graham Niven, a landed proprietor, and Henrietta Julia Niven. David was the last-born of their four children. By the time David was two, his father had gambled away much of his fortune on horse races. Enough money remained so that when World War I erupted in 1914 and Niven's father joined the Berkshire Yeomanry as a lieutenant, he took a valet, an under-gardener, and two grooms with him to attend to his needs. David's sister later recalled her father carrying David upon his shoulders as he waited for the taxi to take him off to war. William Niven was killed during the tragically pointless fighting at Gallipoli.

Niven was sent away to school. He wasn't a good student and often got in trouble over pranks, such as sending a box of dog feces to a sick pal as a get-well gift. Niven was bounced from school to school. Eventually, he wound up in Stowe, a new school, were he continued playing pranks. Once he brought a prostitute to Parent's Day. Stowe's headmaster, J. F. Roxburgh, was aware of the woman's trade, but treated her exactly as he did the other guests. This gentlemanly act made a great impression on Niven. Roxburgh became a father figure. Niven buckled down and became a fair student. Despite being overweight, he also became a good athlete. With Roxburgh's help, Niven entered Sandhurst (Britain's West Point) and became an officer in the British Army.

After a few years of military service, Niven met heiress Barbara Hutton, who invited him to spend Christmas in New York with her. Niven enjoyed Hutton's hospitality and America so much that he resigned his commission. He settled in Hollywood and, while working odd jobs, tried to become an actor.

Niven befriended stars and moguls, but a movie contract eluded him. One day, the H.M.S. *Norfolk*, a British warship, visited Santa Barbara on a goodwill tour. Niven was invited by friends to a party aboard the vessel. He overindulged and awoke to find the ship underway. He also saw something impossible when he peered blearily out a porthole: An eighteenth-century British warship was bearing down upon them. It was the H.M.S. *Bounty*—or, rather, a replica of the *Bounty* that was being used to film the Clark Gable and Charles Laughton version of *Mutiny on the Bounty*. The film studio had thought an encounter between the two British vessels would be a great publicity stunt. The *Norfolk* sent Niven, still dressed in the evening wear he had worn to the shipboard party, over to the *Bounty*, which was headed back to port. The resulting notoriety got Niven his studio contract. His first significant role was in the film he had "crashed"— *Mutiny on the Bounty*.

Other Birthdays
1917 Dinah Shore
1927 Harry Belafonte
1945 Dirk Benedict

1954   Ron Howard
1954   Catherine Bach
1956   Timothy Daly

March 2

1904   Springfield, Massachusetts.

Theodor Seuss Geisel was born. His parents were Henrietta Seuss and Theodor R. Geisel, who worked for the family brewery and was due to become its president—on the very day Prohibition began. Instead, he became Springfield's superintendent of parks, which included managing the city's zoo. Theodor spent many hours there watching the animals. He remarked, "I used to hang around there a lot. They'd let me in the cage with the small lions and the small tigers, and I got chewed up every once in a while."

Geisel attended Dartmouth where he majored in English and demonstrated cartooning skills in the student humor magazine. He then spent a year at Oxford University, and another year traveling through Europe. He planned to become an English professor. In 1927, he married Helen Marion Palmer, a schoolteacher he met at Oxford. After seeing Geisel's artwork, she convinced him that he should become an artist. Geisel began contributing humorous material to magazines. His first success was drawing cartoon ads for the insecticide Flit. All these cartoons had the same tagline: "Quick, Henry, The Flit!" It became a national catch-phrase.

In 1936, while traveling by ship to Europe, Geisel's mind fell into step with the pounding rhythm of the ship's engines. He began stringing together a nonsensical rhyme to fit that rhythm. When he returned to America, he published it, with suitable illustrations, as *And to Think That I Saw It on Mulberry Street.* He used the pen name Dr. Seuss. It was an immediate success.

Dr. Seuss went on to write forty-six children's books, including *The Cat in the Hat, Green Eggs and Ham,* and *How the Grinch Stole Christmas.* His books sold over 100 million copies, but his works were not always appreciated by educators. They thought that words such as *ziffs, nerkles,* and *Grinch,* which Dr. Seuss invented for his stories, would confuse children learning to read. Children enjoyed them thoroughly and suffered no ill effect.

Geisel once observed, "I think I have helped kids laugh in school and at home. That's enough, isn't it?" He also remarked, "I'd rather write for kids. They're more appreciative; adults are obsolete children, and the hell with them."

Other Birthdays
1793   Sam Houston
1919   Jennifer Jones
1931   Tom Wolfe
1942   John Irving
1943   Lou Reed
1949   Eddie Money
1962   Jon Bon Jovi

March 3

1847   Edinburgh, Scotland.

Eliza Grace Bell and Alexander Melville Bell had the second of their three sons, Alexander Graham Bell. Bell's father was an elocution teacher interested in instructing deaf-mutes. He developed the system of lip-reading the deaf still use today. Although Eliza herself was deaf, she refused to learn her husband's system. Bell said of his mother, "It is a great grief when I come home to see her quiet resignation 'under the will of God,' because of an obstinate disbelief in the power of lip-reading." Despite this difference, Bell's parents were a loving couple and lived to an advanced age.

Like their father, the Bell boys were interested in sound. Bell's brothers invented talking toys, but their work ended when they died from tuberculosis, leaving just Alexander. He and his parents moved to Canada, seeking a more healthy climate. Alexander traveled to New England to teach his father's methods and work on his own research. In 1876, he invented the telephone. Bell married a deaf woman, and, like his parents, they were happy and devoted.

Other Birthdays
1911   Jean Harlow
1962   Jackie Joyner-Kersee
1962   Herschel Walker

March 4

1888   Voss, Norway.

Football legend Knute Rockne was born. Rockne's father was a skillful carriage builder. In 1891, he traveled to the World's Columbia Exposition in Chicago to place some of his carriages on exhibition. Rockne's father decided to stay, sending for his family. A talented athlete, young Rockne played football and baseball, ran track, and pole-vaulted but didn't consider pursuing professional sports. Instead, after high school, he went to work for the post office. He ran to stay in shape and, in his fourth year as a postal worker, a couple of his running pals persuaded him to enroll in Notre Dame University. Rockne played on the school's football team, but his athletic abilities weren't noticed at first. Instead, he became known as an excellent student. He was particularly good at chemistry and would have become a chemist but for a single football game.

In 1913, Notre Dame, then a less-than-notable football power, unexpectedly got a chance to play West Point, which had one of the best teams in the country. Rockne and his roommate Gus Dorais, who was Notre Dame's quarterback, racked their brains to come up with some stratagem to defeat West Point. Their innovation was the forward pass. Notre Dame whomped West Point, stunning the nation. Rockne went on to coach for Notre Dame and become one of the game's legends. Before his untimely death in an aircrash in 1931, Rockne had attained a winning average of .897.

Rockne was noted for his rousing pep talks. The most famous of these invoked the memory of George "the Gipper" Gipp, a Notre Dame football star who died unexpectedly. Rockne urged his players "to win one for the Gipper," and they did. Rockne was a hard competitor. He once said, "Show me a good and gracious loser and I'll show you a failure."

Other Birthdays
1913   John Garfield
1939   Paula Prentiss
1953   Kay Lenz
1969   Chastity Bono

March 5

1936   North Hollywood, California.

Actor Dean Stockwell was born into a show biz family. His parents, Harry and Betty Veronica Stockwell, were Broadway actors, and his brother, Guy, also became an actor. Stockwell made his stage debut at seven, with Guy, in a Theater Guild production of *The Innocent Voyage*. He began his film career at nine in *Anchors Aweigh* (1945). He next played the son of Myrna Loy and William Powell in *Song of the Thin Man* (1947). His first significant role was in *The Boy with the Green Hair* (1948). Stockwell also played opposite Errol Flynn in *Kim* (1950). On the first day of shooting for *Kim,* Flynn won fourteen-year-old Stockwell's admiration by cheerfully asking him in front of his mother if had slept with a woman yet.

Later, Stockwell tried grittier roles, such as a thrill-killer in the Leopold and Loeb story *Compulsion* (1959). He has since become a character actor of great skill and was recently featured in the television series *Quantum Leap*.

Other Birthdays
1908   Rex Harrison

1927   Jack Cassidy
1939   Samantha Eggar
1954   Marsha Warfield

March 6

1906   Paterson, New Jersey.

Anthony Cristillo was a member of a devout, Catholic, Italian family. His parents placed his sister in a convent and dispatched him to a seminary to train for the priesthood. It wasn't an occupation he wanted, so, when they died, he left to join his brothers in America, who worked in a dye works. One of his new neighbors was a pretty Irish girl, Helen Rage, nicknamed Lolly. When Lolly turned 18, he married her. In 1903, they had their first child, Anthony. On this date, they had their second son, Louis Francis. Six years later, their only daughter, Marie Katherine, was born.

Of the three children, Louis, called Lou, was the most mischievous. One Christmas, Anthony was practicing his violin when he noticed Lou fetching a glass of water, then another, then, faster, still another. Curious, Anthony followed Lou and discovered that, while demonstrating his new Magic Lantern to a friend, Lou had set the Christmas tree on fire and, now, the living room was ablaze. Fortunately, the Cristillos lived across the street from a fire station, so the fire was extinguished. The family piano was lost, however, and Lou got a paddling.

Once, when a new movie house opened, Lou and Anthony skipped school to see a silent Western, paying their way in with their lunch money. Unfortunately, when the lights came up, their father leaned over their shoulders to ask them how they liked the show. Their punishment didn't dispell Lou's love of movies.

Lou's brother Anthony shared Lou's show business dreams and became a successful band leader. One of his friends, Dorothy Russell, the daughter of Lillian Russell, couldn't remember his first name. She nicknamed him Pat after his hometown, Paterson. The owner of a deli that Anthony patronized had a similar problem with Anthony's last name. He converted Cristillo to Costello. Eventually, everyone called Anthony Pat Costello. Anthony reluctantly accepted his new name. When, in 1927, Lou persuaded his father to let him go to Hollywood to become an actor, he, too, adopted the name Costello.

Lou hitchhiked to save money. He got a job in a film labor gang. One day, when a stunt man failed to show up to do a balcony fall, Lou offered to replace him, despite knowing nothing about stunt work. Lou survived and got more stunt work, but he still couldn't break into acting. After a year, an actress friend suggested Lou go to New York and obtain some training. Lou sadly left Hollywood. He was hitchhiking through St. Joseph, Missouri, when he ran out of money. Fortunately, a local burlesque house was looking for a "Dutch comic." Lou got the job and worked there for a year, becoming a favorite with burlesque audiences. He met Bud Abbott in 1936 (see 10/2/1895). As a team, they became Hollywood stars.

Other Birthdays
1475   Michelangelo
1806   Elizabeth Barrett Browning
1923   Ed McMahon
1943   Bobby Fischer
1945   Rob Reiner
1959   Tom Arnold
1972   Shaquille O'Neal

March 7

1934   Alexandria, Virginia.

Today show weatherman Willard Scott was born. He will turn one hundred years old in the year 2034.

1940   Kenosha, Wisconsin.

Actor Daniel J. Travanti, famed for his role on television's *Hill Street Blues,* was born to an Italian family. He was an excellent student, a high school football star, and Phi Beta Kappa graduate of the University of Wisconsin. Travanti won a fellowship to the Yale School of Drama and began a stage career. He began having difficulty getting parts, however, when his hidden problems with alcohol came to light. In 1973, in Indianapolis, he got the jitters onstage. Apologizing to the audience, he walked off in the middle of the play and joined Alcoholics Anonymous.

After Travanti stopped drinking, he attended Loyola Mary-mount University in Los Angeles. He returned to acting with a role on the television soap opera *General Hospital.* He became a star with his Emmy-winning role as Captain Frank Furillo on *Hill Street Blues.*

Other Birthdays
1849   Luther Burbank
1875   Maurice Ravel
1942   Tammy Faye Bakker

March 8

1943   London.

Lynn Redgrave was born. She grew up to be a plump young woman. She planned to become a chef until her actor father, Sir Michael Redgrave, pushed her into acting. In her first major movie, *Georgy Girl* (1966), she played a chubby, ugly-duckling. Afterwards, Redgrave fell into a vicious cycle of gorging and purging. In the 1970s, while traveling to Toronto by airplane, she was seated by comedian Gilda Radner. They started chatting. When they shared stories of their eating problems, Radner began crying. Redgrave says, "She had never talked about it before. Nor had I. But hearing how out of control she was got to me. I decided I had to quit." With counseling, Redgrave recovered and went on to become a svelte diet system spokesperson.

Other Birthdays
1841   Oliver Wendel Holmes Jr.
1891   Sam Jaffe
1921   Cyd Charisse
1945   Mickey Dolenz

March 9

1918   Brooklyn, New York.

Writer Frank Morrison "Mickey" Spillane was born to Irish bartender John Joseph Spillane and Catherine Spillane. Spillane did his first storytelling in grammar school, where his ghost stories terrified his classmates. After an unsuccessful run at becoming a lawyer, Spillane resorted to odd jobs. One of these was as a salesman at Gimbel's during the Christmas rush. A coworker there got him a job writing for comic books. After service in the U.S. Air Force during World War II, Spillane married. He and his wife chose a homesite in Newburgh, New York. They needed $1,000 to buy it, so Spillane took a few weeks and pounded out his first novel, *I, the Jury*. Featuring the tough detective Mike Hammer and lurid sex, it earned enough money to buy the property, but Spillane still had to stretch to pay his bills. He worked as a sales clerk and for the Ringling Bros. and Barnum & Bailey Circus, where he was a trampoline artist and was even shot from a cannon. After a few more novels, Spillane could put away his leotards. Mike Hammer became a hit with readers.

Critics were appalled at Spillane's work. One claimed that Hammer killed fifty-eight antagonists in Spillane's first six books. It didn't help that Spillane let some of his anti-Communist views seep into his work. Spillane said, "I pay no attention to those jerks who think they're critics. I don't give a hoot about reading reviews. What I want to read is the royalty checks." Of his raw style, Spillane said, "Hey, if Shakespeare was selling big today, I'd write like Shakespeare."

Other Birthdays
1934   Yuri Gagarin
1936   Marty Ingels
1940   Raul Julia
1971   Emmanuel Lewis

March 10

1888   Dublin.

William Joseph Shields was born. Under the name Barry Fitzgerald, he became one of Hollywood's favorite character actors. Fitzgerald's father was a newspaperman who had a hard time supporting his large family. He pushed Fitzgerald into the British Civil Service, specifically the Unemployment Insurance Division. It gave security, a solid wage, and some status, but Fitzgerald found his work dull. To relieve his boredom, he spent his free time boxing, swimming, and playing football. He was sociable and had many friends, including the writer James Joyce.

Fitzgerald's brother Arthur eluded the civil service and became an actor at Dublin's prestigious Abbey Theatre. Fitzgerald later said, "I went frequently to the Abbey Theatre, of course, and once when I was invited backstage to meet some of the players, I was roped in to play a walk-on the following week. I played walk-ons frequently, never having the energy to go away and do something useful in my spare time. It became a habit. I got to know the players well and met many notable and interesting people. It was fun, but I didn't take it seriously and neither I nor anyone else thought I had the least talent for the stage."

Fitzgerald's first speaking part was in Sheridan's *The Critic*. He had one line. He was supposed to say " 'Tis meet it should," but he nervously said, " 'Tis sheet it mould." His embarrassment didn't stop him from accepting more roles. He learned his lines at lunch and acted at night under his stage name. For twenty years, Fitzgerald kept up his dual career. He appeared in plays by Synge, Yeats, and Dunsany, becoming more and more a favored player. In 1929, Sean O'Casey wrote the play *The Silver Tassie* specifically for Fitzgerald. When it became a success and went on tour, Fitzgerald finally abandoned his civil service desk to become a full-time actor.

Fitzgerald toured Broadway with the Abbey Players. He got good reviews and Hollywood signed him. His best film role was as the curmudgeonly Catholic priest opposite Bing Crosby's optimistic Catholic priest in *Going My Way* (1944). Fitzgerald and Crosby both won Oscars. Ironically, Fitzgerald was Protestant.

Other Birthdays
1898　Bert Bacharach
1940　Chuck Norris
1958　Sharon Stone
1964　Prince Edward, youngest son of Queen Elizabeth II
1964　Jasmine Guy

March 11

1931　Melbourne, Australia.

Media mogul Rupert Murdoch was born. His parents were Sir Keith Murdoch and Dame Elisabeth Joy Murdoch. Murdoch's father, a famous World War I correspondent, was a prominent publisher, heading *The Melbourne Herald*. Murdoch was sent to Oxford, where he studied political science and economics. In 1952, his father died. Murdoch, who supposed he would be inheriting his father's position, spent two years working as a junior sub-editor for London's *Daily Express* to learn the business. When he returned to Australia, he was stunned to discover that his father actually had a very small interest in the *Herald*. Murdoch's legacy was just two struggling papers. A friend later remarked, "The greatest driving force in Rupert's life is the feeling that his father was cheated."

Murdoch changed the editorial policies of his papers, embracing lurid headlines and sensational stories. He also incorporated as much sex as possible. By 1968, he was worth at least $50 million. He returned to England to buy London's *News of the World* and the *Sun.* He doubled the *Sun's* circulation with such novelties as the daily "Page Three Girl," a topless beauty. Murdoch soon crossed the Atlantic to buy American publications such as the *New York Post, New York Magazine, The Village Voice, TV Guide,* and *Seventeen.* He also moved into television and films, purchasing Fox Studios. Murdoch's latest coups include the wresting of the rights to NFL football from CBS for Fox and persuading several NBC affiliates to switch to his station.

Murdoch is unembarrassed by his tactics. He once said, "A press that fails to interest the whole community is one that will ultimately become a house organ of the elite engaged in an increasingly private conversation with a dwindling club."

Other Birthdays
1903   Lawrence Welk
1934   Sam Donaldson
1950   Douglas "Don't Panic" Adams
1952   Bobby "Don't Worry, Be Happy" McFerrin

March 12

1858   Cincinnati, Ohio.

Adolph Simon Ochs was born. Ochs began his working career as a newsboy peddling papers. At the end of his career, he was still peddling newspapers, but he sold them as the publisher of the *New York Times.*

1946 Los Angeles, California.

Liza Minnelli was born to singer Judy Garland (see 6/10/1922) and filmmaker Vincente Minnelli. Liza made her first film appearance in the final scene of the musical *In the Good Old Summertime* (1946), playing, aptly enough, her mother's infant daughter. Minnelli's parents divorced when she was six. Garland had serious problems with alcohol and drugs, leading her to flirt with suicide. She provided affectionate but spotty mothering. By the time Liza was 11, she had assumed many of the responsibilities of homemaker.

Perhaps realizing that she wasn't the best of parents, Garland turned Minnelli over to a string of boarding schools. Used to her independence, Minnelli fared poorly and, as soon as she was able, set out on her own to build an acting career. Her mother's stardom helped, but Minnelli's own talent earned her recognition. At 19, she won a Tony Award for the Broadway play *Flora, the Red Menace*. She followed this with the movie *Charlie Bubbles* (1968). Her starring role in *The Sterile Cuckoo* (1969) won her an Academy Award nomination, and her role in *Cabaret* (1972) won her the Best Actress Award. She also won an Emmy that year, for a television special.

Minnelli's quick success wasn't without problems. She turned out a number of film bombs, married unhappily, and, like her mother, had problems with substance abuse. Unlike her mother, who died in her 40s, Minnelli received treatment and renewed her career. Judy Garland did live long enough to enjoy her daughter's success. She admiringly remarked, "I think she decided to go into show business when she was an embryo, she kicked so much."

Other Birthdays
1922   Jack Kerouac
1928   Edward Albee
1941   Barbara Feldon
1948   James Taylor
1962   Darryl Strawberry

March 13

1939   Brooklyn, New York.

Rock and roll legend Neil Sedaka was born. Raised in a Sephardic Jewish home, Sedaka showed musical talent early and was selected by Arthur Rubinstein as New York's outstanding young classical pianist. The chubby Sedaka, however, decided that a better way to win his teenage peers' approval was to write rock songs. He scored his first hit in 1955 with "Stupid Cupid," recorded by Connie Francis. Sedaka formed his own group, the Tokens but left after discovering that he worked better alone. His efforts produced such hits as "Breaking Up Is Hard to Do," "Happy Birthday, Sweet Sixteen," "I'm Living Right Next Door to an Angel," and "Calendar Girl." By the time Sedaka was 23 he had made enough money to retire. Perhaps it was the right time for him to do so, as American rock was passing through the British invasion, and his songs were considered old-fashioned. Sedaka kept his hand in by writing songs for the Fifth Dimension.

By 1975, times had changed, and with the help of rocker Elton John, Sedaka staged a comeback. He wrote "Love Will Keep Us Together" for the Captain and Tennille, and himself recorded "Laughter in the Rain" and "Bad Blood." Now in his 50s, Sedaka continues to perform and his audiences still love hearing his old hits.

Other Birthdays
1910   Sammy Kaye
1956   Dana Delany

March 14

1879   Ulm Donnau, Germany.

Albert Einstein was born to businessman Hermann Einstein and Pauline Koch Einstein. Albert was a worry to his parents.

Although he had started playing the violin at six, his speech was still clumsy at nine. He had trouble with mathematics and needed a year's remedial study before he was admitted into Zurich's Federal Polytechnic Academy. He tried to find an academic job when he graduated but was forced to work as a minor clerk in a Swiss patent office in Bern. In his spare time, Einstein wrote "A New Determination of Molecular Dimension." His paper was well received, and the University of Zurich awarded him a Ph.D. based on its significance. In 1916, Einstein published his Theory of Relativity, earning him international recognition as a genius. Nevertheless, Einstein continued to experience difficulty handling everyday life. When he worked at Princeton, he often got lost. He never learned to drive a car and found filling out his U.S. income tax forms impossible.

Einstein, who often had to explain extraordinary things to ordinary people, once said, "Everything should be made as simple as possible, but not simpler."

Other Birthdays
1864   Casey Jones
1933   Michael Caine
1933   Quincy Jones
1947   Billy Crystal

March 15

1767   South Carolina, North Carolina, Pennsylvania, Virginia, Ireland, England, or onboard a ship in the Atlantic Ocean.

Andrew Jackson was born. The location of his birth is uncertain: the most likely contenders are the Carolinas. The Jackson family lived near the border between them, which wasn't officially drawn until later. Political rivals suggested Ireland, England, and shipboard because that would have taken away his American citizenship and rendered Jackson's presidency unconstitutional.

Jackson's parents were Elizabeth Hutchinson Jackson and Andrew Jackson, a tenant farmer from Ireland. They came to America with two small boys and headed straight into the wilderness. The elder Andrew worked hard. Two years later, he died after straining himself lifting a log. Two or three days after this tragedy, his wife gave birth to a son. She named him Andrew Jackson, after her late husband.

Jackson was raised in the crowded household of one of his aunts. When he was five, the local pastor gave him reading lessons. In his illiterate community, Jackson became the public reader. When the newspaper came in the post, he read it aloud to his neighbors. The Revolutionary War filled the papers, and local interest was great. Jackson's two elder brothers enlisted. At 13, Jackson signed up with the militia as a courier.

One brother was soon killed in battle. Jackson and his brother Robert were captured. When they refused to polish a British officer's boots, he slashed the boys with his sword. Jackson wound up with a scar across his cheek. The brothers were imprisoned in a squalid jail, where both contracted smallpox. Robert died, but, after Jackson's mother begged for clemency, Andrew was released and survived.

The Jacksons had endured more than their share of the war, but their participation didn't end with Jackson's release. His mother heard how American prisoners were dying of plague untended on a British prison ship. She decided she had to help, despite the danger. She said goodbye to her sole surviving son, saying, "Andy, never tell a lie, nor take what is not your own, nor sue for slander. *Settle them cases yourself.*" She contracted the plague, died, and was buried with the other plague victims in an unmarked grave.

Jackson grew up a rowdy yahoo before he decided to become a lawyer. In 1791, he married Rachel Robards. They later discovered that her divorce from an earlier husband hadn't become final until two years after she married Jackson. When Jackson went into politics, this incident was used to attack him. Jackson took his mother's advice and fought several

duels, killing one man. He also incurred a chest wound that
ultimately led to his death many years later.

The duels added to Jackson's reputation for toughness.
During the War of 1812, he decisively defeated the British at
the Battle of New Orleans. The victory helped him become the
seventh president of the United States in 1828. During his
campaign, he was vilified by rivals. By then, however, the 60-
year-old veteran had developed a tough hide. Only one attack
stung: His rivals circulated a vicious, untrue story about his
mother. Though she had been dead for four decades, Jackson
still wept.

Other Birthdays
1924   Sabu
1935   Judd Hirsch
1935   Jimmy Swaggart
1941   Mike Love
1961   Fabio

March 16

1926   Newark, New Jersey.

Joey Levitch was born. His father was a vaudevillian, and
Levitch was singing on the Borscht Belt at five. In high school,
Levitch's show biz background led him into cheerleading. His
clowning around was so well received that he dropped out of
school to become a comic. After changing his name to Jerry
Lewis, he played dive after dive with growing success. He was
a well-established comic when, in 1946, he met singer Dean
Martin in Atlantic City. Their pairing turned both into stars.

Although the Martin and Lewis duo made several successful
films, they broke up in 1956, at the height of their popularity.
Both went on to successful solo careers, but Lewis's was
plagued by spectacular ups and downs. Some of his films were
poorly received, while others were successful. When he began
appearing on stage without Martin, he often floundered, but

eventually became a Las Vegas headliner. His charity telethons raised hundreds of millions of dollars to fight muscular dystrophy, though his charitable efforts are challenged by some as patronizing.

Lewis's worst personal problem began in 1965, when a botched pratfall chipped a bone in his spinal column. Lewis was given the pain-killer Percodan, to which he became addicted. By 1973, the addiction was so severe that Lewis says he locked himself in his mansion's bathroom, put a gun to his mouth, and was ready to pull the trigger. Ironically, considering his comic career, he says that only the sound of his children laughing kept him from killing himself. A near-fatal ulcer compounded his physical problems. In 1979, Lewis ended his addiction. Despite open heart surgery in the 1980s, his comic career continues. In 1995, he appeared on Broadway in *Damn Yankees*.

Lewis often has been labeled less than modest. He once said of himself: "I'm a multi-faceted, talented, wealthy, internationally famous genius. I have an IQ of 190—that's supposed to be a genius. People don't like that. My answer to all my critics is simple: I like me. I like what I've become. I'm proud of what I've achieved, and I don't really believe I've scratched the surface yet."

Lewis's films include *The Bellboy* (1960), *The Nutty Professor* (1963), and *The King of Comedy* (1983).

Other Birthdays
1751   James Madison
1912   Pat Nixon
1920   Leo McKern
1927   Daniel Moynihan
1949   Erik Estrada

March 17

1938   Near Irkutsk, U.S.S.R.

Ballet dancer Rudolf Nureyev was born on a train crossing Siberia. Raised in a poor peasant household near the Siberian border, he dreamed of a more graceful life as a ballet performer, but his father mocked his ambitions. Nureyev persisted and, when he was 16, joined a local dance group, which in turn led to an apprenticeship in the *corps de ballet* at the Ufa Opera House. This sparse training encouraged him to buy a one-way ticket to Leningrad to audition for the famed Kirov Ballet School. Nureyev didn't have enough money to pay his fare home, so it was fortunate that he was accepted on the spot. He became Kirov's foremost student, touring internationally with the troupe before taking advantage of a stop in Paris to defect. He was soon paired with British prima ballerina Dame Margot Fonteyn and became a world-renowned star.

Of his late start in ballet, Nureyev said, "Those who have studied from the beginning never question anything. For me, purity of movement wasn't enough. I needed expression, more intensity, more mind."

Other Birthdays
1919   Nat "King" Cole
1949   Patrick Duffy
1951   Kurt Russell
1954   Lesley-Anne Down
1964   Rob Lowe

March 18

1963   New York City.
Vanessa Williams, the first black Miss America and the first Miss America to resign, was born. She gave up her title after nude photos of her and another woman appeared in *Penthouse* magazine.

Williams's parents were both public school music teachers. They raised Williams and her brother in a Catholic household in the suburban community of Millwood, New York. Williams played French horn and piano and was a bit of a singing star at her high school. She decided to try show business, and the nude photos were taken while she was attempting to establish herself. Assuming that the photos would never appear, she entered a beauty contest to gain public attention. She worked her way up the pyramid of contests to the Miss America crown, but just weeks before her reign was to end, the photos were printed. Williams was forced to resign by pageant officials. She lost $2 million worth of endorsements, two scheduled appearances on Bob Hope specials, a starring role in the Broadway show *My One and Only*, and the job of hosting the Macy's Thanksgiving Day Parade. Williams struggled to rebuild her career and, in the 1990s, succeeded, with a hit album.

Other Birthdays
1837   Grover Cleveland
1911   Smiley Burnette
1926   Peter Graves
1927   George Plimpton
1941   Wilson Pickett
1964   Bonnie Blair

March 19

1947   Greenwich, Connecticut.

Glenn Close was born into a wealthy family. She was a tomboy who loved playing with animals on her family's 500-acre estate, which had been in the family for twelve generations. This pleasant life changed when Close was seven. Her father, a noted surgeon, opened a clinic in the Belgian Congo (now Zaire). Close and her three siblings spent their childhoods bouncing between Africa, Connecticut, and Europe. Close says of the abrupt move, "It is something I find very difficult to talk about in an interview. It was ultimately something that had a rather traumatic effect on our family." Close, however, has a positive opinion of her parents. "My father is a dreamer who has put a lot of his dreams into reality....My mother is *very* down-to-earth. She's the most unmaterialistic person I know."

Close attended a Swiss boarding school, then was enrolled in the expensive private school Rosemary Hall in Greenwich, where she became interested in the theater. After graduating from William and Mary, she went into regional theater, toured with the super-wholesome singing group Up With People, then broke into Broadway with the successful musical *Barnum*. Her next role was as Garp's mother in the film *The World According to Garp* (1982). Her other films include *The Big Chill* (1938), *The Natural* (1984), and *Fatal Attraction* (1987).

Close had long hoped to be a movie star. As a child, she fantasized about being discovered by Walt Disney. It was a natural choice. She says, "The only movies we were allowed to see were Walt Disney!"

Other Birthdays
1848   Wyatt Earp
1860   William Jennings Bryan
1894   "Moms" Mabley
1928   Patrick McGoohan
1936   Ursula Andress
1955   Bruce Willis

March 20

1828   Skien, Norway.

Norwegian playwright Henrik Ibsen, author of *A Doll's House* and *Hedda Gabler*, was born the son of Marichen Altenburg Ibsen and Knud Plesner Ibsen, a prosperous merchant who owned a general store. Ibsen was his parents' second son (the first died in infancy). His parents had four more children. The family lived well until 1834, when Ibsen's father declared bankruptcy. They sold most of their possessions. Ibsen's father could find only odd jobs and often had to accept money from friends and relatives. He grew bitter and abusive. Ibsen's mother withdrew, hiding from the outside world. Young Ibsen must have felt little regret when he left home on December 27, 1843, to become a druggist's apprentice.

Ibsen at first studied medicine, but the theater soon attracted his interest. In 1851, he became the manager and official playwright of the newly built National Theater at Bergen. He went on to write such masterpieces as *Peer Gynt, A Doll's House*, and *The Master Builder*. Unsurprisingly, Ibsen's plays focused on real-world social problems.

Things might have turned out quite differently for Ibsen. One of his brothers chose a different escape from poverty, and sought his fortune in California during the Gold Rush. Whether he found it or not is unknown—he was never heard from again.

Other Birthdays
1907   Ozzie Nelson
1920   Werner Klemperer
1922   Carl Reiner
1928   Fred Rogers
1931   Hal Linden
1939   Brian Mulroney
1948   Bobby Orr
1950   William Hurt
1957   Spike Lee
1958   Holly Hunt

March 21

1685   Eisenach, Germany.

German baroque composer Johann Sebastian Bach was born. His mother was Elizabeth Laemmerhirt, whose fur trader family loved music and regularly held family sing-alongs. His father was Johann Ambrosius Bach, one of a set of twins. Johann Ambrosius played strings in his town band. Johann Sebastian Bach (it was a family tradition to give sons the first name Johann) was the youngest of Elisabeth and

Ambrosius's eight children, four of whom died in childhood. In 1694, Elisabeth herself died. Ambrosius remarried, but, just months afterwards, he, too, was dead, and it was left to Johann Sebastian's oldest brother, Johann Christophe, 24, to raise the family.

Johann Sebastian Bach shared his parents' musical interests and became a Lutheran church organist. He displayed a startling capacity for composing, and produced organ pieces for church services and concerts. This attracted the attention of Prince Leopold and Bach became his court musician. Despite his voluminous output, Bach was overshadowed by more fashionable composers. His work was discarded as old-fashioned after his death in 1750. It wasn't until the composer Mendelssohn revived Bach's work in 1829 that Bach was recognized as one of the greatest composers. His precise, nearly mathematical pieces don't please everyone, however: French novelist Colette called him "a divine sewing machine."

Bach's efforts were probably aided by his parochialism. He had nothing to distract him. He never traveled outside of Germany, read very little, and showed no interest in any of the arts other than music.

Late in the nineteenth century, a rather confused music fan asked composer William Schwenck Gilbert if Bach was still composing. He replied: "No, madam, he's decomposing."

Other Birthdays
1806   Benito Juarez
1869   Florenz Ziegfeld
1903   Edgar Buchanan
1929   James Coco
1944   Timothy Dalton
1962   Matthew Broderick

March 22

1887   New York City.

Tailor Sam Marx and wife, Minnie, had their first child, Leonard. He was an active child who was fascinated by the penny-ante poker games his father staged in their tenement household. As soon as Leonard was allowed, he joined in, eagerly pawning his possessions to stay in the games. A mathematical whiz who could multiply large numbers in his head, Leonard used this talent to calculate odds. In addition to his number-crunching skill, Leonard could mimic any of the many ethnic accents of New York. It came in handy in his perambulations of the city: No matter what neighborhood he was in, he could avoid being beaten up, which was how strangers usually were welcomed, by appearing to be a local. Leonard had a lightning-fast gift of gab. He could go into any poolroom and, in minutes, set up a hustle.

Such a young man would have been enough excitement for any family, but the Marxes had four more extraordinary sons. Adolph Marx, born in 1888, was dreamy, with a relaxed charm that made everyone like him. He had a hearty appetite and planned to become a butcher so he would always eat well.

Brother number three, born in 1890, was Julius. He was bored by gambling and, although he loved jokes, he also loved literature. He was a serious student who hoped to become a doctor. He was nervous in company and covered his anxiety with aggressive putdowns.

Brother number four, born in 1897, was Milton. He was the sensible one who helped his brothers with their business affairs. Brother number five, born in 1901, was Herbert. He was good-looking, but, being the youngest, he always struggled to keep up with his older brothers, and the strain often showed. Still, he could fill in for any of them in their joking and make them laugh at his imitations of their antics.

These boys might have led mundane lives but for their mother, Minnie, who knew that there was big money in show business. She said, "Where else can people who don't know anything make a living?" She also knew that her boys had talent. Leonard played the piano. Adolph taught himself how to play his grandmother's harp. Julius could strum a guitar. Minnie pushed Leonard, Julius, Milton, and Adolph into forming a singing group called The Four Nightingales.

One night in the small Texas town of Nacogdoches, a runaway mule lured their audience right out of the theater. After the crowd returned, the brothers angrily went berserk, insulting the town and everyone in it. The audience loved it, and The Marx Brothers were born. Their antics brought them to Broadway in 1923 in *I'll Say She Is*. This, in turn, led to further stage success and then Hollywood. Milton became their manager, while Herbert, who was pigeonholed as their straight man, left to become an agent and successful manufacturer.

According to one of several explanations, the Marx brothers came up with their unique names after a discussion of how other vaudeville performers were giving themselves names like Boffo and Supremo. Leonard was named Chicko, later shortened to Chico by a typesetter's error on a poster, because he loved "chicks." Adolph became Harpo, because of his harp. Julius became Groucho, because of his grouchy ways. Milton became Gummo because he liked chewing gum. And, finally, Herbert became Zeppo for no discernible reason at all.

Other Birthdays
1908   Louis L'Amour
1914   Karl Malden
1920   Werner Klemperer
1923   Marcel Marceau
1930   Pat Robertson
1931   William Shatner
1948   Andrew Lloyd Webber
1952   Bob Costas

March 23

1906   San Antonio, Texas.

Lucille Fay LeSueur was born. Her mother was Anna Bell Johnson, a pretty Irish-Swedish girl. Her father was contractor Thomas LeSueur, a handsome French-Canadian. LeSueur had trouble finding work and one day just left town. Anna divorced him and married Henry Cassin.

Cassin ran a theater in Lawton, Oklahoma. Lucille, nicknamed Billie because of her tomboy ways, loved watching the vaudevillians and copied their acts, especially the dancers'. At six, Billie severely cut her foot. After two operations, the doctor told her parents that she would walk with a limp for the rest of her life and would never dance again. Cassin refused to agree, inspiring Billie to completely overcome the handicap. However, Billie's life soon took a turn for the worse. While playing in their cellar, Billie discovered a sack of gold coins an embezzler had hidden there. Suspicion fell upon Cassin as an accomplice. Though a trial vindicated him, he could no longer remain in Lawton. Cassin sold his theater and bought a hotel in Kansas City, Missouri. When this failed, Cassin and Anna divorced.

Anna was a harsh mother to Billie. She beat the girl severely for minor misbehaviors and placed her in a convent grammar school, where Billie worked as a servant to pay her way. After finishing the eighth grade, Billie was sent to work in a boarding school, where she labored all day in return for a high school education. She was beaten with a broom handle by the school's female principal for the slightest reason. The beatings stopped when one of the school's rich students asked Billie on a date. The principal thought Billie's looks would attract more students to the school. Billie learned that her beauty had practical value. After graduation, Billie worked in a department store. She took a stab at college, but her high school education had been a sham and she was unprepared. She left school to become a dancer. After a few clerking jobs, she made it into a chorus line, which led to a film contract.

At first, Billie used the stage name Lucille LeSueur, but her studio decided it sounded too much like "LeSewer." They held a contest to name Billie. The winner was a handicapped woman from Albany, New York. She got $500. Billie hated the winning entry, complaining, "It sounds like 'Crawfish!'" Still, she kept it. Billie's new name was Joan Crawford.

Other Birthdays
1857   Fannie Farmer
1900   Erich Fromm
1912   Wernher von Braun
1953   Chaka Khan
1954   Moses Malone

March 24

1930   Beech Grove, Indiana.

Actor Steve McQueen, best remembered for his roles in *The Great Escape* (1963) and *Bullitt* (1968), was born. His pretty 19-year-old mother was Julian McQueen, who suffered from alcoholism. His father was Terrence William McQueen, who abandoned the family shortly after Steve's birth. The boy proved too much for Julian, so she turned him over to his great-grand-uncle, Claude Thompson, a reserved but kind man. Unfortunately, Julian insisted on later reclaiming her son, removing him from a stable home.

Julian dated a series of men who abused Steve. When she remarried, her son was in the way, but instead of returning him to Thompson, she sent the child to a home for wayward boys, which was essentially a reform school. Like a Dickensian character, McQueen was often left alone at the school over holidays.

Eventually, Julian again reclaimed her son and this time moved him to Greenwich Village. By then, McQueen had become interested in acting, and, despite the encumbrance of his alcoholic mother, he succeeded. His first movie lead was in the classic horror movie *The Blob* (1958). The lead in the television series *Wanted: Dead or Alive* made him a star. Ironically, one of the show's fans was McQueen's father, who wondered whether the actor was his son but never pursued the question. In 1959, McQueen began looking for his father. Unfortunately, McQueen's mother had never liked the name Terry and had rechristened her former husband Bill, after his middle name. When McQueen finally tracked down Terry, he had been dead for three months. This incident fed McQueen's disgust with his mother. Nevertheless, when she died in 1965, he felt great guilt over failing to reconcile with her.

Howard Koch said of McQueen, "Early in his life he developed a toughness and a calculated determination, first perhaps for survival, later for his professional ambitions.... And the arrogance which motivates some of his actions is mitigated by the charm of that quick half-smile which assures us that, at bottom, he is a 'good guy.'"

Other Birthdays
1874   Harry Houdini
1887   Fatty Arbuckle
1954   Robert Caradine
1970   Lara Flynn Boyle

March 25

1920   On this historic date, in the community of Winston-Salem, North Carolina, an epoch-making event transpired that set to naught all the other events of that day. Howard Cosell was born.

The son of Polish-Jewish immigrants, Cosell was raised in Brooklyn, New York. He claims to have started talking at nine months, and many of his nonfans claim he never stopped. Cosell observed of his parents, "They didn't give me looks, but they gave me an absolute monopoly on brains and talent." Cosell used these gifts to earn a law degree at New York University. It was as a lawyer in 1953 that Cosell got into broadcasting. ABC radio employed him to host a panel of Little League baseball players to interview professional athletes. He did so well that ABC hired him as a sports commentator.

Cosell adopted a flowery, egocentric, machine-gun style that didn't please everyone. Joe Namath observed, "He's the kind of guy who, when he meets someone, says very loudly, 'This must be a great day for you—meeting me.'" Frank Gifford, who worked with Cosell for years on *Monday Night Football,* remarked, "Howard was like the little girl with the little curl in the nursery rhyme: When he was good, he was very, very good, and when he was bad, he was horrid. By and large, Howard and I had a great time together (even though you couldn't tell that from the way he bad-mouthed me in the ABC hallways and carved me up in his books)....Most of all Howard was funny—sometimes when he tried to be. If we sat together on an airplane, he'd summon the stewardess and intone: 'Young lady, would you bring this man a cocktail along with your phone number? You are about to become blessed among women. This man has stupendous sexual prowess.' I can't count the number of times I felt like a piece of luggage that was too big to fit under the seat."

Other Birthdays
1934   Gloria Steinem
1940   Anita Bryant
1942   Aretha Franklin
1947   Elton John
1965   Sarah Jessica Parker

March 26

1931   Boston.

Actor and director Leonard Nimoy, famed for playing Spock on television's *Star Trek,* was born, the second son of Russian-Jewish immigrants. His father was a hard-working barber who spent years giving 75¢ haircuts. Nimoy's parents wanted better for their sons. Nimoy's older brother obligingly went to college and became a successful engineer, but Nimoy took a different path. Frustrated with his mundane life, he scraped together train fare to Los Angeles and left home at 18 to become an actor. His folks weren't happy. Nimoy says, "They didn't want me to be an actor. That was the worst thing I could possibly do. My folks didn't sneak across the borders of Russia into Poland and make their way to the United States in order for their kid to be a bum....They wanted me to be a doctor or lawyer...hang out a shingle."

Their fears must have seemed well-founded at first. Nimoy wasn't an instant sensation in Hollywood. He spent fifteen years playing character roles, such as a green Martian in the 1952 low-budget movie serial *Zombies of the Stratosphere*, before Gene Roddenberry offered him the role of Spock after seeing him play a military cadet on the television show *The Lieutenant* (Martin Landau and DeForest Kelley were also considered for the role). Nimoy was interested in Spock's inner struggle between his logical and emotional sides but was concerned about being typecast as an oddball. When he asked Roddenberry why Spock needed pointed ears, Roddenberry replied that he wanted the viewers to be reminded every time they saw Spock's ears that the cast were in an interplanetary situation. Nimoy accepted the role and became a cultural icon.

The character wasn't without controversy, though. NBC network officials thought a pointy-eared, greenish alien who resembled Satan would alienate advertisers in the Bible Belt, so, in the initial publicity photos, Spock's ears were airbrushed to remove the points. After the sponsors were lined up, the points went back on.

Nimoy's parents were pleased with his success. Of his father, Nimoy says, "He never acted like he knew the first thing about what *Star Trek* was about. [He would say] 'I don't know. People like it. I don't know what it is.'" Nevertheless, he proudly kept a picture of his son as Spock in his barber shop and, when kids saw it and asked for a Spock haircut, he happily obliged—still for just 75¢.

Other Birthdays
1874   Robert Frost
1911   Tennessee Williams
1930   Sandra Day O'Connor

1934   Alan Arkin
1939   James Caan
1942   Erica Jong
1950   Martin Short
1957   Leeza Gibbons
1960   Marcus Allen
1960   Jennifer Grey

March 27

1924   Newark, New Jersey.

Jazz singer Sarah Vaughan was born. Her parents loved music and happily provided Vaughan with piano lessons. She soon joined her mother in the Mount Zion Baptist Church choir. When Vaughan turned 18, she entered the raucaus, weekly amateur contest at Harlem's Apollo Theater on a dare. She sang "Body and Soul." Pianist and bandleader Earl Hines witnessed the performance and said, "She just came out there cool as a cucumber, never moved a muscle, and just sang." Vaughan won the contest. Hines hired her to sing with his band. She performed with them through the 1940s, then went solo. Her first hit was "It's Magic," recorded in 1947.

Vaughan received many rave reviews and compliments, but the best probably came from Frank Sinatra. He said, "Sassy sings so good, I want to cut my wrist with a dull blade, and let her sing me to death."

Other Birthdays
1899   Gloria Swanson
1931   David Janssen
1939   Judy Carne
1942   Michael York
1970   Mariah Carey

March 28

1955   Chockie, Oklahoma.

Singer Reba McEntire was born. McEntire learned rodeo barrel-riding from her father, Clark McEntire, a rancher and rodeo steer-roper. She learned to sing from her mother, Jacqueline McEntire, a teacher and singer. McEntire gave her first money-making performance at age five. Her family was following the rodeo circuit and had stopped in Cheyenne, Wyoming. McEntire saw her brother earn a nickel singing for a tourist. She promptly launched into a rendition of "Jesus Loves Me," earning her own nickel. She went on to work her way through college singing.

In 1974, McEntire sang "The Star-Spangled Banner" at the National Rodeo Finals in Oklahoma City. Her performance attracted the interest of a songwriter. Within a year, she had made a demo tape and signed a recording contract. In 1980, she scored her first hit with "(You Lift Me) Up to Heaven." McEntire has won twenty-eight major country western awards, including two Grammys.

McEntire credits her parents for her success, saying, "My parents taught us responsibility early. Once, my sister Alice came in so late Daddy was already up cooking breakfast. He waited until she got sound asleep and then woke her up, told her he needed help with the cattle that day, and he worked her butt off."

Other Birthdays
1868   Maxim Gorki
1914   Edmund Muskie
1921   Dirk Bogarde
1924   Freddie Bartholomew

March 29

1918   Kingfisher, Oklahoma.
Billionaire merchant Sam Walton was born. After getting an economics degree, he went to work for J. C. Penney. When he felt confident of his retail skills, he bought a Ben Franklin franchise in Newport, Arkansas. He managed it well, opening fifteen more stores with his brother. In 1962, he opened the

first Wal-Mart. His strategy was simple. Walton knew that rural customers had few shopping choices. Walton aggressively placed large stores carrying a wide variety of cheap goods into rural markets. In twenty years, he owned close to 2,000 stores.

Walton personally inspected his stores and offered profit sharing to his employees. He did everything he could to encourage his workers to excel. For example, in 1983, he promised to dance in a grass skirt on Wall Street if they exceeded a profits goal. They did and Walton did the hula for an audience of stockbrokers.

Other Birthdays
1790   John Tyler
1859   Oscar Mayer
1867   Cy Young
1878   Albert Von Tilzer, composer of "Take Me Out to the Ball Game"
1916   Eugene J. McCarthy
1917   Man O' War
1918   Pearl Bailey
1937   Billy Carter
1943   Eric Idle
1943   John Major
1963   Hammer
1976   Jennifer Capriati

March 30

1937   Richmond, Virginia.

Warren Beatty was born to psychology professor Ira Owens Beaty and Kathlyn MacLean Beaty (Warren added the second *t* when he became an actor), who raised him in Arlington, Virginia. Warren's sister, who is three years older than he, is Shirley MacLaine. Beatty was an athletically and intellectually gifted kid, becoming both captain of the football team and class president. He left Northwestern University after just one year, however, to pursue a career in acting. After a few roles on the stage, Beatty got a contract with MGM, but this led nowhere until film director Elia Kazan cast him in *Splendor in the Grass* (1961). Beatty became a star. He also became an infamous womanizer.

Shirley MacLaine observed of her brother, "The difference between us is sex. I can take it or leave it. But my kid brother... Sex is the most important thing in his life. It's his hobby, you could say."

Other Birthdays
1880   Sean O'Casey
1930   John Astin
1930   Peter Marshall
1945   Eric Clapton
1957   Paul Reiser

March 31

1927   Near Yuma, Arizona.

Farm labor organizer Cesar Chavez was born. He was one of five children. His Mexican-American parents were poor migrant workers who had lost their farm during the Depression. On a good day, they could earn 50¢. Chavez attended sixty-five elementary schools as a child. Still, he finished high school. He was picking apricots near San Jose when a labor organizer recruited him into the labor movement. Chavez became head of the United Farm Workers. His presidency was highlighted by the successful grape boycott of 1970. Undoubtedly, the low point occurred when he purged all non-Hispanics from the UFW leadership.

Chavez once said of his efforts to improve life for migrant workers, "For many years I was a farm worker and, well, personally—and I'm being very frank—maybe it's just a matter of trying to even the score."

Other Birthdays
1929   Liz Claiborne
1934   Shirley Jones
1935   Richard Chamberlain
1948   Albert Gore
1948   Rhea Perlman

April 1

1905   Elizabeth City, North Carolina.

Clara Hale, better known as Mother Hale, was born. Orphaned at 16, widowed at 27, she cleaned houses and theaters in New York City to support her four children, then turned to raising foster children. She raised forty before retiring at 63. Hale's retirement didn't last long. Her daughter Lorraine Hale was passing through a poor neighborhood when she saw a drug-addicted woman drop her two-month-old infant. Lorraine persuaded the woman to give her the baby and Hale took it in. Word spread that Hale was taking in babies free of charge. Soon, dozens of drug-addicted babies were left with her. With no training, Hale achieved a 90 percent success rate at getting the drug-affected children through childhood. Hale said, "We hold them and touch them. They love you to tell them how great they are, how good they are. Somehow, even at a young age, they understand that. They're happy, and they turn out well."

One might have expected New York City authorities to do everything they could to help Hale. They did just the opposite, harassing her with red tape. It was only after Hale became a celebrity (Ronald Reagan cited her in his 1985 State of the Union address for her work with AIDS-infected children) that she had enough clout to keep the bureaucrats at bay.

1932   El Paso, Texas.

Mary Frances Reynolds was born to Maxene and Ray Reynolds. Mary's father, a railroad carpenter, moved to California looking for work. He went hungry and slept on benches before he could afford to send for his family. Nevertheless, this was probably the best place in the world to bring his daughter.

Mary Reynolds loved singing and played the French horn in her high school band. At 16, she entered the Miss Burbank beauty contest. One of the judges was impressed by the way she applauded for the other contestants, then was further impressed by Reynolds's performance. She danced and lip-synched to a popular Betty Hutton recording. When her borrowed high heels proved too tight, instead of quitting, she gamely continued barefoot, winning the contest. The impressed judge was a talent scout for Warner Brothers Studio. He signed Mary Reynolds and changed her name to Debbie Reynolds.

Unfortunately, Reynolds's first film was a disaster, and Warner's dropped her. However, the film made it easier for her to obtain a contract with MGM. Reynolds's big break came when she appeared in MGM's *Two Weeks With Love* (1950), in which she sang the novelty song "Abba Dabba Honeymoon." It sold 2 million copies and led to her costarring role in *Singin' in the Rain* (1952).

Other Birthdays
1815   Otto von Bismarck
1883   Lon Chaney
1886   Wallace Beery
1939   Ali MacGraw

April 2

1805   Odense, Denmark.

Hans Christian Andersen was born to Anne Marie and Hans Andersen. Anne Marie was illiterate and had had a miserable childhood. Andersen said, "When she was little, her parents had hounded her out to beg, and when she couldn't do that, she had spent a whole day sitting weeping under a bridge. My childish imagination saw that so distinctly that I wept over it too."

Anne Marie was a superstitiously devout Christian, while Andersen's father, a cobbler, questioned Christian precepts, including the existence of the Devil. When he came to breakfast one morning with scratches on his arms, Anne Marie was certain the Devil had tormented him during the night to prove that he existed. Anne Marie must have thought it a judgment when he went insane and died when Hans was 11 years old.

Andersen's mother labored as a washerwoman until she married a second cobbler. Andersen worked in a cloth factory to help out. He sang while he worked, until his work mates pulled down his pants to see if he was a girl. At 14, he tied together a bundle of clothing and left for Copenhagen, where his singing won him the patronage of an Italian opera singer and the director of the Dutch Royal Theater. Andersen studied music and dance, and started writing. At 17, he published his first story. Two unremarkable books followed before Andersen published a very successful book of fairy tales. He went on to write nearly 200 fairy tales, including "The Ugly Duckling" and "The Emperor's New Clothes."

After Andersen left home, his mother's second husband died. Andersen sent her money, but she used it to soothe herself with drink. She died in 1834. Andersen said, "Although I should never be able to make her last days bright and carefree, she had died in the happy belief of my good fortune, that I was *someone*."

Andersen had only one encounter with his mother's family.

When he was a small boy, he was sent to visit his aunts in Copenhagen. The boy didn't understand why they were reluctant to see him until much later, when he realized that they were running a bordello. It was an ironic incident, for unlike his entrepreneurial relatives, Andersen died a virgin.

Andersen once observed, "Every man's life is a fairy tale written by God's fingers."

Other Birthdays
1908   Buddy Ebsen
1914   Alec Guinness
1920   Jack Webb
1945   Linda Hunt
1948   Emmylou Harris
1955   Dana Carvey

April 3

1961   Brooklyn, New York.

Comedian Eddie Murphy was born. His father was a New York City cop who moonlighted as a comic. He died when Murphy was eight. Murphy's mother remarried and he was raised in a prosperous neighborhood on Long Island. Murphy first felt the thrill of entertaining in the third grade. He says, "I had a potbelly, brown frame glasses, and a bald head. One day, Mr. Wunch came into class and said that whoever made up the best story would win an Eskimo Pie....It was my first performance. And guess who won the pie!" By the time he was 20, Murphy was performing on *Saturday Night Live*.

Other Birthdays
1924   Marlon Brando
1924   Doris Day
1934   Jane Goodall
1942   Wayne Newton
1944   Tony Orlando
1958   Alec Baldwin

April 4

1908   Greensboro, North Carolina.

Edward R. Murrow was born to Roscoe and Ethel Murrow. He was raised in Washington, where his father worked as an engineer for a logging company. After college, Murrow worked for an international student organization, then became a foreign correspondent for CBS radio. His reports from London during World War II set the standard for broadcast journalism. Journalist David Halberstam said of Murrow: "The right man in the right place...a rare figure, as good as his legend." Murrow advised Charles Kuralt, "Just because you speak in a voice loud enough to be heard over television by 16 million people, that doesn't make you any smarter than you were when you spoke loudly enough to be heard only at the other end of the bar."

The *R* in Edward R. Murrow stood for Roscoe, but Murrow's first name was originally Egbert. He so hated having his brothers call him Egg that he changed his name to Edward.

Other Birthdays
1915   Muddy Waters
1932   Anthony Perkins
1946   Craig T. Nelson
1965   Robert Downey Jr.

April 5

1900   Milwaukee, Wisconsin.

Spencer Tracy was born. While Carrie Tracy gave prayerful thanks for her second son, her husband, John Tracy, bought the house a drink in every Irish saloon in town. Spencer Tracy's boyhood was troubled. He tried to burn down the house after an argument with his father. He loved fighting and wandered from neighborhood to neighborhood looking for opponents.

Because of truancy, bad behavior, and poor performance, he went through fifteen schools before finishing the eighth grade. He later said he only went to school so that he could learn to read movie subtitles. One day, he met Pat O'Brien, who wanted to be an actor. Although Tracy thought acting sissified, O'Brien convinced him that an actor's life was lucrative and fulfilling, but it would be years before either did anything about their dream.

Tracy entered Milwaukee's Marquette Academy because O'Brien attended. Tracy did well, but, when the United States entered World War I, he enlisted in the U.S. Navy, with his brother and O'Brien. The war wasn't very interesting for Tracy; he never got sea duty. After the war, Tracy attended Ripon College. Because of his naval service, Tracy was older than the other students. The drama teacher, looking for mature-appearing actors, cast him in a play. Tracy discovered that he had a talent for acting and proceeded to exploit it. For a public speaking course, he delivered an emotional description of the brief, tragic life of his sister. He had his class in tears, despite the fact that the "sister" was entirely fictional. Tracy joined the debating team and, during a debating tour, auditioned for New York's American Academy of Dramatic Arts. He was immediately invited to attend. Amazingly, he discovered that his friend O'Brien had also been accepted.

Tracy and O'Brien roomed together in a cheap apartment, subsisting on meager veterans' benefits. Tracy got them their first roles in a production of Karel Capek's *R.U.R.* Tracy and O'Brien played robots. The pair then went on to join different traveling theater groups. Tracy married the leading lady of his first company, and they had a baby boy. They named him John, after Tracy's father. Tragically, the boy was born deaf. According to Jimmy Cagney, Tracy somehow blamed himself for his child's handicap. Tracy went on a savage bender. There were many more over the years. His son's handicap also caused Tracy to buckle down. He worked hard to become a better actor. As anyone who has seen his movies can affirm, he became a very good one, indeed.

Tracy's long-time companion Katharine Hepburn observed, "He never gussied it up. He just did it, he let it ride along on its enormous simplicity. That's what was absolutely thrilling about Spencer's acting." Tracy observed of the lean days before he became successful, "There were times my pants were so thin I could sit on a dime and tell if it was heads or tails."

1908   Lowell, Massachusetts.

Bette Davis was born. Lowell was populated mainly by textile mill workers, but the Davis family were not blue-collar types. Bette's upper-class father, Harlow Morrell Davis, graduated from Harvard Law School and became a well-to-do patent lawyer. Bette's mother, Ruth Favor Davis, was also a blue blood. Both parents could trace their families back to the Pilgrims. Indeed, there was even a Salem witch cackling from one of the family tree's more crooked branches.

While Harlow was dispassionate, Ruth was emotional. When Ruth became pregnant with Bette just after their marriage, Harlow wanted her to have an abortion because he was still in school and couldn't afford a child. Ruth refused. A second daughter, Barbara, was soon added to the family. Harlow treated Ruth and the children with cold hostility. Soon, Harlow and Ruth divorced.

Although Harlow became a wealthy attorney, Ruth received little alimony. She turned her hand to any work she could find and bitterly taught her daughters to distrust men. Barbara, whom Ruth neglected when she discovered that Bette had more talent, developed mental problems, failed at whatever work she tried, and never married happily. Bette, whom Ruth pushed into show business, became aggressive and self-involved. Although Bette succeeded professionally, winning Academy Awards for Best Actress for *Dangerous* (1935) and *Jezebel* (1938), and performing in such classics as *All About Eve* (1950) and *Petrified Forest* (1936), she was divorced four times, and her own daughter grew distant and wrote a severely critical book, *My Mother's Keeper*, about Bette's poor mothering. Bette said, late in life, "I always knew I would end up an old woman alone on a hill."

Other Birthdays
1871   Pop Warner
1916   Gregory Peck
1934   Frank Gorshin
1941   Michael Moriarty

April 6

1937   Bakersfield, California.

Merle Haggard was born. His parents were poor farm laborers who lived in a converted boxcar. Haggard's father, who played fiddle, died when Haggard was nine. Haggard reacted badly. At 10, he hopped a freight train. He was brought home, but ran away again and again. Haggard says, "I was a pretty wild kid. I love excitement. I'm not proud of what I did. I wouldn't recommend it to anyone else, but I do believe I benefited from my experiences."

At 14, Haggard was jailed for suspicion of armed robbery. By 17, he had spent two years in reform school. At 21, he had been sentenced to three years in San Quentin after an unsuccessful burglary. He'd been so drunk at the time that he had burglarized a nightclub that was still open. After prison, Haggard became an electrician's helper, playing guitar at the local country club on the side. In 1963, he recorded "All of My Friends Are Gonna Be Strangers." It became a top ten hit, launching Haggard's country western career. In 1969, he recorded "Okie From Muskogee," which firmly positioned him as a star.

Haggard credits his parents for his success: "My folks always told me how happy they were the day I was born. They may not have had much money, but they sure had lots of love to give."

Other Birthdays
1937   Billy Dee Williams
1944   Michelle Phillips
1947   John Ratzenberger
1952   Marilu Henner

April 7

1915   Baltimore, Maryland.

Eleanora Fagan Holiday was born. She later wrote, "Mom and Pop were just a couple of kids when they got married. He was 18, she was 16, and I was three." Holiday's father was a poorly paid guitarist who passed his love of music on to his daughter. He nicknamed her Bill, which she altered to Billie after her favorite movie star, Billie Dove.

Billie Holiday certainly could have used some film fantasy in her life, which was filled with horrible incidents. She shared a bed with her great-grandmother in the Holiday home. One night, the old lady affectionately wrapped an arm around Holiday, then died. By the time the girl awoke, the woman's grip had stiffened, and Holiday couldn't shake loose. The corpse's arm had to be broken to free Billie. Then, at 10, Holiday was raped by a neighbor. Somehow, a judge decided that this was a reason to send Holiday to a reform school. When she returned to her family, she began running errands for a brothel and not long after joined the profession herself. She was arrested and imprisoned. After her release, Holiday tried earning money singing. Her first venues were slummy, but her voice won her better bookings. In time, she was performing in concert with such jazz legends as Benny Goodman, Artie Shaw, and Count Basie.

Unfortunately, the pressures of show business and her horrific background proved too much for Holiday. She died in 1959 of heart and liver disease induced by drug abuse.

Other Birthdays
1897   Walter Winchell

1928   James Garner
1939   Francis Ford Coppola
1960   Buster Douglas

April 8

1912   Oslo, Norway.

Champion figure skater Sonja Henie was born. Her parents were Selma and Hans Wilhelm Henie, a prosperous wholesale fur merchant and one-time champion bicyclist. Thanks to their support, Henie got an early start on a successful life. In 1918, she received a pair of skates for her birthday. Henie, who was already receiving dance lessons from a former teacher of the legendary ballerina Anna Pavlova, showed great aptitude for skating. Her parents hired tutors and by the time Henie was eight, she was the children's figure skating champ of Oslo. At nine, she was the Norwegian national champ in her age group. At 10, her parents sent her to London to study with the famed Russian ballerina Karsavina. At 12, Henie won an Olympic bronze medal in free-skating competition. She went on to win gold medals in the 1928, 1932, and 1936 Olympics. She was also world champion for the years 1927 to 1936. Her graceful skating style, heavily influenced by ballet, became the standard.

In 1936, Henie made an exhibition tour of the United States. Her father, who had become her manager, arranged for movie mogul Darryl F. Zanuck of Twentieth Century-Fox to see Henie skate. He gave her a five-year movie contract. Her first film, *One in a Million* (1936), was a hit. Henie made ten successful films before leaving the movies to form her own ice show. Her private life wasn't entirely romantically successful, but was financially rewarding. Henie married three times, each time to a millionaire.

In later years, Henie skated for exercise but didn't perform. She explained, "The ice is so much colder these days."

Other Birthdays
1918   Betty Ford
1963   Julian Lennon

April 9

1926   Chicago.

Hugh Marston Hefner was born. His father was a minister who gave him an ordinary Midwestern upbringing. When Hefner was rebuffed by his female schoolmates because of his unimpressive appearance, he "reinvented" himself by changing his hair, clothing, and manner. His new image won him friends. The rejection Hefner suffered may also have raised the importance of success with women for him—his life eventually centered on pursuing them.

After high school, Hefner spent two years in the U.S. Army. Upon his discharge, he worked as a clerk, then earned a bachelor's degree in psychology from the University of Illinois. Hefner married his high school sweetheart and had two children, then went to work for *Esquire* magazine, where he earned $60 a week. He seemed destined for a modest white-collar existence, but when his request for a $25 weekly raise was refused, he quit and, with a few hundred dollars, set up *Playboy*.

Hefner purchased the rights to some nude photographs of Marilyn Monroe. With these for his centerfold, the magazine was a success. Hefner built a $200 million fortune. In 1959, he divorced his wife, but kept in touch with his children. His daughter Christine now runs his corporation. Hefner has changed as he has aged. He has remarried and is busy with his second family.

Hefner once philosophised, "If a man has a right to find God in his own way, he has a right to go to the Devil in his own way also."

Other Birthdays
1929   Michael Learned

1933   Jean-Paul Belmondo
1954   Dennis Quaid

April 10

1903 New York City.

Clare Boothe Luce was born. A prominent conservative, Luce was an advocate of women's rights. She said of her chorus girl mother, "My mother threw a brick through a window on Fifth Avenue during the first suffrage rage. And she was very proud because she was taken to the station house with a number of other women and very disappointed when she wasn't put in jail. Many people consider that she was the most unladylike creature. I think I inherited my own views on the freedom of women quite naturally." Luce's father was a violinist who deserted his family when Luce was nine, leaving them in a precarious financial state. Luce's mother chose a wealthy man for her second husband and instructed her daughter in the importance of money in marriage.

During World War I, Luce attended a posh finishing school, where a suffragette teacher drilled her students in uniform. The teacher told Luce, "Clare, I think you will go far. You have talent and so on. But always remember only two things you need: confidence in yourself and confidence in God and *She* will protect you." After graduation, Luce went into politics at 18. She appeared in newsreels in goggles and flying togs, tossing handbills from a biplane for the National Women's Party.

Despite her feminist views, Luce tried to be a conventional wife when her mother arranged her marriage to George Tuttle Brokaw in 1923. The marriage didn't work—they divorced in 1929—but Luce received a large settlement that allowed her to pursue literary interests. She became a journalist for *Vogue*, then for *Vanity Fair*. In 1935, she married wealthy publisher Henry Robinson Luce and turned to playwriting. Her best effort was the 1936 play *The Women*, which became a classic film. Luce served as a Republican member of Congress during the 1940s. In the 1950s, she became ambassador to Italy. She continued to be a force in conservative journalism till her death in 1987.

Luce observed of the Democratic Party, "Its leaders are always troubadours of trouble; crooners of catastrophe.... A Democratic President is doomed to proceed to his goals like a squid, squirting darkness all about him." Of men, she said, "A man's home may seem to be his castle on the outside; inside, it is more often his nursery."

Other Birthdays
1921 Chuck Connors
1929 Max von Sydow
1932 Omar Sharif
1936 John Madden
1938 Don Meredith
1951 Steven Seagal

April 11

1913 Paris.

Oleg Loiewski-Cassini was born to Countess Marguerite Cassini and Count Alexander Loiewski, an Imperial Russian diplomatic attaché. They brought their son home to Russia to raise. The young Oleg was to become a nobleman, but, in 1917, the Russian Revolution changed his future. After seeing a teenaged cousin hauled out of his house and shot by the Communists for the crime of being a military cadet, Cassini's family fled Russia, leaving their wealth behind.

Oleg described his father as a dandy. His mother was also fashion-conscious. Oleg's maternal grandfather had been the Czar's ambassador to the United States. His mother had been his hostess in Washington, D.C. A trendsetter and a friend of Alice Roosevelt, she designed her own dresses, spoke six languages, smoked cigarettes in public, was one of the first women to win an auto race, and was much admired by the young Franklin Roosevelt. She found the handsome Count Loiewski more suitable and married him. They had two sons.

When Loiewski returned to Russia to fight for the Czar, Oleg's mother was left alone for a year to support her sons. She opened a boutique in Switzerland and shared a house with another dispossessed aristocratic couple. When Oleg's father rejoined them following the failure of Czarist forces, he wasn't much help. He fantasized about destroying the Bolsheviks and refused to accept employment he deemed beneath him while insisting on luxuries. The family moved to Florence, where Cassini's mother opened a second, successful boutique.

The Countess gave her sons lessons in every aristocratic art and sport. She even hired an ex-colonel of the Imperial Guard to tutor Oleg in gentlemanly conduct. He instructed Oleg: "Your clothes and appearance are crucial to your position in the world—but, equally important, when you are well-dressed, you *feel* better, more confident and assured about yourself."

Cassini worked for his mother, designing clothing. In the 1930s, her boutique failed and anti-foreign sentiment in Italy made life unpleasant. On the way home from a dinner party, police arrested Cassini for not carrying identity papers and held him for three days in a cell so filthy that he stood the entire time. To rescue the family's finances and secure their social position, Cassini reconciled himself to marrying a beautiful heiress. When the couple and a chaperoned group of friends were to go on a ski trip, however, Cassini's heiress couldn't attend. A lovely brunette could. Cassini persuaded her to nocturnally visit his hotel room several times. These trips weren't as discreet as they should have been. A gossip quickly spread the scandal. Cassini lost his heiress, became a social outcast, and wisely decided to try new surroundings. He left for America.

Cassini's aristocratic background and talent made him a great success in the United States. He became a costume designer in Hollywood, then a renowned couturier with celebrity clients. The most notable of these was Jacqueline Kennedy. It was Cassini who put the pill box hat on her head.

Other Birthdays
1932   Joel Grey
1939   Louise Lasser
1964   Bret Saberhagen

April 12

1947   Indianapolis, Indiana.

David Letterman was born to florist Joseph Letterman and his wife, Dorothy. The couple also had two daughters. Letterman's family lived in Broad Ripple, a suburb of Indianapolis with a small-town atmosphere. Letterman says, "The house I grew up in was nuts because I was there. I was a maniac.... I was always picking fights, starting trouble. I don't think there was a single meal where my mother didn't have to say, 'All right, David. If you can't behave, take your plate and eat outside.'"

Of his career choice, Letterman says, "I couldn't do math, I couldn't learn German. So instead of college courses, I was getting put into things like *general merchandising*. Then one day I realized, 'I'm just as smart as my friends. But while they're studying calculus, I'm sittin' here reading a book about how to make a pleasing display of canned goods.' So I took a class in speech and just loved it. I thought, 'Wait a minute: I can actually get a grade here, just standing up and telling stories?' That was real insight to me. So I thought, 'How do you apply this?' And when I found out you could study broadcasting in college, I thought, 'Holy cow! There you go! It's a miracle! What's next?' And what was next was figuring out how to get on the radio."

After attending Ball State University, where he was fired from a disc jockey job on the college radio station for making up humorous biographies for classical composers, Letterman became a television weatherman. He sprinkled his forecasts with glib humor, describing hail as being as big as "canned hams." The ham comment, reportedly, got him fired. He then became a radio disc jockey. A friend recalls how he and Letterman would get together to watch Johnny Carson's *The Tonight Show*. Letterman remarked that he could do better punchlines.

In 1975, Letterman moved to Los Angeles, where he tried stand-up comedy. Letterman's friend Jay Leno introduced him to Jimmy Walker, who hired Letterman as a writer. Bob Hope and Paul Lynde also bought his material. Letterman got a job with Mary Tyler Moore's CBS variety show *Mary*. When that show folded, Letterman returned to stand-up. An appearance on Johnny Carson's *The Tonight Show* led to an invitation to substitute host. Letterman did so with such success that he was given his own morning talk show in New York City. This failed, but, in 1982, after Tom Snyder's *Tomorrow* show was canceled, network executives gave him *Late Night With David Letterman*. In 1993, a contretemps with NBC after the retirement of Johnny Carson and a massive salary offer drew Letterman to CBS, where his Emmy-winning *Late Show* became the victor in the late night wars.

Despite becoming a big-time show biz celebrity, Letterman corresponds regularly with hometown friends and has quietly helped many of his past neighbors. He also funded a scholarship for *C* students at his alma mater, Ball State.

Letterman has remarked, "I just keep waiting for someone to tap me on the shoulder and say, 'Okay, buddy, give us the money back.'"

Other Birthdays
1922   Tiny Tim
1946   Ed O'Neill
1950   David Cassidy
1956   Andy Garcia
1971   Shannen Doherty

April 13

1743 Shadwell, in the foothills of Virginia's Blue Ridge Mountains.

Thomas Jefferson, author of the Declaration of Independence and the third president of the United States was born to Peter Jefferson, a prosperous planter, and Jane Randolph Jefferson, a member of an aristocratic family. Thomas was their firstborn. They had seven more children, of whom two died in infancy. Jefferson's father was hardworking but had a yen for politics that kept him away from home. Jefferson's mother was left behind. As their home was on the frontier, she was in some danger of Indian attack. In 1757, Peter Jefferson's hopes for political success ended when he suddenly died.

Peter Jefferson left his family provided for, but perhaps the anxiety of raising a family on her own made his wife unpleasantly stern. In later years, Thomas Jefferson, while expressing interest in the well-being of his siblings, showed little interest in his mother's welfare. She died in 1776 and never saw her son's success.

Jefferson served as vice president before becoming president. One day, he was traveling unattended through Baltimore. When he dismounted at a tavern to secure a room for the night, the tavern keeper thought the dusty Jefferson was some common farmer and turned him away brusquely. Later, someone told the tavern keeper who Jefferson was. He sent a servant after Jefferson to explain and beg him to return. Jefferson replied, "Tell him that I value his good intentions highly, but if he has no room for a dirty farmer he shall have none for the Vice President."

Other Birthdays
1873 Theodore Morse, who wrote the song "M-O-T-H-E-R"
1909 Eudora Welty
1919 Madalyn Murray O'Hair
1945 Tony Dow
1970 Rick Schroder

April 14

1935   Butcher Hollow, Kentucky.

Loretta Lynn was born the second of eight children of a coal miner who died of black lung disease. Lynn purchased a Sears Roebuck guitar when she was very young. After teaching herself to play, she began writing country western songs. At 13, Lynn married moonshiner Oliver "Mooney" Lynn Jr. Lynn became a mother within a year (she had her first grandchild before she was 30). Mooney went from radio station to radio station trying to convince disc jockeys to play Lynn's recordings. Eventually, he succeeded and Lynn became a regular on Nashville's *Grand Ole Opry*. In the 1970s, she and Conway Twitty became country music's top duo. Loretta and Mooney Lynn went on to have a total of five children (one died) and fourteen grandchildren.

Lynn once said, "If you have heard that there is a woman in your man's life, if you don't know for sure, you can live with it. But if you know for sure, you can't live with it. So I don't want to know for sure. I just go on guessing and singing about it."

Other Birthdays
1904   John Gielgud
1925   Rod Steiger
1941   Julie Christie
1941   Pete Rose

April 15

1874   Blenheim Castle.

Lord Randolph Churchill and his Brooklyn-born wife, Jenny Jerome Churchill, had their first child, Winston Churchill. The boy was born seven months prematurely after their wedding because of an "imprudent" and jarring ride Lady Churchill took in a pony cart. Lord Randolph's father, the Duke of Marlborough, initially refused to give his permission for his son to marry Jenny. Fanny, the Duchess of Marlborough, also disliked her. It hadn't helped matters that Lord Randolph had proposed just three days after meeting Jenny. She later wrote that British aristocrats considered an American woman "a strange and abnormal creature with habits and manner something between a Red Indian and a Gaiety Girl." The Duke permitted the marriage only after Lord Randolph promised to follow the Duke's wishes and enter politics.

In keeping with British aristocratic custom, young Churchill was raised by a nanny and dispatched to a boarding school as soon as possible. Despite this treatment, or perhaps *because* of the glamorizing distance it imposed, the boy was devoted to his mother, and she, in turn, doted on him when he was home on holidays. Lord Randolph, however, was a remote father. Churchill could remember only one close conversation with him. Their relationship was further marred when Lord Randolph began to lose his mind due to syphilis. The disease eventually killed him. Churchill followed his father into politics after an adventurous career in journalism.

Churchill said of his mother, "My mother made a brilliant impression upon my childhood life. She shone for me like the evening star—I loved her dearly, but at a distance."

Other Birthdays
1452 Leonardo da Vinci
1894 Bessie Smith
1933 Roy Clark
1933 Elizabeth Montgomery
1951 Heloise B. Reese, household-hinter Heloise

April 16

1867 Millville, near New Castle, Indiana.
Aviation pioneer Wilbur Wright was born. His brother, Orville was born on August 19, 1871, in Dayton, Ohio, where the family had moved. Their father was Bishop Milton Wright

of the United Brethren in Christ. Bishop Wright was a stern fellow. At a religious conference in Indiana in 1870, a college president addressed the assembly: "I believe we are coming into a time when we will see, for example, wonderful inventions. I believe men will fly through the air like birds." To this, Bishop Wright angrily replied: "This is heresy, this is blasphemy; I read in my Bible that flight is reserved for the angels. We will have no such talk here in my area."

Apparently the Wright brothers didn't listen. After receiving a brief education and setting up a bicycle shop in Dayton, they developed an interest in aviation. They took a methodical approach, reviewing all of the literature available and constructing a wind tunnel to test designs. On December 17, 1903, after Orville won a coin toss, he flew the first heavier-than-air flying machine, and Wilbur flew second.

The Wrights telegraphed their sister Katherine back in Dayton, Ohio: "SUCCESS FOUR FLIGHTS THURSDAY MORNING ALL AGAINST TWENTY-ONE MILE WIND STARTED FROM LEVEL WITH ENGINE POWER ALONE AVERAGE SPEED THROUGH AIR THIRTY-ONE MILES LONGEST 59 SECONDS INFORM PRESS HOME CHRISTMAS."

Katherine ran to the local newspaper office. She excitedly cornered the editor and showed him the telegram. He read it, then smiled and said, "Well, well, isn't it nice that they will be home for Christmas."

1889 London

Charlie Chaplin was born. His mother was singer Lily Harley. Lily had gone onto the stage as a teenager and, at 18, had eloped to Africa with a nobleman twice her age. Something about the nobleman or Africa disagreed with her, for she quickly returned to the English stage. In 1886, she married actor Charles Hill Chaplin. They had two sons, Sydney and Charlie, during their four-year marriage, which ended when Charlie's father left his family. At first, Lily's earnings kept the family in comfort, but when she lost her voice, the family wound up living in an attic. Charlie worked in a barbershop as a janitor while his brother, Sydney, delivered telegrams. Lily scratched out pennies sewing. She eventually developed mental problems, and the boys were sent to orphanages and workhouses during their mother's trips to institutions. Charlie went into vaudeville and, while touring in America, was spotted by movie producer Mack Sennett. It wasn't long before he was earning millions. Charlie used some of his money to bring his mother to America, where she received better treatment.

At the height of his fame, Chaplin impersonation contests were held around the world. As a joke, Chaplin entered one. He came in second.

Chaplin said in his later years, "Life is a tragedy when seen in close-up, but a comedy in long-shot."

Other Birthdays
1921   Peter Ustinov
1924   Henry Mancini
1935   Bobby Vinton
1947   Kareem Abdul Jabbar
1954   Ellen Barkin

April 17

1923   Dakota City, Iowa.

Harry Reasoner was born. His parents were schoolteachers, both of whom died when Reasoner was a teenager. They had hoped he would get a higher education, but Reasoner left college to serve in the army during World War II. After the war, he worked as a drama critic for the *Minnesota Times*. He was fired when he gave a bad review to a New York production touring Minnesota. He later observed, "The theory was that you couldn't criticize them or they'd stop coming." Reasoner took a stab at writing fiction, but when his novel, *Tell Me About Women*, did poorly, he turned to news reporting. CBS

News hired him as a radio broadcaster in 1956. He moved into television journalism, rising to become an anchor and one of the founding correspondents of *60 Minutes*.

Reasoner became known for his unaffected approach to his business. He said, "Journalism is a kind of profession, or craft, or racket, for people who never wanted to grow up and go out into the real world. If you're a good journalist, what you do is live a lot of things vicariously, and report them for other people who want to live vicariously."

Other Birthdays
1918   William Holden
1951   Olivia Hussey

April 18

1857   Near Kinsman, Ohio.

Clarence Darrow was born. With just a year of law school, he passed the Ohio bar exam, in 1878. After moving to Chicago, he became a junior law partner of John Peter Altgeld, who became governor of Illinois. Darrow first snagged headlines when he defended the Haymarket Riot bombers in 1887. Altgeld helped Darrow become a counsel for the city of Chicago, then an attorney for the Chicago and North Western Railway. Darrow abruptly left the railroad to defend Eugene V. Debs, president of the American Railway Union, who had been jailed for contempt of court during the Pullman strike of 1894. Darrow went on to defend in numerous high-profile cases, including the Leopold and Loeb thrill-killing and the Scopes "Monkey" Trial.

Darrow was known for his acerbic character. He said, "The first half of our lives is ruined by our parents and the second half by our children." The famed attorney also observed, "The trouble with law is lawyers."

Other Birthdays
1922   Barbara Hale

1946   Catfish Hunter
1946   Hayley Mills
1954   Rick Moranis
1963   Conan O'Brien

April 19

1935   Dagenham, Essex, England.

Five-foot-two entertainer Dudley Moore was born to a British Railways electrician and a secretary. Moore's left leg was shorter than his right, causing him to limp, which prompted classmates to christen him Hopalong. Moore compensated by developing a clownish sense of humor and by immersing himself in music. Educated at the Guildhall School of Music and Drama and at Oxford's Magdalen College, Moore toured with an orchestra before teaming up with fellow Oxfordians Peter Cook, Alan Bennett, and Jonathan Miller to create the comedy revue *Beyond the Fringe*. The offbeat revue was a hit. Moore and Cook left to perform on their own. They appeared on stage, recorded comedy albums, and made their first movie, *The Wrong Box* (1966). Moore went solo in the 1970s. The films *10* (1979) and *Arthur* (1981) were his biggest hits.

After the short Moore was romantically linked to statuesque Susan Anton, Joan Rivers quipped, "She has hickies on her knees."

Other Birthdays
1933   Jayne Mansfield
1933   Dick Sargent
1946   Tim Curry

April 20

1893   Bruchard, Nebraska.

Harold Clayton Lloyd, who would become famous as the bespectacled comic hanging from a clock face high above the street, was born to Elizabeth (Fraser) Lloyd and James Darsie

Lloyd, who went by the nickname Foxy. Foxy was a man of many occupations. He sold Singer Sewing Machines door-to-door, managed a hardware store, worked as a photographer, and ran a restaurant. His most frequent occupation was shoe salesman. Each career change usually caused a change in location. Harold spent his youth bouncing from small town to small town. One would think that this would cause him to dislike his father, but Harold was devoted to Foxy and disliked his mother. She seems to have been both jealous and scornful of her husband.

To help support his family, Harold mowed yards, stoked furnaces, sold newspapers, delivered telegrams, and peddled popcorn on trains. Because of these enterprises, he did poorly in school. One thing Harold did get from his mother was an interest in acting. Elizabeth had wanted to be an actress and she'd travel miles to see even a paltry show. She read Shakespeare to Harold to put him to sleep and encouraged him to put on plays for his friends.

Harold's first appearance onstage was arranged by his mother and his elder brother, Gaylord. Elizabeth had pushed Gaylord onto the stage, and now he got Harold a minor role in a production of *Macbeth*. Harold loved it.

At age 12, while living in Omaha, Harold met a real, big-time actor, John Lane Connor. Harold was fascinated by astronomy at the time. An astrologer had plastered her windows with charts of the planets and Harold was, along with a crowd, absorbed in examining them. When a fire engine came clattering down the street and the others went to watch the fire, Harold stayed put. Connor spotted him and wondered what kind of boy would prefer the solar system to a fire. They chatted, and Connor wound up boarding with the Lloyd family. Connor was a producer as well as an actor, and he soon was using Harold in his plays. The chance meeting on an Omaha street eventually led to Hollywood stardom for Harold Lloyd. His films include *Grandma's Boy* (1922), *Why Worry?* (1923), and his most famous film, *Safety Last* (1923), which included the hair-raising clockface scene.

Other Birthdays
1941   Ryan O'Neal
1949   Jessice Lange
1961   Don Mattingly

April 21

1926   England.

Queen Elizabeth II was born to Lady Elizabeth Angela-Marguerite Bowes-Lyon and Prince Albert, the second in line to the throne after Prince Edward. After meeting at a dance, Albert had decided he wanted Lady Elizabeth for his wife. Albert's father, King George V, told his son, "You'll be a lucky fellow if she accepts you." She did, and they were married in Westminster Abbey in 1923. Elizabeth was their first child. They had a second daughter, Margaret, in 1930, and lived a quiet life until Edward, who had become king, abdicated to marry Wallis Simpson. Albert became King George VI and young Elizabeth the heir to the throne.

Elizabeth and her sister were raised by their Scots governess, Miss Marion Crawford. During World War II, their parents sent them to the country, away from the bombing, while they themselves stayed in London to show solidarity with the city's people. Teenaged Elizabeth insisted on doing her part for the war effort and became a military driver. When the war ended in 1945, she and Margaret made a small, incognito excursion into the victory celebration. This was probably the closest Elizabeth would ever be to her people. In 1952, her father died, and Elizabeth became queen.

As a small child, Elizabeth was asked what she wanted to be when she grew up. The polite little girl answered, "I should like to be a horse."

Other Birthdays
1915   Anthony Quinn
1935   Charles Grodin

1947   Iggy Pop
1951   Tony Danza
1958   Andie MacDowell

April 22

1937   Neptune, New Jersey.

Jack Nicholson was born. His father deserted Nicholson's mother before Jack was born, leaving her to scratch out a meager living. For a time, she ran a beauty parlor out of her living room. Nicholson, an overweight child, developed an interest in fantasy and a sharp sense of humor to deflect taunts. He turned down an engineering scholarship to the University of Delaware to go to Los Angeles and try his hand at acting. To support himself, he sold toys, hustled pool, answered fan mail for MGM's *Tom & Jerry* cartoon show, and served as a firefighter with the California Air National Guard. Of the last occupation, he has said, "In my asbestos suit, I used to walk into the flames. It gave me the most wonderful 'high,' this feeling of being otherworldly." Nicholson got parts in television and twenty Roger Corman low-budget horror films. After fifteen years, his break came with the filming of *Easy Rider* in 1969. It made him a cult hero. He went on to win an Oscar for *One Flew Over the Cuckoo's Nest* (1975).

In the 1990s, a story about Nicholson was going around Hollywood. It is probably not true, but it is still in character with Nicholson's devilish reputation. Reportedly, while in Cannes, a pretty French woman was interviewing Nicholson, who allegedly said, "You know, in the old days, after 20 minutes of this, I would have tried to screw you." The French woman giggled and replied, "Oh, that is funny—20 years ago you tried to screw my mother."

Other Birthdays
1908   Eddie Albert
1928   Aaron Spelling

1938   Glen Campbell
1946   John Waters
1961   Byron Allen

April 23

1928   Santa Monica, California.

Bank manager George Temple and his wife, Gertrude, had two sons, but when two of Gertrude's friends had cute little girls, Gertrude determined to have a daughter of her own. On this date, the stork cooperated and Shirley Jane Temple was born.

Gertrude had wanted an artistic child, so while she was pregnant she read aloud, listened to classical music, watched romantic movies, visited museums to meditate on art, and went to the beach to enjoy its natural beauty. After Shirley's birth, Gertrude kept the radio on most of the time and danced to popular tunes beside her baby's crib. Almost as soon as Shirley began walking, she, too, began dancing. Her mother enrolled her in a dance school when she was three. A talent scout spotted Shirley at the school. When he pointed her out, Shirley decided she didn't like the looks of him and grabbed a piano leg, refusing to budge. Eventually, she was coaxed forward. By the time she was six, Shirley was a star, and by age 10, she had won an Academy Award. As for Gertrude's friends' cute little girls, one of them became Shirley's stand in.

Of her Depression-era success, Shirley has said, "I was in a class with Rin Tin Tin. People were looking for something to cheer them up, so they turned to a dog and a little girl." Fame was not without its drawbacks. Shirley also observed, "I stopped believing in Santa Claus when my mother took me to see him in a department store, and he asked for my autograph."

Other Birthdays
1940   Lee Majors

1942   Sandra Dee
1960   Valerie Bertinelli

April 24

1934   Richmond, Virginia.

Shirley MacLaine (in her most recent incarnation) was born to psychology professor Ira Owens Beaty and Kathlyn Mac-Lean Beaty. MacLaine's younger brother is actor Warren Beatty. MacLaine got her start in show business when her parents sent her to a dance instructor. They thought dance lessons would improve the ducklike waddle she had as a child.

MacLaine liked dance so much that, after high school, she headed for Broadway to become a professional dancer. She made her way into the chorus of the long-running hit *Pajama Game*. When, in 1954, the star injured her ankle, MacLaine stood in for her. A producer in the audience was mightily impressed with MacLaine's talent and gave her a film contract. MacLaine made several classic films, including *The Apartment* (1960), *Irma La Douce* (1963), *Sweet Charity* (1969), and *Terms of Endearment* (1984), for which she won an Oscar.

MacLaine has become as famous for her odd paranormal interests as for her acting. Dean Martin remarked, "Shirley— I love her, but her oars aren't touching the water these days."

1942   Brooklyn, New York.

Barbra Streisand was born. Her father died when she was fifteen months old. Her mother remarried, but the marriage ended when Streisand was 13. Her stepfather was, according to Streisand, emotionally unsupportive. She says, "I never had a conversation with him." She is also critical of her mother, although, Streisand says, "she did the best she could. And without her pushing me into, let's say the school system, it might not have sparked this rebellion inside of me to do the opposite." Streisand says she felt "unseen" as a child, but adds that if it had been otherwise, "I might not have been an artist. I might not have had the need to express myself, to live in my imagination. I might have had a whole other life."

Streisand's first show business success was at eighteen when she won an amateur contest in a Greenwich Village bar. She worked in a Chinese restaurant to support herself while she studied acting. Her first stage appearance, in a supporting role in *I Can Get It for You Wholesale*, was well received. It got her the lead in *Funny Girl*, which made Streisand a star.

In a Barbara Walters interview, Streisand related how her stepfather attended a performance of *Funny Girl*. He sent candy backstage afterwards, and she kept the jar for two decades, long after his death, before throwing it out one day after looking at it and deciding "I don't need this any more."

Other Birthdays
1893   Leslie Howard
1936   Jill Ireland

April 25

1939   Bronx, New York.

Al Pacino was born. He was raised in the South Bronx by his divorced mother and his grandparents. An exuberant boy, he reenacted scenes from his favorite films, jumping from one tenement roof to another in imaginary chases. Pacino decided he wanted to become an actor halfway through high school and promptly dropped out. Most dropouts wind up in some dead-end occupation. Pacino, however, made his way into an off-Broadway comedy, William Saroyan's *Hello Out There*. He got big laughs in his first stage role. Pacino reacted contrarily. The laughter unsettled him, and he couldn't return to the stage for a year. When he did, it was in the play *The Indian Wants the Bronx*. It was a success, and Pacino made the transition to films. His most notable film role was as Michael Corleone in the *Godfather* trilogy.

Other Birthdays
1874   Guglielmo Marconi

1918   Ella Fitzgerald
1932   Meadowlark Lemon

April 26

1933   San Antonio, Texas.

Carol Burnett was born. Her father ran a movie theater and her film-loving mother was watching *Rasputin and the Empress* when she went into labor. She named her daughter after Carole Lombard. Burnett's childhood was marred by parental alcoholism. Her parents wisely turned her over to her grandmother and great-grandmother to raise. Burnett would later recall that her great-grandmother could always make her laugh by popping out her false teeth and giving her a toothless grin. Burnett and her grandmother went to live with Burnett's mother in Los Angeles but the older woman remained Burnett's primary caregiver.

Burnett grew up in a tiny apartment. She attended UCLA, where she studied English and theater. In 1954, impatient to start a show business career, she left school for New York City. After six years of chasing parts, Burnett appeared on Broadway in *Once Upon a Mattress*. She was soon a regular on the *Garry Moore Show*. With the help of her husband, Joe Hamilton, Burnett starred in a television version of *Once Upon a Mattress* and a television variety special. In 1966, Hamilton produced *The Carol Burnett Show*, and Burnett became a comedy superstar. Her end-of-the-show signature of pulling her ear was a tribute to the grandmother who had reared her. Burnett continued the gesture long after her grandmother died.

Burnett once remarked of a play she was starring in, "I'm in bed with Burt Reynolds most of the time in the play. Oh, I know it's dirty work, but somebody has to do it."

Other Birthdays
1893   Anita Loos
1942   Bobby Rydell

April 27

1822   Point Pleasant, Ohio.

Jesse and Hannah Simpson Grant had a son. The parents were unsure what to name him. Hannah wanted Albert. An aunt wanted Theodore. Other names were suggested. When no agreement could be reached, lots were drawn. Hannah's parents won. Her father decreed Hiram. Her mother added Ulysses. Hiram Ulysses Grant was known to his mother as Lys. His enemies called him Useless. When he won an appointment to West Point, a clerk recorded his name as "Ulysses Simpson Grant." His fellow cadets jokingly called him Uncle Sam, which was shortened to Sam. Grant learned to like his new name. U. S. Grant had a nice sound for a U.S. Army officer.

Grant's career was, at first, unspectacular. He got bad grades at West Point. Although he performed well during the Mexican-American War, he was asked to resign following charges of excessive drinking. He married but had little luck supporting his family. For a time, he was reduced to selling firewood on a streetcorner. When the Civil War broke out, he had difficulty getting a command, but, when he did, he led the Union Army to victory and earned his way into the White House.

Grant's mother was sober, quiet, and mystically religious. She believed that God decreed the outcome of all events. For example, when neighbors reported her infant son was crawling around where horses could trample him, she didn't rush to his aid, confident that God would save him if he were meant to be saved. She never visited him at the White House and never made a fuss when he visited her. She was at her most demonstrative when Grant returned from the Civil War. She greeted him in her apron with "Well, Ulysses, you've become a great man, haven't you?"

Other Birthdays
1922   Jack Klugman

1927   Coretta Scott King
1932   Casey Kasem
1959   Sheena Easton

April 28

1941   Valsjobyn, Sweden.

Ann-Margret was born. Her father was Gustav Olsson. In the 1940s, he came to America to make his fortune. It was five years before he could send for his wife and daughter. Unfortunately, soon after they arrived, Olsson became an invalid. His wife worked as a receptionist at a funeral home to support the family. Part of her pay was the privilege of living in the funeral home. While her parents slept in the place's dining room, Ann-Margret slept on a small bed in the mourning room beside a casket.

Ann-Margret dropped out of college to become part of George Burns's Las Vegas Act. In 1961, she got her first film role, playing Apple Annie's daughter in *Pocketful of Miracles*. More film roles followed, including the Elvis Presley film *Viva Las Vegas* (1964). In the late 1960s, she and Roger Smith of *77 Sunset Strip* were married. He abandoned his career to manage hers, but she didn't have much critical success until she made *Carnal Knowledge* (1971), which earned her an Academy Award nomination. In 1972, she accidentally fell twenty-two feet from a Lake Tahoe stage during a rehearsal. She suffered a concussion, broke her left arm and jaw, and also fractured many bones in her face. At first, it seemed she would be disfigured, but a talented surgeon restored her looks and she returned to the stage in three months. Three years later, Ann-Margret earned another Academy Award nomination as Best Actress for *Tommy* (1975).

1950   New Rochelle, New York.

Jay Leno was born. His father, Angelo Leno, was an Italian-American insurance salesman who sold policies in Harlem, and his mother, Catheryne, was a Scottish girl who had left home for America when she was just a teenager. Leno was a classroom clown. His fifth-grade teacher sent a note home that read: "If Jay spent as much time studying as he does trying to be a comedian, he'd be a big star."

Leno worked his way through college doing stand-up comedy at bar mitzvahs, birthday parties, nursing homes, and strip clubs. He got his first break when Jimmy Walker hired him to write for the television show *Good Times*. Leno gave friend David Letterman his first break by introducing him to Walker, who hired Letterman as a gag writer. When Letterman got his own show, he returned the favor by frequently booking Leno on it. Leno credits Letterman with his early success. Both remain friendly, despite the fact that Leno, instead of Letterman, won the job of replacing Johnny Carson on the *Tonight Show*.

When Leno's mother died and his father died soon after, Leno eulogized both on his program. Leno recalled how his father always did the right thing and reminisced about his mother's quirky personality. When Leno told his mother that Sylvester Stallone was getting $10 million for just twelve weeks' work, she replied, "Well, what is he going to do the other 40 weeks?"

Other Birthdays
1758   James Monroe

April 29

1899   Washington, D.C.

Composer "Duke" (Edward Kennedy) Ellington was born to James Edward and Daisy Kennedy Ellington. James had worked as a butler at the White House before becoming a blueprint-maker for the U.S. Navy. It was a good job, and Edward had a comfortable home. His mother doted on him, encouraging him to dress well and behave in a refined manner, thereby earning himself the nickname Duke. She wanted him to obtain a musical education, but Ellington didn't like his music teacher and soon quit. He preferred sneaking into the burlesque show and hanging out in poolrooms. Ironically, it was in the latter that he got interested in playing piano. Poolrooms were social centers in those days and usually had a piano with which patrons entertained each other. Ellington used his minimal training to plink out tunes and found that it "was a good way to get a girl to sit beside you and admire you as you played." He practiced at home on his family's player piano, copying ragtime piano rolls. He formed his own band, began composing, and became a legendary jazzman.

Other Birthdays
1863   William Randolph Hearst
1933   Rod McKuen
1955   Jerry Seinfeld
1958   Michelle Pfeiffer
1970   Andre Agassi

April 30

1933   Abbott, Texas.

Willie Nelson was born to Ira and Myrle Nelson. His mother left the family when Nelson was six months old and his mechanic father turned him over to his grandparents. They were churchgoing people with a love of music. Nelson got his first guitar from his blacksmith grandfather when he was five. He taught himself to play by listening to the *Grand Ole Opry*. He and his sister began playing at local dances. To the horror of his grandmother, Nelson was performing in honky-tonks in the sixth grade. After high school, Nelson enlisted in the U.S. Air Force. A back injury forced him out. He took a brief stab at college, then worked as a disc jockey and sold encyclopedias and vacuum cleaners door-to-door while spending nights playing in bars.

Nelson married, but his marriage was troubled. He says of

his wife, "She was a full-blooded Cherokee and every night with us was like Custer's Last Stand. We'd live in one place a month, then pack up and move when the rent would come due." They optimistically moved to Nashville, Tennessee, where Nelson hoped to sell his songs. When he had no success, he grew so dispirited that, after a night of drinking, he lay down in a street and waited for a car to run him over. Fortunately, that didn't happen. Another binge ended when he woke up to find that his wife had sewn him up in a sheet and was beating him with a broomstick. She left, taking his clothing and their children.

Perhaps Nelson's hard luck added authenticity to his soulful country songs. He sold one called "Family Bible" for $50. It became a number one hit. He sold "Night Life," one of the most recorded country songs, for $150. Nelson got no royalties for either, but they proved he could write.

Nelson's second marriage was as troubled as his first. His drinking and promiscuity destroyed it. A third marriage was happier and, after buying an old bus, he began touring, playing country fairs and dives. In 1973, he recorded his first successful album, *Shotgun Willie*. His next, *Red-Headed Stranger*, included Nelson's signature hit, "On the Road Again." Nelson's career skyrocketed. It wasn't long before he was entertaining at the White House, where he claims to have relaxed by smoking marijuana on the roof. Unfortunately, he had terrible business skills. The Internal Revenue Service claimed he owed them $34 million. The interest on the debt alone added $5,000 a day to his tax debt. With the help of friends, a grueling tour, and the IRS, who lowered his bill to $9 million, Nelson recovered.

Nelson has said, "To write songs, I usually need a reason. Like not having any money."

Other Birthdays
1925   Cloris Leachman
1944   Jill Clayburgh
1961   Isaiah Thomas

May 1

1923   Brooklyn, New York.

Joseph Heller was born. He was the youngest of three children. When his father, a bakery truck driver, died when Heller was five, Heller's mother raised her family on her own in an ethnically mixed Coney Island neighborhood. After high school, Heller worked as an insurance company clerk until the Japanese bombed Pearl Harbor. Heller enlisted in the U.S. Army Air Corps and became a B-25 bombardier stationed in Corsica with the 488th Squadron, 340th Bombardment Group. He flew sixty bombing missions over Italy and France.

After the war, Heller used the GI Bill to attend New York University. He then earned a master's degree in American literature at Columbia and studied English literature at Oxford on a Fulbright scholarship. While still an undergraduate, Heller began publishing short stories. Though a promising writer, he abruptly stopped writing. He later said, "I wanted to write something that was very good and I had nothing good to write. So I wrote nothing."

After an unpleasant stint teaching composition at Pennsylvania State University, Heller went into a New York ad agency and spent a decade in that business. When he published *Catch-22*, it enjoyed little success until, during an interview, S. J. Perelman was asked if he'd read anything good lately. Perelman mentioned *Catch-22* and helped turn Heller into a prominent figure in American literature.

Catch-22 was based on Heller's war experiences. His early bombing missions encountered little opposition. He says, "I was *sorry* when nobody shot at us. I wanted to see a sky full of flak and dogfights and billowing parachutes. War was like a movie to me until, on my 37th mission, we bombed Avignon and a guy in my plane was wounded. I suddenly realized, 'Good God! They're trying to kill me, too!" War wasn't much fun after that.... After Avignon, all I wanted to do was go home." This event inspired a key scene in *Catch-22*.

Other Birthdays
1909   Kate Smith
1917   Glenn Ford
1918   Jack Paar
1930   Richard Riordan
1939   Judy Collins
1962   Bobcat Goldthwait

May 2

1903   New Haven, Connecticut.

Benjamin Spock was born. His father was Benjamin Ives Spock, a sedate corporate lawyer. His mother, Mildred Spock, was a strict disciplinarian who walloped her children with little provocation. To toughen them up, she had them sleep, both summer and winter, in an unheated tent on the roof of their home. Spock later described her as "a very moralistic, opinionated, domineering person. As soon as a child got past the age of one and started showing an inclination toward independence, she would move in to squelch it. That happened to every child in my family. I am sure that as I searched into psychiatry and psychoanalysis I was motivated by the feeling that there must be pleasanter ways to bring up babies than the way I had been brought up."

Perhaps due to his stern mother, Spock had difficulty learning to speak and had numerous phobias, including fear of fire engines, a lion he supposed lived in the bushes by his house, and a large Italian woman who dug dandelions from neighborhood lawns. He grew up shy, but with a dandyish streak. After attending Yale, he studied pediatrics at Columbia. It took him years to establish a practice, but he became more and more confident of his ideas concerning child-rearing.

In 1946, Spock published *The Common Sense Book of Baby and Child Care*. It became the manual for the parents of the Baby Boom generation. Spock claimed excessive control destroys the child's spirit. Some parents took this injunction to the extreme, abandoning all restraint. Spock countered that children also needed a framework of discipline to feel secure. It is interesting to note that Spock's own two sons criticized him for failing to show affection.

Other Birthdays
1901   Bing Crosby

May 3

1898   Kiev, Ukraine.

Golda Mabovitz was born the seventh of eight children to Bluma and Moshe Mabovitz. Moshe, a woodworker, sold his tools and emigrated to Milwaukee, Wisconsin, planning to send back money so his family could follow. It took three years for him to scrape together their fare. Meanwhile, Bluma worked in her father's tavern and sold bread door-to-door. Even when the money came, the family's trip wasn't simple. They needed false passports (Bluma had to pass for half her age), and before they even got to the boat their luggage was stolen. When Bluma and the kids arrived in Milwaukee, she found that Moshe's business wasn't prospering. All he could afford was a single rented room.

Bluma took charge. She borrowed money from a moneylender and opened a grocery. The children went to work as well. Golda's sister, Shana, got a factory job, but when her mother insisted she also work in the grocery and dump her boyfriend, Shana left home. Bluma and Golda also quarreled. Golda hoped to become a teacher, but her mother didn't want her to go to high school because she needed her in the grocery. When Bluma arranged a marriage for Golda to a rich man twice her age, she ran away to live with Shana. Curiously, after Shana and Golda quarreled, Bluma welcomed Golda home, stopped insisting on the arranged marriage, and allowed Golda to study teaching, although she did steam open the letters Golda got from her boyfriend.

Golda did become a teacher and eventually married. The girl who successfully battled her domineering mother also became a Zionist leader and, under the name Golda Meir, prime minister of Israel.

Other Birthdays
1469   Niccolò Machiavelli
1906   Mary Astor
1947   Doug Henning

May 4

1929   Brussels, Belgium.

Audrey Hepburn-Ruston was born to a Dutch baroness and an Anglo-Irish banker, who abandoned his family when Audrey was six. When World War II broke out, Audrey was at school in England, but her mother thought she wouldn't be safe there and brought her home just before the Nazi occupation. Audrey lost family members, was reduced to surviving on tulip bulbs, and helped the Resistance by carrying messages in her ballet shoes. After the war, she studied ballet in Amsterdam. She dropped Ruston from her name and went to London's West End to become an actress. She enjoyed limited success until 1951, when Colette selected her to play the title role in the Broadway production of *Gigi*. In 1953, she won an Oscar for Best Actress for her first American film, *Roman Holiday*.

Hepburn went on to a series of roles that highlighted her grace and beauty, but she didn't forget her wartime deprivation. She once said, "Your soul is nourished by all your experiences. It gives you baggage for the future—and ammunition." Hepburn set aside the baggage and used the ammunition to give her strength. A relief agency fed her when she was starving, so she became a spokesperson for UNICEF, traveling the world to publicize their efforts to feed children. Hepburn was in Somalia, bringing the attention of the world to the starvation there, just months before she died of cancer in 1993.

Other Birthdays
1956   Pia Zadora
1959   Randy Travis

May 5

1942   Red Bay, Alabama.

Country singer Tammy Wynette was born (her real name is Wynette Pugh). She was raised in Tupelo, Mississippi, in poverty, sometimes picking cotton. Later she became a beautician but wasn't satisfied, so she traveled to Nashville and took a stab at singing. She soon convinced recording executives of her talent, recording thirty-two number one songs, including "Stand by Your Man," the biggest country single ever, and "D-I-V-O-R-C-E."

Wynette's success hasn't been untroubled. She has had five husbands and, in 1978, was the victim of a bizarre kidnapping and nearly killed. Wynette has also suffered severe medical problems, going through nineteen surgeries and, at one time, was considered a terminal case by her doctors. Wynette says, "My life has been a soap opera."

Other Birthdays
1913   Tyrone Power
1937   Colin Powell
1943   Michael Palin

May 6

1856   Vienna, Austria.

Sigmund Freud was born to Jakob Freud, a wool merchant, and Amalie Nathansohn Freud. The couple had seven more children after Sigmund, but he was always his mother's favorite. She was certain he would be a great man and indulged him at the expense of his siblings. Freud responded with an unusually strong attachment to her. After being spurned by a girl when he was 16, Freud developed a crush on his mother and didn't show any interest in other women until he was 26.

Amalie became peculiar as she aged. She refused to understand the inflation that plagued Germany after World War I. She insisted that her daughter, who spent her life caring for Amalie, was wasting money when she couldn't buy goods at prewar prices. Freud and his brothers had to slip their sister money to pay Amalie's bills. Amalie also thought she was much younger-appearing than her years. At 90, she refused the gift of a shawl because she thought it would make her look old. At 95, she complained that a newspaper photo of her was a bad reproduction: "It makes me look a hundred!"

1915   Kenosha, Wisconsin.

Richard and Beatrice Welles had a son, George Orson Welles. Richard had earned a fortune by inventing a bicycle headlight and later a mess kit used during World War I. He once bought a hotel because he liked the service, then kicked out all the guests because he didn't like them. Unlike the precocious Orson, Orson's younger brother, Dickie, hid in his room and, whenever someone spoke to him, could only stammer a reply. Dickie was institutionalized at 23 as a profound schizophrenic.

Welles had a flock of eccentric aunts. One bathed only in ginger ale because she couldn't afford champagne. Another went jogging behind her chauffeur-driven limo tied to it by a long rope so she wouldn't slow her pace. Another amused herself doing card tricks after her magician husband ran off. Still another disappeared in China. Probably the oddest aunt of the group went about in a riding outfit and red wig. When she met a friend, she would politely doff the wig. Orson's paternal grandmother cursed his parents' marriage, then turned her mansion's ballroom into a miniature golf course, which she later replaced with a black magic chapel. Welles remembered peeking in and seeing piles of dead birds and a bloodstained altar.

Perhaps the grandmother's curse worked. Beatrice and Richard divorced when Welles was six. More probably, their divorce could be blamed on Richard's drinking and Beatrice's affair with her mother's physician, Dr. Maurice Bernstein. Bernstein became a mentor to Orson. He introduced Welles to every important musician who passed through Chicago. Through these connections, Welles got his first show business role. At three, he appeared in the opera *Madame Butterfly.* Bernstein also introduced Welles to the magician Houdini, who taught him some magic.

Welles was tutored at home and spoke only with adults. He desperately wanted to be seen as an adult. He lowered his voice, smoked cigars, drank mixed drinks, and even used makeup to put lines on his face. But despite these devices,

Welles remained a child. On his eighth birthday, his mother, who was ill, called him into her room. She admonished him to be sure to blow out all the candles on his cake, because while he might have many cakes in the future, he would never again have precisely that number of candles to blow out. Welles succeeded in extinguishing the candles but in the process forgot to make a wish. He would regret this the rest of his life when his mother died soon afterwards at 40.

Welles had a tumultuous career that reached remarkable heights before fading into a long decline. He remarked, "I started at the top and have been working my way down ever since."

Other Birthdays
1895   Rudolph Valentino
1856   Robert Peary
1931   Willie Mays

May 7

1901   Helena, Montana.

Frank James Cooper, who would later be known as Gary Cooper, was born. The future cowboy star spent much of his childhood actually punching cattle on his family's ranch. This gave veracity to his rustic image, but Cooper was more than a rustic. His prosperous family sent him to England to get an expensive private education. He loved art and hoped to become a political cartoonist. Unable to find work with a newspaper, he supported himself by working as an extra and as a stunt man in movies. His cowboy past got him lots of jobs. Sometimes he actually had more than one role in the same movie. It was later claimed by film historians that he sometimes played the Indian shooting at the settler and, in the next cut, the settler tumbling from his horse.

Cooper saw others becoming wealthy stars and decided to try for better parts. He hired agent Nan Collins, who gave him the name Gary, after her Indiana hometown. Collins got him his first big role in *The Winning of Barbara Worth* (1926). However, what may well have been his real big break was a romance with "It" girl, Clara Bow. He impressed her with his capabilities, and she got him a part in one of her films. The part was small, but the romance spread his name all over Hollywood. Cooper went on to many starring roles and many other star romances, including Marlene Dietrich, Lupe Velez, and Patricia Neal. Director Howard Hawks said, "If I ever saw him with a good-looking girl and he was kind of dragging his feet over the ground and being very shy and looking down, I'd say, 'Oh-oh, the snake's gonna strike again.'"

Other Birthdays
1833   Johannes Brahms
1840   Pyotr Ilyich Tchaikovsky
1885   George "Gabby" Hayes
1919   Eva Perón

May 8

1884   Lamar, Missouri.
    Martha and John Truman had a son, Harry Truman. Raised on the family farm in Independence, Missouri, he was a good student but his parents were too poor to send him to college, and his bad eyesight kept him from gaining admission to a military academy. Instead of becoming a college student, Truman got work as a bank clerk in Kansas City. After five years, he grew dissatisfied with his meager prospects and returned to his family's farm. He left in 1917 to fight in World War I as an artillery first lieutenant in the Missouri National Guard. He proved a good officer, cool under fire and considerate of his men. After the war, he married Bess Wallace and became a haberdasher. When this business failed in 1921, he was left deep in debt and desperately in need of a job. Thomas J. Pendergast, Democratic boss of Kansas City, obliged.

"Boss" Pendergast was impressed with Truman's war record and his membership in a Baptist church, the Masons, and the American Legion. Pendergast needed men with useful associations, clean records, and honest faces to front for his corrupt administration. He took Truman on as Jackson County overseer of highways. Pendergast moved him upward through county government, then, in 1934, backed Truman in a successful bid for U.S. senator.

Truman made a name for himself on the Senate Committee to Investigate the National Defense Program. That committee investigated fraud in defense contracts—an ironic way for Truman, the Pendergast man, to distinguish himself. In 1944, Franklin Roosevelt needed a vice presidential running mate. He favored William O. Douglas, but the big city bosses preferred Turman, the reliable cog in the Pendergast machine. Douglas became a Supreme Court Justice. Truman got the vice presidency and, when Roosevelt died, became president.

Truman once remarked, "As long as I have been in the White House, I can't help waking at 5 A.M. and hearing the old man at the foot of the stairs calling and telling me to get out and milk the cows." He also observed, after years of a crowded, public life, "You want a friend in this life? Get a dog."

Other Birthdays
1847   Oscar Hammerstein
1926   Don Rickles
1932   Sonny Liston
1964   Melissa Gilbert

May 9

1936   Salford, Lancashire, England.

Albert Finney was born. His father was a Lancashire bookmaker who, along with the colorful characters associated with horse racing, gave Finney valuable examples for the ne'erdo-well characters he later played. After training at the Royal Academy for Dramatic Arts, Finney was offered a film contract. Unlike most young actors who would leap at such an opportunity for quick fame and fortune, he chose to work on stage instead, appearing with the Birmingham Repertory Company and at the Old Vic. This stage experience helped make his first starring film appearance, in *Saturday Night and Sunday Morning* (1960), a startling success. In 1963, he appeared in both the well-received Broadway play *Luther* and the popular movie *Tom Jones*. Again Finney defied conventional wisdom. In a *New York Times* interview he later said, "People told me to cash in on my success while I was hot. But what I wanted to do then was go around the world. . . . Captain Cook had been a hero of mine when I was a kid."

After a year of traveling, Finney returned to acting with his skills undiminished. He rolled up a string of successful stage appearances and starring roles in such varied films as *Scrooge* (1970), *Gumshoe* (1971), *Murder on the Orient Express* (1974), *Annie* (1982), *The Dresser* (1983), and *The Browning Version* (1994).

Finney once received an honorary doctorate of letters from a well-known British university. He called his father to brag a little bit. "Doctor of letters, eh?" his father wryly countered. "You never even send me a postcard."

Other Birthdays
1860   J. M. Barrie
1918   Mike Wallace
1946   Candice Bergen
1949   Billy Joel

May 10

1899   Omaha, Nebraska.

Fred Astaire was born Frederick Austerlitz. His career began in 1911, when his mother forced him and his sister, Adele, into vaudeville as a dance team. The brother and sister act broke box office records in London and New York City before Adele quit the team in 1932 to marry. Astaire worried about his future without his talented sister. A bad screen test didn't help his confidence. A studio executive observed, "Can't act. Can't sing. Can dance a little." Fortunately, other studio executives saw more in the thin, balding dancer. He made hit film after hit film in his forty-year career.

Mikhail Baryshnikov said, "What do dancers think of Fred Astaire? It's no secret. We hate him. He gives us a complex because he's too perfect. His perfection is an absurdity. It's too hard to face."

Other Birthdays
1922   Nancy Walker

May 11

1888   Temum, Siberia.

Leah and Moses Baline had a son, Irving, one of eight siblings. At that time, Jewish families in Russia were constantly in dread of Cossack attacks. When the Baline's house was burned, they left for New York City, where Moses could find only part-time work as a cantor. He gave Hebrew lessons and worked long hours in a Kosher slaughterhouse. The labor proved too much, and Moses died in four years, leaving Leah, who couldn't speak English, to support the family.

Leah began by breaking up the family's brass samovar and selling the pieces to scrap dealers. Her children took odd jobs. Irving, who went by the nickname Izzy, quit school at eight to peddle newspapers. He hoped to earn enough to get his mother a new rocking chair. Izzy also sang in saloons. Although he couldn't read music, he taught himself to play the black keys of the piano to accompany himself. His mother was horrified by the dives he worked in and once stormed into a particularly low place to drag him home. When Izzy told her he wanted to become a singing waiter, she drew the line. Izzy obeyed for a while, then ran away from home.

Izzy got the singing waiter job and also worked as song-plugger, but he made a success of himself when he started writing songs. A printing error on the sheet music for one of his songs gave his name as "I. Berlin," and Izzy became Irving Berlin. Although he never learned to read music, Berlin became one of America's foremost popular composers. His hits included "Alexander's Ragtime Band," "Oh, How I Hate to Get Up in the Morning," "Always," "White Christmas," and "God Bless America."

Berlin didn't forget his mother. She got her new rocker, and, one evening, a cab drew up in front of her East Side apartment and took her to a mansion, complete with servants. Berlin had bought her a new home to put the rocker in.

Berlin once observed, "The toughest thing about success is that you've got to keep on being a success."

Other Birthdays
1892   Margaret Rutherford
1904   Salvador Dali
1912   Phil Silvers

May 12

1820   Florence, Italy.

Florence Nightingale was born to William and Frances "Fanny" Smith Nightingale, who had married in 1818, then gone on an extended honeymoon across Europe. The trip was so long that the wealthy couple's first child was born as they traveled. Since the baby girl was born in Greece, they named her Parthenope. They brought her along as they continued their leisurely trip. In Italy, they had a second daughter, who unlike poor Parthenope, got a more sensible, geographic name: Florence.

The Nightingales returned to England and settled down to a

luxurious life. Although the girls had governesses, their father also helped educate them. Fanny was more concerned that they marry well, and to insure this arranged parties, a presentation at court, and outings. Though kindly and generous, Fanny couldn't understand when Florence showed an interest in humanitarian activities. She was horrified when Florence decided to become a nurse. Florence later said, "[It] was as if I had wanted to be a kitchen maid."

Florence Nightingale persisted in her ambition and, when war broke out in the Crimea, she organized hospitals, saving thousands of lives and launching the reform of hospital care. Fanny changed her mind about Florence's career. She said of a reception given to honor Florence: "The like has never happened before, but will, I trust, from your example gladden the hearts of many future mothers."

Other Birthdays
1925   Lawrence P. "Yogi" Berra
1936   Tom Snyder
1937   George Carlin
1950   Bruce Boxleitner
1966   Stephen Baldwin

May 13

1924   New York City.

Beatrice Arthur was born. Arthur studied acting at New York's School for Social Research. Her first major role was as Lucy in a 1954, off-Broadway production of *The Threepenny Opera*. She went on to a number of stage hits, winning a Tony for her supporting role in *Mame*. On the television screen, she has had two hits, *Maude* and *The Golden Girls*.

Arthur, who is a brunette and five-foot-ten, once said, "All this time I've just wanted to be blond, beautiful—and five feet two inches tall."

1950   Saginaw, Michigan.

Steveland Morris Hardaway was born. Under the name Stevie Wonder, he became a rhythm-and-blues singing star, despite being born blind. At 10, Wonder had mastered the piano, bongos, guitar, and harmonica and, at 12, he was working in Motown. He quickly made it to the top forty with tunes such as "I Was Made to Love Her," "My Cherie Amour," and "Uptight."

Wonder is modest about his success. He once said, "How can you even think of being conceited—with the universe as large as it is?"

Other Birthdays
1907   Daphne du Maurier
1914   Joe Louis
1939   Harvey Keitel

May 14

1944   Modesto, California.

Filmmaker George Lucas was born. Lucas originally wanted to be a racecar driver, but this dream ended when a little premature racing in high school resulted in a near-fatal crash just two days before graduation. Lucas switched to moviemaking. After attending USC, he became a protege of Francis Ford Coppola, who financed his first film *THX-1138* (1971) and his first big success, *American Graffiti* (1973). Lucas was one of the best-paid directors in Hollywood before he turned 30. His *Star Wars* films were among the biggest money-making films ever made.

Lucas says of his films, "I'm not out to be thought of as a great artist. It's a big world and everybody doesn't have to be significant."

Other Birthdays
1936   Bobby Darin
1948   Meg Foster

May 15

1856   Chittenango, New York.

L. Frank Baum was born. He spent the first half of his life struggling to find a niche for himself. He worked as a journalist in South Dakota, then moved his family to Chicago. He had little success until he compiled a children's book titled *Father Goose* in 1899; however, it was his second book, *The Wizard of Oz*, published in 1900, that made him famous. He wrote thirteen more Oz books and dozens of other children's books, but poor investments strained his finances. In his later years, he lived in Los Angeles, where his attempts to build what would have been the world's first theme park failed. Baum was comforted by the fact that Oz and its inhabitants had entertained generations of children around the world.

Baum got the name for his fictional kingdom from a file cabinet label in his office. It read "O–Z."

Other Birthdays
1905   Joseph Cotten
1953   George Brett

May 16

1905   Grand Island, Nebraska.

Henry Jaynes Fonda was born to Herbeta and William Fonda. Henry and his two sisters were raised in Omaha, where their father opened a printing company. As a child, Henry was shy and small. After high school, he hoped to work his way through the University of Minnesota, where he planned to study journalism. Part-time jobs with the phone company and a settlement house, however, proved too much. He was forced to drop out of school.

Fonda was unsure what to do next. Then, a family friend, Dorothy Brando, suggested he audition for a play she was producing for the Omaha Community Playhouse. Fonda got the part and decided he wanted to be an actor. His father didn't approve, so Henry got a job as a file clerk after the play's run ended. When the Playhouse offered him the lead in their next production, he happily quit. His father was furious. Fonda's mother worked out a compromise, whereby he would keep his day job and rehearse on weekends and in the evenings. Still, father and son didn't speak for weeks.

Before the curtain went up, Fonda experienced a nervous thrill. He said, "The short hair on the back of my neck felt like live wires and my skin tingled. That was the first time I realized what acting meant. It also dawned on me that for a self-doubting man, this was the answer. Writers give you the words and you can become another person."

Fonda's family was in the audience and witnessed his first standing ovation. Later, at home, his father silently sat with his nose in his newspaper while Fonda's mother and sisters lavished praise on Fonda. This went on for quite some time, until one sister ventured a minor criticism. The elder Fonda peered over his paper and said, "Shut up. He was perfect." Fonda would remember that as the best review of his career.

Fonda later admitted that he was too shy to refuse Dorothy Brando when she asked him to audition. Dorothy Brando had another, less shy, but successful protege—her son Marlon.

1919   West Allis, Wisconsin.

Wladziu Valentino Liberace was born to French horn player Salvatore Liberace and Frances Zuchowski Liberace. Liberace's father had played with John Philip Sousa's band and the Milwaukee Symphony Orchestra but disapproved of his son's interest in the piano. Liberace's mother was a farm girl of Polish extraction. She insisted that Liberace and his three siblings be raised in the same rural circumstances that she had been. Unfortunately, the employment opportunities for a French horn player in rural Wisconsin were small. Liberace's mother opened a grocery store to support the family. Salvatore's unemployment had one benefit. It allowed him to teach his children music. Young Liberace decided he wanted to be a concert pianist even before he started school.

Liberace's desires were nearly cut short—quite literally—when he injured a finger. It became infected and his doctor recommended amputation. Liberace's mother refused to allow the amputation and treated his finger with an old-fashioned poultice. Fortunately, the infection disappeared. Liberace returned to his musical studies and won a scholarship to the Wisconsin College of Music.

Liberace became a fine classical pianist, but he also loved pop tunes. He finished his first recital with a rendition of "Three Little Fishies." In the 1950s, he became a popular, flamboyant fixture on television. He gradually progressed from placing a candelabrum on his grand piano to donning fanciful costumes loaded with feathers and sequins. When a London critic described him as "fruity," he successfully sued. Of such negative comments, Liberace said, "They've got me crying—all the way to the bank." He later added, "Wisecracks lifted my income from $150 a week to more than $2 million a year. You know the bank I used to go crying to? Now I own it."

Other Birthdays
1952   Pierce Brosnan
1955   Debra Winger
1966   Janet Jackson
1969   Tracey Gold
1970   Gabriela Sabatini
1973   Tori Spelling

May 17

1956   Wilmington, North Carolina.

"Sugar" Ray Leonard was born to Cicero and Getha Leonard. They named him after jazz great Ray Charles, hoping he would become a musician. The fifth of the couple's seven children, he grew up in a poor, mixed suburb of Washington, D.C. Leonard was a shy kid who sang in the church choir. His father described him as "a funny sort of kid", who "always hung back." He said, "It used to worry me. All my other boys were into something, but not Ray...not until boxing."

Leonard started boxing at age 14. After a walloping 145 amateur victories and only 5 losses, he won Gold Medals at the 1975 Pan American Games and the 1976 Olympics. He went on to a profitable professional career, becoming welter-weight champ in 1979.

Other Birthdays
1911   Maureen O'Sullivan
1936   Dennis Hopper
1970   Jordan Knight

May 18

1912   Canonsburg, Pennsylvania.

Pierino Roland Como, better known as Perry Como, was born the seventh son of a seventh son, and his mill hand father had thirteen children in all. Consequently, it was of great importance that each child become self-sufficient. Perry did his part by opening his own barber shop at 14, where he sometimes entertained his customers with songs. After one pleasing tune, a customer suggested Como audition for a professional band. Como took his advice and was hired. His first hit song, "Till the End of Time," was soon recorded. He took a shot at making movies, but his laid-back style didn't go over well. He went back to recording and released hit song after hit song. His television variety show for Kraft did so well that, when he decided to quit series television, Kraft paid him $25 million for seven specials.

Como hits include "Hot Diggety Dog Diggety," "Catch a Falling Star," and "It's Impossible."

1920   Wadowice, Poland.

Karol Wojtyla was born. His parents were working-class people, and his hometown was a grim factory city. His mother died when he was three. When Wojtyla was a teenager, he lost his older brother, and his father died when Wojtyla was 21. Despite these losses, Wojtyla was a high-spirited young man. A good athlete, he enjoyed soccer and was also a good student, studying both Greek and Latin. He considered becoming an actor. His clean-cut good looks, which certainly helped him earn the admiration of his female associates, might have made him a success at that trade, but World War II intervened.

Perhaps the terrors of war changed Wojtyla. He abandoned dreams of acting and enrolled in an underground seminary to study for the priesthood. When he passed out anti-Nazi pamphlets, the Nazis put his name on an arrest list, and Wojtyla was forced to hide until the war ended. Ordained in 1946, he continued his studies in Rome, winning degrees in philosophy and theology. He returned to Poland to become a professor at the Catholic University of Lublin and in 1967 was made a cardinal. Despite the surveillance of the Secret Police, he courageously challenged Poland's Communist rulers and rose to archbishop of Krakow. In 1978, after fifty hours of deliberation, Wojtyla was elected pope, making him the first non-Italian to become pope in four hundred and fifty-five years and the first Polish pope ever. He adopted the name John Paul II to honor his immediate predecessor, Pope John Paul.

In 1992, *Time* magazine revealed that on June 7, 1982, John Paul II met with Ronald Reagan at the Vatican and secretly planned a campaign to destroy Communism in Eastern Europe. Funneling money and equipment from western labor unions, the National Endowment for Democracy, and the CIA through the Catholic Church into Poland, they supported the successful anti-Communist uprising led by the Solidarity movement. The revolution spread to other Iron Curtain countries and eventually to the Soviet Union itself.

Pope John Paul II once said, "There is but one thing more dangerous than sin; the murder of man's sense of sin."

Other Birthdays
1872   Bertrand Russell
1919   Margot Fonteyn
1946   Reggie Jackson

May 19

1897   Bisaquino, Sicily.

Frank Capra was born. He celebrated his sixth birthday deep in the bowels of a steamer bound for America. On their thirteenth day at sea, his father carried him out on deck and pointed to the Statue of Liberty, saying, "Look at that! It's the light of freedom!"

The Capra family settled in Los Angeles. Neither Capra's father nor mother could read or write, so the best work they could find was demanding physical labor. Capra's father became a fruit picker and his mother, a factory worker. Frank also worked but studied as well, graduating from the California Institute of Technology in 1918 with a degree in engineering, just in time for World War I. He could have gotten a draft exemption and worked in a munitions factory, but he enlisted in the army (and later reenlisted in 1941 for World War II). In San Francisco, Capra taught mathematics to artillerymen and nearly died during the 1918 influenza epidemic that killed thousands of servicemen.

After the war, Capra couldn't find work, so he traveled the country by freight car, earning money by singing. When a bootlegger learned he was an engineer, he offered Capra $20,000 to design stills, but Capra refused, wanting nothing to do with crooks. A little bit of crookedness, however, got him his start in films. Capra saw a newspaper ad seeking an experienced film director. He claimed to be one and got the job. Later, he admitted his falsehood, but by then he had proven that he could direct. Indeed, in 1934, his movie *It Happened One Night* earned five Academy Awards, setting a record that lasted forty-one years.

Capra is best remembered for his 1946 film *It's a Wonderful Life*. It was poorly received when it was released and led to the failure of Capra's film company, Liberty Films. Capra went on to other films but never enjoyed as much artistic freedom. In a mix-up, the copyright for the film was allowed to expire. When television stations in need of holiday fare discovered that they didn't have to pay anyone to show it, the film was soon being aired everywhere. Time had graced it with an atmosphere of nostalgia, and the film that had failed at the box office became a family favorite.

Other Birthdays
1925   Malcolm X
1935   David Hartman
1941   Nora Ephron
1952   Grace Jones

May 20

1946   El Centro, California.

At 18, Jackie Jean Crouch married Johnny Sarkisian to escape poverty and an abusive father who had once, in a drunken rage, tried to gas her and her siblings to death. Sarkisian, however, was a disappointing husband and their marriage failed. After their break-up, Crouch discovered she was pregnant. Crouch's mother persuaded her to get an abortion. Crouch got all the way to the abortionist's table before she changed her mind. She went back to Sarkisian and named her daughter, born on this date, Cherylynn. Sarkisian abandoned his family within a year.

As a child, Crouch had sung hillbilly songs for nickels in bars across the Southwest. She turned to show business to support her daughter. She managed to get a juicy role in the 1949 film *The Asphalt Jungle* but was replaced by the then-unknown actress Marilyn Monroe just before shooting began. Cherylynn also began acting up as a teenager. At 15, she was dating movie star Warren Beatty. She soon dropped out of high school. At 18, Cherylynn, who had shortened her name to Cher, met and married record promoter Sonny Bono (see 2/16/1935).

Sonny proved a better husband than Crouch's mates. He masterminded a successful duo rock career with hits like "I Got You Babe" and "The Beat Goes On." When their careers abruptly bottomed out, and they were forced to pay the bills performing in bowling alleys, Bono revamped their act and negotiated a throwaway summer replacement show, *The Sonny and Cher Comedy Hour,* with CBS. The show clicked but their marriage, after producing a daughter, broke up in front of 20 million viewers, when Cher had an affair (off-screen) with record producer David Geffen. A second affair, with rocker Greg Allman, produced a second child, a second marriage, and a second divorce. Cher was later romantically linked to a number of younger men.

Cher's career progressed steadily upward while Bono's declined. She became a successful actress, winning an Academy Award nomination for her supporting role in *Silkwood* (1983) and continued recording hit songs. Bono eventually rebounded. He became a restaurateur, mayor of Palm Springs, and a U.S. congressman.

Other Birthdays
1908   Jimmy Stewart
1944   Joe Cocker
1958   Ronald Reagan Jr.
1959   Bronson Pinchot

May 21

1916   New York City.
Harold Robbins was born on this day. Or at least this is Robbins's best guess—he isn't sure where or when he was born. Shortly after his birth, his mother deposited him on the steps of a Catholic orphanage in New York's tough Hell's Kitchen. He

was christened Francis Kane but renamed himself Harold Robbins after one of his foster parents, druggist Harold Rubin.

Robbins's lack of roots never slowed him down. He dropped out of school at 15 to work as a grocery clerk. Noticing a shortage of canned vegetables, he had a hunch that he could make a lot of money anticipating such shortages. He took flying lessons, rented a plane, and flew to Kentucky, where he bought up options on as many crops as he could. The large vegetable canneries began buying to fill shortages, making Robbins a millionaire by the time he was 20. He moved into sugar speculation, but his fortune evaporated when Franklin Roosevelt froze sugar prices. Robbins managed to get a job for $27 a week as a shipping clerk for Universal Pictures. By detecting a pattern of illegal freight overcharges, he saved Universal $37,000. The studio rewarded him by placing him in charge of planning and budgets. As an executive, he read many film scripts and was convinced that he could write better ones. In 1948, he penned the best-selling novel *Never Love a Stranger* and has written many bestsellers since, including *The Carpetbaggers*, a thinly veiled version of Howard Hughes's life, which sold over 6 million copies. His annual income has been estimated at nearly $2 million.

Robbins always took a very pragmatic view of writing, disdaining more artistic work. He once said, "Hemingway's stupid book comes out and they make a big fuss out of this old man and the stupid dead shark, and who cares?"

Other Birthdays
1917   Raymond Burr
1944   Janet Dailey
1953   Mr. T
1957   Judge Reinhold

May 22

1907   Dorking, Surrey, England.

Laurence Olivier was born. Olivier later wrote of his earliest memories of his father: "The slight disgust he felt at his first viewing of me seemed to me and, I feel sure, to my mother, to last all my boyhood until my heaven, my hope, my entire world, my own worshipped Mummy died when I was 12." Olivier's strongest recollection of his mother was of her frequent spankings. He wrote: "From the age of five until I was nine my Mummy had, more often than it pleases me to remember, to quell the natural anguish which she suffered at what was to her the dreaded prospect of spanking me for one inveterate and seemingly irresistible sin, that of lying; it was apparently impossible for me to resist this temptation. It was a compulsion in me to invent a story and tell it so convincingly that it was believed at first without doubt or suspicion." Olivier claimed that he finally broke his habit of lying to spare his mother the distress of punishing him. He added: "If my wonderful Mums had lived to watch me at work, at times more glowingly fortunate than I would have dared to imagine, I have sometimes wondered whether she might not have come to the conclusion that those years of habitual lying were due to an instinct for some initial practice in what was to become my trade. Let it not be thought that I am attempting to find any excuse whatever for my early wicked tendencies, but it might, as is said west of the Atlantic, it might well figure."

Olivier's first stage role was at 15 in a school production of *The Taming of the Shrew*. He played Katherine.

Other Birthdays
1813   Richard Wagner
1859   Arthur Conan Doyle

May 23

1933   London.

Actress Joan Collins was born. Her father was a theatrical booking agent, so it isn't surprising that she got her first acting job at age nine in a production of Ibsen's *A Doll's House*. At 19, she began performing in films in parts ranging from ambitious queen in *Land of the Pharaohs* (1955) to lady-in-waiting-who-gets-the-guy in *The Virgin Queen* (1955) to saucy showgirl in *The Girl in the Red Velvet Swing* (1955). By the 1960s, Collins was playing in lesser films such as *Tales From the Crypt* (1972) and *Empire of the Ants* (1977). All this changed in 1981, following the success of the TV soap opera *Dallas,* when the networks rushed to introduce more steamy sagas of life among the rich and beautiful and nasty. Tapped for the role of Alexis on *Dynasty,* Collins quickly became television's foremost female villain.

Actor Stewart Granger remarked of Collins, "She's common, she can't act—yet she's the hottest female property around these days. If that doesn't tell you something about the state of our industry today, what does?"

Other Birthdays
1934   Robert A. Moog
1951   Anatoly Karpov
1954   Marvin Haglar

May 24

1819   Kensington Palace, London.

Queen Victoria, the longest-reigning British monarch, was born. She was the daughter of Victoire, Duchess of Kent, and Edward, Duke of Kent, the fourth son of George III. Victoria's father died when she was an infant. Her mother, under the influence of business advisor Sir John Conroy, sought to dominate Victoria and sheltered her from the world. Conroy hoped to become wealthy when Victoria ascended to the throne, and Victoria's mother wanted power. To their disappointment, Victoria firmly asserted herself when she became queen at 18.

Although Victoria's reign is known as an era of prudery, Victoria and her husband, Albert, had a happy married life that produced nine children. When her doctor advised her to refrain from having more, she reportedly said, "Oh, Sir James, can I have no more fun in bed?" Despite her marriage, Victoria remained uninformed about many sexual matters. When presented with the antihomosexual Criminal Law Amendment in 1885, she removed every reference to females. Victoria simply didn't believe women did such things.

1941   Duluth, Minnesota.

Robert Zimmerman was born. He loved music and headed for Greenwich Village to become a folk singer when he turned 20. He caught the fad right on the rise. His odd voice was unimportant because his lyrics said all the right things. After renaming himself after poet Dylan Thomas and recording his anti-war tune "Blowin' in the Wind," Bob Dylan became wealthy as the voice of a generation of would-be social reformers.

Dylan didn't always return his fans' devotion. He once said, "Just because you like my stuff doesn't mean I owe you anything."

Other Birthdays
1943   Gary Burghoff
1944   Patti LaBelle
1945   Priscilla Presley
1955   Roseanne Cash

May 25

1929   Brooklyn, New York.

Opera star Beverly Sills (real name Beverly Miriam Silverman) was born. She began singing as a preschooler. As "Bubbles," she starred on WOR radio's *Uncle Bob's Rainbow House* and on *Major Boews' Capital Family.* By the time she was seven, she knew twenty-three arias and had sung in one of the first singing commercials. At 15, she had mastered twenty operatic roles. At 16, she was touring with a Gilbert and

Sullivan company. Despite this early experience, it took her eight auditions to become a member of New York's City Opera in 1955. She soon proved that she was a "good hire."

New Yorker Sills says, "New York is run by hookers who married well."

Other Birthdays
1927   Robert Ludlum
1943   Leslie Uggams
1955   Connie Sellecca

May 26

1907   Winterset, Iowa.

Marion Mitchell Morrison was born to Mary and Clyde Morrison.

After Clyde and Mary had a second child, Robert, they bought a drug store. The couple wasn't happy and started to fight over the business. The arguments had a bad effect on Marion, who threw tantrums and repeatedly ran away. At five, he hopped a freight train and was miles from home before he was found. When he was seven, the family moved to a farm near the Mojave Desert in California, where they barely managed to survive. In 1916, Clyde's father died and left a small estate, which the Morrisons used to move to Glendale, California.

Marion had a hard time at school. He was shy and small, a ready target for bullies, who teased him about his name. He spent his free time with books and held down a number of part-time jobs, including one in a Glendale movie studio, to help out his family. While kids in other towns played cowboys and Indians, Glendale kids played cowboy-actors and Indian-actors. Marion's job gave him a certain cachet with his playmates. Marion slowly overcame his shyness and made many friends.

A new nickname—Duke—also helped give Marion confidence. He owned an Airedale dog who, after a summer of playing with Marion, followed the boy to school in the fall. School authorities sent such dogs to the pound, so Marion left his dog at a firehouse while he was in school. The firemen liked the dog and knew his name, Duke, but couldn't remember Marion's name. They started calling the dog Little Duke and the boy Big Duke. Marion's pals shortened this to "Duke."

Duke did well in high school but was labeled a prankster after he stole a foul-smelling chemical from his father's drug store and stank up the entire school. He was also known to drink bootleg liquor on weekends. Duke's reputation kept his neighbors from letting their daughters date him, but he couldn't afford dates anyway. He could only enter the University of Southern California, where he planned to study law, after winning a football scholarship and getting part-time work as an extra and prop-mover in a Hollywood studio. When he lost his football scholarship, he desperately struggled to stay in school, donating blood so often that he was barred from the blood bank. After being evicted from his fraternity, he lived over a friend's garage. Duke spent the next summer working at the studio, frantically saving his money. When he still couldn't pay for college in the fall, he decided to become a full-time prop man. As a new worker, Duke was given the less-desirable tasks, including handling props for the dictatorial director John Ford.

Ford loved to humiliate crew members. He set up a shot to catch Duke in frame and then berated him for "spoiling" the shot. He forced Duke to march up to an actor dressed like a German officer, have an Iron Cross pinned to his chest, bend over in a football set position, and then submit to having Ford boot him in the butt. Apparently, this cemented in Ford's brain the fact that Duke had been a football player, for, when Ford later filmed a football film, he hired Duke to act. He did well. The studio changed his name to John Wayne and placed him in cheap serials and singing cowboy films. His voice and guitar strumming were supplied by another actor. Wayne was so embarrassed when fans asked him to sing that he refused to continue and was replaced with Gene Autry. After years of minor roles, Wayne became a star in 1939 through John Ford's classic *Stagecoach*.

In 1971, Wayne observed, of his stage name, "I didn't have any say in it, but I think it's a great name. It's short and strong and to the point. It took me a long time to get used to it, though. I still don't recognize it when somebody calls me John."

Other Birthdays
1920   Peggy Lee
1948   Stevie Nicks
1949   Hank Williams Jr.
1951   Sally Ride

May 27

1923   Fürth, Germany.

Henry Kissinger was born. Because of his Jewish heritage, he was beaten by Nazis on his way to and from school. His family fled Germany for New York in 1938. During World War II, Kissinger served in the U.S. Army in Europe, making sergeant. After the war, he attended Harvard, where he obtained his Ph.D. His writings caught the eye of Nelson Rockefeller, and Kissinger became Rockefeller's foreign policy advisor during Rockefeller's unsuccessful bid for the presidency in 1968. This service got the attention of Richard Nixon, who brought Kissinger into his administration as an advisor and then secretary of state. Kissinger won a Nobel Prize for his 1973 Vietnam peace agreement, which ultimately proved worthless when North Vietnam ignored it and conquered South Vietnam.

Kissinger once said, "The nice thing about being a celebrity is that when you bore people, they think it's their fault."

Other Birthdays
1878   Isadora Duncan

1911 Vincent Price
1935 Lee Meriwether
1936 Lou Gosset
1965 Todd Bridges

May 28

1944   Atlanta, Georgia.

Rhythm-and-blues singer Gladys Knight was born. When she was four, she sang with an adult choir at her church. At eight, she won the first prize of $2,000 on Ted Mack's *Original Amateur Hour.* At nine, Knight was touring with brother Merald and cousins William Guest and Edward Green backing her up as the Pips.

Success for Knight's group was not immediate. They were often cheated by club owners, one of whom pulled a gun when they tried to collect their pay. The group recorded their first hit, "Every Beat of My Heart," in 1961, but it wasn't until 1966 that they got a Motown recording contract. Even then, they were given only second or third choice of songs and they eventually sued the company for nonpayment of royalties. They scored another hit in 1967 with "I Heard It Through the Grapevine." It finally won the group financial success. With a new contract with Buddah Records, they recorded such hits as "I've Got to Use My Imagination," and "Midnight Train to Georgia."

Other Birthdays
1888   Jim Thorpe
1908   Ian Fleming
1957   Kirk Gibson

May 29

1903   Eltham, a suburb of London.

Avis Hope, the daughter of a Welsh sea captain, and William Henry Hope had the fifth of their seven children, Leslie Townes Hope. When his name, reversed for role call, led his schoolmates to nickname him Hopeless, he renamed himself Bob Hope.

William Hope was a stonemason who enjoyed drinking a little too much. The reduced demand for stone-cutting caused him to migrate to the United States in 1906. He worked hard and brought his family over in 1908. The Hopes settled in Cleveland, where Avis took in boarders to help make ends meet when her husband's drinking limited their income. The boys had part-time jobs. Bob caddied at a local golf course, worked in a butcher shop, sold shoes, hustled pool, and peddled papers. Once, the millionaire John D. Rockefeller bought one of Bob's 2¢ newspapers with a dime. Bob had no change, so he told the oil baron that he would trust him until the next day and gave Rockefeller his dime back. Rockefeller insisted Bob take the dime and bring him change. Bob fetched the change from a nearby store. Rockefeller took it and kindly admonished the boy: "Always deal in cash." Perhaps the advice came in handy, for Bob, after trying journalism, boxing, and teaching dance, went into show business and, in part through wise investments, became one of its wealthiest stars.

Woody Allen once said, "If I wanted to have a weekend of pure pleasure, it would be to have a half-dozen Bob Hope films and watch them, films like _Monsieur Beaucaire_ and _My Favorite Brunette_. It's not for nothing that he's such a greatly accepted comedian. He is a great, great talent, a guy who has been able to combine a thin story with great jokes."

Other Birthdays
1630   Charles II
1917   John F. Kennedy

May 30

1964   Ashland, Kentucky.

Christina Claire Ciminella was born to Diana and Michael Ciminella. Diana had become pregnant at 17 while still in high school and had considered suicide. The couple married and Christina was born the week of Diana's graduation. They later had a second daughter, Ashley. After Michael finished college, he became a video producer in Los Angeles. When the Ciminella marriage ended in 1972, Diana went back to her maiden name, Judd, and changed her first name to Naomi, from the Bible story of Ruth and Naomi. Christina changed her name to Wynonna, from the pop song "Route 66."

Naomi managed a health store, worked as a secretary, and modeled before moving her daughters back to Kentucky. She was afraid they were becoming too Hollywoodized. In Kentucky, the family lived in a small house without electricity or phone. Wynonna, 12, amused herself with a toy plastic guitar, and Naomi sang along while working around the house. In 1978, the Judds moved back to California, where Naomi finished getting a nursing degree. Wynonna was a rebellious teenager, often arguing with her mother. Wynonna said, "It was like tying two cats' tails together." Once, Naomi locked her out of the house in just her slip. Occasionally, Wynonna was packed off to relatives until things calmed down. Despite these difficulties, she showed talent, winning a high school talent show at 16.

To amuse themselves, Naomi and Wynonna tape-recorded themselves singing several songs. They learned how to harmonize à la country by listening to a $1 album by a duo called Hazel and Alice. One day, Naomi was assigned to nurse a girl injured in a car wreck. Her father was a record producer. When the girl recovered, Naomi gave him a copy of the tape. He was impressed and signed them. After a few months of training, the Judds recorded the top twenty hit "Had a Dream (For the Heart)." They followed it with the number one hit, "Mama He's Crazy."

Wynonna and Naomi worked out their differences while touring by bus. This closeness was supportive when, in 1991, Naomi discovered she had contracted chronic active hepatitis while working as a nurse, forcing her into early retirement. Fortunately, it seems to be in remission. Wynonna has scored two platinum albums on her own. In 1994, Wynonna shocked her fans by announcing that she was pregnant and that she wasn't going to immediately marry the baby's father, Nashville boat dealer Arch Kelley III.

Other Birthdays
1901   Cornelia Otis Skinner
1908   Mel Blanc
1936   Keir Dullea
1943   Gale Sayers

May 31

1930   San Francisco, California.

Clint Eastwood was born. His father was a hard-working laborer who supported his family well. Eastwood did poorly in school but shared his father's work ethic, cutting timber, fighting fires in Oregon, pumping gas, and working in a steel mill. In 1950, he was drafted into the U.S. Army, where he taught swimming. One of his Army buddies was actor David Janssen, who suggested Eastwood try acting. When Eastwood left the service, he went to Hollywood and snagged a contract with Universal Studios. They paid him $75 a week to appear in such films as *Tarantula* (1955), in which he played a pilot napalming a giant spider. These roles ended after eighteen months when a studio executive decided that Eastwood's Adam's apple was too big and fired him.

Eastwood dug swimming pools and pumped more gas while chasing parts in television. In 1959, he was visiting a friend at the CBS studio when a producer spotted him having lunch in the cafeteria. The producer cast Eastwood as Rowdy Yates in television's *Rawhide*. In 1964, Eastwood was offered $15,000 to make a low-budget, Italian-Spanish-German "spaghetti Western." Eastwood claims he took the job to get a free trip to Europe. Whatever the reason, Sergio Leone's *A Fistful of Dollars* (1964) was a hit. Eastwood's quick-shooting Man

With No Name—and practically no dialogue—made him a superstar.

Other Birthdays
1908   Don Ameche
1943   Joe Namath
1965   Brooke Shields

EM

June 1

1926   Los Angeles, California.

Film cutter Gladys Monroe Baker Mortenson gave birth to a daughter, Norma Jeane. Her mother composed the name by combining the names of film stars Norma Talmadge and Jean Harlow. Years later, Norma Jeane would change her name to Marilyn Monroe.

Marilyn's birth certificate listed Edward Mortenson, a Norwegian-American killed in a 1929 motorcycle wreck, as the father. Mortenson, Gladys's second husband, is a figure of some mystery. Marilyn would later say that he was not her real father. Rumor had it that an affair ruined Gladys's marriage to Mortenson and that Marilyn was the product of that affair. Marilyn recalled her mother showing her a photo of a smiling man with a pencil mustache and a slouch hat. Her mother said the man was Marilyn's father. The man reminded Marilyn of Clark Gable. A recurring fantasy of Marilyn's was that her father actually *was* Gable. Marilyn retained this fantasy until the end of her life, even after playing opposite Gable in *The Misfits* (1962).

Glady's father, Otis Monroe, died in an asylum of paretic dementia, the insanity that accompanies the final stage of syphilis. Her mother, Della, also died in an asylum. Della was a religious fanatic who, Marilyn later said, had tried to smother her with a pillow when Marilyn was 13 months old. Gladys turned over the care of Marilyn to foster parents. When Marilyn was seven, Gladys went into a profound depression that ended in a murderous rage when she supposedly attacked a friend with a knife. Gladys was strapped to a stretcher and sent off to the same asylum where her mother had died. She was occasionally released, but Marilyn, from age 11 to 16, was raised by Gladys's friend Grace McKee Goddard and her husband.

When Marilyn's guardians decided to move to the East, Marilyn, 16, stayed behind to marry aircraft worker Jim Dougherty at the beginning of World War II. Dougherty joined the merchant marine and was sent to New Guinea. Marilyn went to work in a defense plant. She wrote him many letters and welcomed him home with a stay at the La Fonda Hotel while he was on leave. Dougherty later fondly recalled a black net nightgown Marilyn had worn for this occasion, but he also remembered that she had started drinking. When his leave ended, Dougherty went back to the Pacific and Marilyn to her factory.

In 1944, army photographer David Conover (whose commanding officer was Captain Ronald Reagan) came to Marilyn's factory to take photos of girls for *Yank* magazine. Marilyn, now 18, posed in her coveralls on the assembly line. Impressed with her good looks, Conover offered her $5 an hour to model. The factory paid only $20 a week. Soon, Marilyn was busy modeling full-time and planning a movie career. When she couldn't be with Dougherty for his Christmas leave in 1945, he demanded she give the work up. He was in China when he received divorce papers.

Marilyn later said, "I used to think as I looked out on the

Hollywood night, 'There must be thousands of girls sitting alone like me, dreaming of becoming a movie star. But I'm not going to worry about them. I'm dreaming the hardest.'"

Other Birthdays
1801   Brigham Young
1926   Andy Griffith
1934   Pat Boone

June 2

1944   New York City.

Composer and pianist Marvin Frederick Hamlisch was born. His parents, Lily and Max Hamlisch, an accordionist with his own band, raised Hamlisch on Manhattan's Upper West Side. At age five, young Hamlisch was plinking out tunes he heard on the radio on the family's piano. At six, he began taking lessons. At seven, he became the youngest student ever admitted to the Julliard School of Music. He won a scholarship to that school after an audition during which he performed the adroit musical stunt of transposing "Goodnight Irene" into any key his auditioners requested.

At Julliard, Hamlisch trained to become a concert pianist. Before reaching his teens, he was giving recitals. However, he soon gave up that avenue of performance. Nervous tension before the concerts caused him to vomit and he lost weight. He says, "By the time I was 13 or 14, it became obvious it was going to kill me." Hamlisch switched his attention to composing. When a high school chum began dating Liza Minnelli, Hamlisch provided her with a tune he wrote while working as a music counselor at a girl's camp in Lake Geneva, New York. Called "Travelin' Man," it was later recorded by Minnelli on her first album. Minnelli introduced Hamlisch to a Broadway vocal arranger, who hired him as his assistant.

Hamlisch worked on the musicals *Funny Girl*, *Fade Out-Fade In*, and *Henry, Sweet Henry*. He also worked as a rehearsal pianist for television. During this time, Hamlisch scored his first hit, the cheerful *Sunshine, Lollipops, and Rainbows*, which he wrote when he was 17. However his big break came after he graduated from college.

Hamlisch was playing at a party staged by Hollywood movie mogul Sam Spiegel when he heard that Spiegel was about to film *The Swimmer* (1968). Three days later, Hamlisch showed up at Spiegel's door with a score. Spiegel hired him and Hamlisch moved to Hollywood where he wrote music for such films as *Take the Money and Run* (1969), *Bananas* (1971), *The Way We Were* (1973), and *The Sting* (1973).

Hamlisch won three Academy Awards. He also worked on music for television and Broadway—most notably, *A Chorus Line*.

Other Birthdays
1938   Sally Kellerman
1941   Stacy Keach

June 3

1925   The Bronx, New York.

Tony Curtis was born. His real name was Bernard Schwartz, but he changed it after being hired by Universal Studios. Curtis was so eager to get into films that he signed his film contract without reading it. It was a semislavery deal, but Curtis ruefully observes today, "That's how I got started in movies. Agreeing to anything. And that's what it takes." Curtis thinks it was worthwhile. He recently observed, "Everywhere I go people put a smile on their face and are glad to see me...it couldn't be nicer."

Although Curtis had good looks, he had a couple of theatrical deficiencies. He was short for a leading man, but, more significantly, he had a harsh Bronx accent. Studio executives were stunned when Curtis, as a sheik upon an Arabian charger, carried the leading lady to the top of a sand dune and grandly declaimed: "Yonda lies da castle of my fodda!"

Other birthdays
1906   Josephine Baker
1911   Paulette Goddard
1915   Leo Gorcey

June 4

1936   Winnetka, Illinois.

Actor Bruce Dern was born into a prosperous and prominent family. His grandfather had been the governor of Utah, his great-uncle the writer Archibald MacLeish, and his parents the owners of a department store chain. Dern was sent to the University of Pennsylvania, where he excelled in track. His family had plans for him, but, after Dern saw his first James Dean movie, he dropped out of college and took off for Hollywood to become an actor. He succeeded, becoming famous for his villainous roles. His films include *The Cowboys* (1972), *Silent Running* (1971), *The Great Gatsby* (1974), and *Coming Home* (1978).

Dern says, "I've played more psychotics and freaks and dopers than anyone.... Actually, I don't even drink—much less take drugs."

Other Birthdays
1880   Clara Blandick
1924   Dennis Weaver
1928   Dr. Ruth Westheimer

June 5

1934   Hugo, Oklahoma.

Journalist Bill Moyers was born. His parents, John Henry and Ruby Johnson Moyer, raised him in Marshall, Texas. Moyers's father was a laborer; Bill once said of him "to this day, I cannot remember him saying an ugly thing about anybody." As a boy, Moyers listened to Ed Murrow's wartime broadcasts and was inspired to take a job as a cub reporter for Marshall's *New Messenger* at age 15. A second inspiration was a crowd-swaying speech in 1948 by Lyndon Johnson, then in the House of Representatives. In college, Moyers spent a summer on Johnson's staff addressing envelopes. He impressed Johnson and was soon handling all of his mail.

Johnson persuaded Moyers to transfer from the small college he was attending to the more prestigious University of Texas at Austin. Moyers became the assistant news editor for KTBC Radio and Television, the broadcasting facility Johnson owned under his wife's name. After graduation, Moyers attended the University of Edinburgh on a fellowship, then Southwestern Theological Seminary, where he earned a divinity degree in 1959. Moyers actually served as a Baptist minister in a small town for a short time before becoming an aide for the now–Senator Johnson.

Moyers helped Johnson during the 1960 presidential campaign, then became deputy director of the Peace Corps in the Kennedy administration. When Kennedy was assassinated in 1963, Moyers was in Dallas. He rushed to Johnson's side and was soon made press secretary.

Moyers became known for his close, admiring relationship with Johnson, who was notoriously hard on subordinates and prone to raucous jibes at their expense. At lunch once, Moyers managed to get a dig back at the president. Moyers, the ex-minister, was saying grace. Johnson suddenly hollered, "Speak up, Bill! I can't hear a damn thing!" To this, Moyers replied, "I wasn't addressing you, Mr. President."

After Johnson left office, Moyers became the publisher of *Newsday* magazine. He left it in 1970 to become a regular feature on public television.

Moyers once observed, "There are honest journalists like there are honest politicians. When bought, they stay bought."

Other birthdays
1723   Adam Smith
1883   John Maynard Keynes

June 6

1954   Brooklyn, New York.

Librarian Jacqueline Fierstein and handkerchief manufacturer Irving Fierstein had their second son, Harvey Forbes Fierstein. The Fiersteins, who had emigrated from Eastern Europe, were very supportive of their children and, when Harvey, at age 13, told them he was gay, they accepted it without fuss. Fierstein was, consequently, untroubled by his sexual orientation. He was, however, troubled by his weight. As a teenager, he weighed over 240 pounds. In part to hide himself behind a different persona, Fierstein began performing as a female impersonator at sixteen in gay nightclubs while studying art at the Pratt Institute. Fierstein's specialty was his impersonation of Ethel Merman. Andy Warhol was so impressed that he cast Fierstein as an asthmatic lesbian cleaning woman in Warhol's *Pork,* which opened Off-Broadway in 1971. Fierstein went on to a string of demanding Off-Broadway shows, which sweated 80 pounds from his frame and strained his voice so much that his gravelly tones have become his trademark.

In 1976, Fierstein was nearly driven to suicide by a failed two-year romance. To escape depression, he turned to writing. The result was *Torch Song Trilogy,* three one-act, semi-autobiographical, serio-comedic plays centered on a gay man's ordinary life struggles. In 1982, it earned him the first two of the three Tony Awards he has won for his play writing. Fierstein has also appeared in several movies, most notably as Robin Williams's brother in *Mrs. Doubtfire* (1994).

In an interview with Michiko Kakutani of the *New York Times,* Fierstein said of his parents, "We were brought up with the feeling that the family unit was everything and something as minuscule as my being gay was not going to disrupt that." Of the recurring theme of his work, that gays want the same things out of life as heterosexuals, he has remarked, "I'm a human being first and gorgeous second."

1956   Stockholm, Sweden.

Tennis star Bjorn Borg was born. He started playing tennis in 1964 after his clothing salesman father won a tennis racket in a Ping-Pong tournament. Seven years later, Borg won the junior championship at Wimbledon.

Other Birthdays
1949   Robert Englund
1955   Sandra Bernard

June 7

1958   Minneapolis, Minnesota.

Prince Rogers Nelson was born. He is known as Prince despite his efforts to rename himself after a cryptic, unpronounceable symbol.

Prince's father was a jazz musician who left his family when Prince was seven. Prince left home at twelve after a disagreement with his stepfather. He moved in with his aunt, who booted him out when his guitar playing drove her crazy. A high school classmate said of Prince, "He was weird in high school. He was always alone. He'd run the other way when he saw people. He wore black all the time. He didn't like being short so he wore black platform shoes. Prince used to cut classes to hang around the music room. One time kids just stood around him and watched him play. Everyone was impressed. While we were struggling to play just one instrument, he could play five with ease."

Prince wound up living in a friend's basement. His friend's mother took care of him and encouraged his musical interests. He formed a band and, at seventeen, got a recording contract with Warner Brothers Records. Prince's first two albums weren't successful. When his group was booked to open for the Rolling Stones in 1981, the audience booed until Prince's band left the stage. Prince looked like he was going nowhere until he decided to spice up his music with massive dollops of sex. Suddenly, he was hot. His next album, *Dirty Mind*, was a hit, as was his following album, *1999*.

Prince still lives in Minneapolis and has kept many of his old friends. He has changed in other ways, however. Once described as a geeky kid brutalized by bullies and without a girlfriend, he now associates with famed beauties and has, on occasion, reportedly zoomed through Minneapolis's streets naked on his purple motorcycle.

Other Birthdays
1848   Paul Gauguin
1909   Jessica Tandy
1940   Tom Jones
1952   Liam Neeson

June 8

1935   Brooklyn, New York.

Joan Rivers was born. Her father was a well-regarded doctor in Larchmont, New York. Her mother was of a wealthy family. Perhaps such successful parents made Joan Rivers ill at ease as a child. She was overweight, shy, and sensitive. She was also bright and, at 19, graduated Phi Beta Kappa from exclusive Barnard College. Rivers was soon married and working as a fashion coordinator. However, she was unhappy in her marriage and her career. She left both in 1958 to try stand-up comedy.

For seven years, Rivers played dives. Then, in 1965, she got her first shot at the big time when Johnny Carson booked her for his *Tonight Show*. She was a hit and, by 1973, she was headlining in Las Vegas. In 1984, she became Carson's substitute host. Rivers made headlines in 1986 with her surprise announcement that she was hosting her own talk show opposite Carson for the Fox network. That show was canceled after a short run. Soon afterwards Rivers's husband, Edgar Rosenberg, killed himself. Rivers managed to make a comeback in daytime television when she moved onto a shopping channel with her own show in 1993.

Rivers quips, "I was born in 1962. True! And the room next to me was 1963."

Other Birthdays
1867   Frank Lloyd Wright
1925   Barbara Bush
1936   James Darren
1940   Nancy Sinatra

June 9

1961   Edmonton, Alberta.

Michael A. Fox was born. His father was an officer in the Canadian Army and Fox was raised on a succession of military bases. He became a gregarious, self-possessed kid. After his family settled in Vancouver, Fox used his charm to win his way into Canadian television. He was reasonably successful and decided to go to Los Angeles to further pursue his career after changing his middle initial to *J* to avoid being styled "Michael, a fox." He won a few roles, but, by the time he was 20, he was selling his furniture to stay ahead of a $30,000 debt. Fox was saved from financial disaster when, in 1982, he was cast for the *Family Ties* television show. His success there led to other successful roles for Fox, most notably the *Back to the Future* trilogy.

Other Birthdays
1892   Cole Porter
1963   Johnny Depp

June 10

1922   Grand Rapids, Michigan.

Frank Gumm and his wife, Ethel, had a third daughter, Frances. Frank, the son of a wealthy Tennessee family, managed a movie theater and sang in his church choir. Ethel played the piano to accompany the silent films Frank showed. In those days, vaudeville still played movie theaters, and the Gumm girls were soon performing as "The Gumm Sisters with Baby Frances." Frances, just two-and-a-half years old, was the darling of their small-town audiences. Her siblings called her "Little Miss Leather Lungs" because of her louder-than-anybody-else's voice. The family seemed happy; however, Frank's work with the choir brought unsavory speculation that he was homosexual. The family couldn't remain in Grand Rapids. Ethel hoped to get her girls to Hollywood, but the closest they managed was Lancaster, a small California desert town sixty miles from Los Angeles. Using this as a base, Ethel and the girls toured the country.

Frank and Ethel's marriage didn't flourish in the desert. The girls, especially Frances, missed their father during their tours. They associated these trips with their mother, who pushed them to develop their talents. Frances's resentment turned to hatred when she discovered her mother with another man. This affair didn't break up the Gumm's marriage, but, again, rumors about Frank made it necessary for him to leave town. This time, however, his family didn't go with him. Instead, Ethel took her girls to Los Angeles by herself. Frank visited often, and it was in his company in 1935 that Frances auditioned for MGM.

MGM studio executive Billy "Square Deal" Grady was vacationing at Lake Tahoe when he first saw Frances. In order to be able to write off his vacation as a business trip, he offered her the audition. MGM thought she was too fat but loved her voice. They signed her under her new stage name, Judy Garland. In her first film, she played a hillbilly. The film bombed. Her next chance was in *Broadway Melody of 1938*, in which she sang the classic song "Dear Mr. Gable." She was just 15, but the public loved it, and she was soon paired with Mickey Rooney (see 9/23/1920) in a series of successful films.

Although Judy had professional success, she had little personal happiness. Her father died just weeks after she signed her contract. She never lost her antipathy for her mother, calling her the Wicked Witch of the West and blaming her for the breakup of a happy homelife that had never existed. Worst of all, eager to see Judy lose weight and anxious to extract as much work out of her as possible, the studio provided Judy with powerful drugs. Before she was 16, she was taking Benzedrine, Dexedrine, and Dexamyl. These bad habits led to Judy's early death. One observer said, "She shot up like a rocket and came down like a charred stick."

Other Birthdays
1889   Sessue Hayakawa
1895   Hattie McDaniel
1933   F. Lee Bailey

June 11

1935   Milwaukee, Wisconsin.

Gene Wilder was born Jerome Silberman. Wilder came to comedy young. After his mother suffered a heart attack, he tried to cheer her up with comedy skits when he was only six. By the time he was 13, he was appearing at the Milwaukee Playhouse as Balthazar in *Romeo and Juliet*. He studied at the Old Vic Theatre School in England but was drafted before he could put his training to use. He asked to serve in a psychiatric hospital. He said, "I chose the job because it seemed most applicable to acting. I've always been drawn to roles of emotional cripples." After his discharge, Wilder tried Broadway. He got a few parts, but his break came when, in his 30s, he was cast at the neurotic accountant opposite Zero Mostel in Mel Brooks's *The Producers* (1968). The Oscar-winning satire featured musical numbers with a Hitlerian theme. It made Wilder a star. He went on to more hit films, including, *Blazing Saddles* (1974), *Young Frankenstein* (1974), and *Stir Crazy* (1980).

Other Birthdays
1913   Vince Lombardi
1936   Chad Everett
1945   Adrienne Barbeau
1956   Joe Montana

June 12

1932   Sylacauga, Alabama.

Jim Nabors was born. The son of a small-town Southern policeman, he achieved fame playing the boobish Gomer Pyle on *The Andy Griffith Show*, a television program about a small-town Southern policeman. In reality, Nabors was a well-educated graduate of the University of Alabama with a degree in business administration. After college, he became a clerk for the United Nations in New York, then a film cutter for NBC in Los Angeles. Proximity to the world of show business fueled Nabors's ambitions to become an entertainer. He put together an act blending his operatic voice and rural Southern humor for comic Bill Dana, who helped Nabors get on Steve Allen's *Tonight Show*. He caught Andy Griffith's eye, and Griffith invited him to audition for a one-time role as a gullible gas jockey on his show. Nabors was so well-liked that he became a regular and his character was spun off to create the popular *Gomer Pyle, USMC* series. Nabors also became a successful recording artist, known for his renditions of pop standards, gospel tunes, and opera favorites. His version of "Amazing Grace" was a particular crowd pleaser.

Other Birthdays
1924   George Bush

1928   Vic Damone
1929   Anne Frank

June 13

1893   Oxford, England.

Mystery writer Dorothy Sayers was born. Her father was the Reverand Henry Sayers, chaplain and headmaster of the Choir School at Wolsey College. Her mother was Helen Mary Sayers, the daughter of a solicitor. When Sayers was born, Henry was 40 and Helen was over 30. This was a bit old in the 1890s, so perhaps it was appropriate that they named their daughter Dorothy, which means "a gift from God."

Henry, a classical scholar and musician, was noted for being dull. After her father's death, Dorothy remarked that because he was the owner of a Victorian walrus mustache, she had never seen her father's upper lip. However, Henry clearly loved his family. She wrote: "He bored [mother] to death for nearly 40 years, and she always grumbled that he was no companion for her—and now she misses him dreadfully."

Other Birthdays
1892   Basil Rathbone
1903   Red Grange
1926   Paul Lynde
1953   Tim Allen
1962   Ally Sheedy

June 14

1811   Litchfield, Connecticut.

Harriet Beecher Stowe was born. A mother of seven she wrote *Uncle Tom's Cabin* between household chores, and popularized the abolition of slavery. The story was soon adapted for the stage, becoming a favorite for many years. Eventually, a version was produced in the Soviet Union. The

Soviets had to make one substantial change, however. In the original adaptation, when the heroine Little Eva dies, she is shown ascending to Heaven. The Communists were atheists and could hardly include this divine reward. Instead, they had Little Eva survive. Then she goes to work in one of the People's cement factories.

Other Birthdays
1909   Burl Ives
1921   Gene Barry
1946   Marla Gibbs
1946   Donald Trump
1969   Steffi Graf

June 15

1937   Littlefield, Texas.

Country singer Waylon Jennings was born. His father was a hard-working truck driver, and Jennings hoped to avoid a similar life through music. At 14, he dropped out of high school to get into radio. He was soon the youngest country western disc jockey in America. Fellow Texan Buddy Holly took an interest in Jennings, producing Jennings's first country album, which was quite successful. After Holly's death, Chet Atkins became Jennings's mentor and persuaded him to move to Nashville. Jennings went on to a wild career, selling 28 million albums and marrying four times.

Jennings leads a more abstemious life today. He broke his cocaine addiction and a six-pack-a-day smoking habit in the 1980s, now avoids sugar because of the onset of adult diabetes, rarely eats red meat because of heart bypass surgery in 1981, and shuns caffeinated coffee. He also battles carpal tunnel syndrome, which he blames on years of guitar strumming. The father of seven, he now has seven grandchildren. Jennings credits his current wife of twenty-five years, Jessie Colter Jennings, for helping him settle down.

Ironically, in 1959, Jennings was supposed to fly with Holly, Richie Valens, and J. P. "Big Bopper" Richardson in the ill-fated airplane that crashed and killed all three stars. Jennings gave up his seat in the crowded plane so that the others could make the trip.

1961   London.

George Alan O'Dowd was born (some sources give June 14) the third of his working-class parents' six children. Under the stage name Boy George, he went on to become one of the classic gender-bending rock stars of the 1980s.

George showed an independent streak early in life, attending his Catholic school in his mother's high heels, scarf, and hat. The school seems to have taken this in stride, but, when, at 15, George dyed his brown hair orange, they expelled him. George worked as a fruit picker, a department store window dresser, and a printer before finding a steady job in a trendy London clothing store. He spent his time off in avant-garde night spots. His outlandish outfits, which, by then, included everything from neo–Teddy Boy to blue-haired punk, made him a bit of a notable. Friends were delighted by his bouffant hairdo and harem girl outfit. They raved at his black leather biker ensemble with rouge and bright red lipstick. In 1981, the new wave band Bow Wow Wow signed him on as their lead singer. Shortly thereafter, George formed his own band, Culture Club. Their first album, *Kissing to Be Clever*, was a spectacular success. George's biggest hit was "Karma Chameleon," but he soon faded from prominence. In 1986, it was revealed that he had a serious heroin problem. Since then, Boy George has cleaned up, and his performance of the title song in *The Crying Game* (1992) brought him renewed fame.

Other Birthdays
1932   Mario Cuomo
1958   Wade Boggs
1963   Helen Hunt
1973   Neil Patrick Harris

June 16

1890   Lancashire, England.

Stan Laurel was born. After being an understudy for Charlie Chaplin he had a low-key career acting in silent comedy films. By 1927, Laurel had become a director for Hal Roach. In one of the films he directed, *Get 'em Young*, Oliver Hardy played the lead, a meek butler. When Hardy burned his arm while preparing a leg of lamb, Laurel jumped into the butler role to keep the film on schedule. When Hardy recovered, Roach insisted that Laurel stay in the picture. He didn't want to throw away the film shot earlier. The script was rewritten and both actors appeared. The film was successful, and Laurel and Hardy became a team. They made 104 films together.

Laurel once observed, "Ollie and I had different hobbies. He liked horses and golf. You know *my* hobby—and I married them all." Indeed, Laurel was married eight times. This wasn't quite as shocking as it seems, for the eight marriages involved only four women.

Other Birthdays
1937   Erich Segal
1938   Joyce Carol Oates
1943   Joan Van Ark

June 17

1917   Steubenville, Ohio.

Dino Crocetti was born. He dropped out of high school and worked as a day laborer before deciding that singing was a better way to earn a living. Under the name Dean Martin, he became a star, teaming up with comic Jerry Lewis. When they split, Martin went on to a successful singing and acting career, recording several hits, starring in a series of successful films, and performing in a long-running, successful television variety show.

Martin is noted for drinking. Joey Adams joked, "I

wouldn't say Dean has a drinking problem, but his major concern in life is what wine goes with whiskey."

1946   Brooklyn, New York.
  Songwriter Barry Manilow was born. He was an only child, with a truck driver father who abandoned his family. Despite growing up in a tough neighborhood, by age seven, Manilow had fearlessly mastered the accordion, the number-two bully-attractor after the violin. Manilow says, "I grew up wanting to be Nelson Riddle." This dream was advanced on his bar mitzvah, when he received a piano.
  Manilow paid his way through college and a year at the Julliard School of Music by working in the CBS mailroom. The first song he sold was the theme for the late night movie on a local television station. In his mid-20s, Manilow got a job as a pianist in Manhattan's Continental Baths, a posh gay bathhouse. This might not have seemed like a promising job, but just weeks after he started work, Bette Midler made an appearance at the bathhouse, spotted Manilow, and hired him. He coproduced Midler's Grammy-winning album *The Divine Miss M* and arranged her singles "Do You Wanna Dance?" and "Boogie Woogie Bugle Boy." He then recorded his own hit, "Mandy." It led to a string of hits, including "I Write the Songs," "Looks Like We Made It," "It's a Miracle," and "The Copacabana."

Other Birthdays
1904   Ralph Bellamy
1951   Joe Piscopo

June 18

Liverpool, England.
  Beatle Paul McCartney was born. His mother, a midwife, died when McCartney was a teenager. His father, a cotton

salesman and part-time musician, gave his son a guitar to distract the grieving boy. Well-behaved and quiet, McCartney diligently practiced, learning the then-popular "Skiffle" music. At 14, he attended a church festival, where he met John Lennon, 16, whose band the Quarrymen was performing at the event (see 10/9/1940). McCartney and Lennon were soon composing songs together. After eight years of obscurity, they became the most successful composers of their generation.

In 1994, a tape of the Quarrymen performing on the day Lennon met McCartney was auctioned off for over $100,000. A man, who had been experimenting with a tape recorder at the time, had taped the band and kept the recording for nearly thirty years.

Other Birthdays
1901   Jeanette MacDonald
1913   Sammy Cahn
1942   Isabella Rossellini

June 19

1954   Springfield, Missouri.

Actress Kathleen Turner was born. Because of her father's foreign service career, Turner grew up in Canada, Cuba, Washington, D.C., Venezuela, and London. Of this rambling childhood, Turner has said, "Unstable? No, my mother would kill me if I ever said that. I loved it." Travel had the advantage of providing fresh starts. She has said, "The parts of myself I hated in Caracas I didn't have to be in London. Our parents told us we could become whatever we wanted because we were smart, well educated and willing to work. And we swallowed it."

Turner studied acting in college, earning an MFA. Her first agent doubted her potential, citing her low voice. Turner says, "I told him, my voice was exactly why I'd be hired, because it was different." After starting in television soap operas, Turner became a superstar in the film *Body Heat* (1981). Turner's sultry voice was perfect for the role of the murderous wife.

Other Birthdays
1896   Wallis Simpson, Duchess of Windsor
1902   Guy Lombardo
1903   Lou Gehrig
1919   Louis Jourdan
1962   Paula Abdul

June 20

1909   Hobart, Tasmania.

Australian marine biologist Theodore Flynn and his wife, Marelle, had been heading to Antartica aboard the research ship *Aurora* when it was discovered that Marelle was pregnant. Theodore continued with the expedition, but Marelle disembarked at Hobart, and on this date their son, Errol Leslie Thomson Flynn, was born.

Errol Flynn, who would become a swashbuckling hero in Hollywood, had a rebellious nature. He once said to his mother, "Every time you come near me you only want to wash me!" His sharp-tempered mother often held him by a fistful of hair while whacking his bottom. At seven, he ran away from home. His mother later said, "We suffered agonies of anxiety for three days and nights. He was found miles away where he went and offered himself for work at a dairy farm. He asked only five shillings a week as wages, saying that would do him as he 'never intended to marry.'"

Flynn's grandfather was a merchant sea captain whose sea stories enchanted Flynn. He stowed away on his grandfather's ship, only to be returned to his mother's smacking hand. In a sense, Flynn spent the rest of his life running away from his mother. After a colorful chain of occupations, which included soldier of fortune, jewel thief, and sheep castrater, he found success in the movies at 26, with his starring role as a pirate in Warner Brothers' *Captain Blood* (1935). He went on to many adventurous roles and great fame, yet Flynn still had some nearly fatal problems with his mother.

After Flynn bought an estate in Jamaica, his parents went to live there. Flynn instructed them to build a 1000-foot-long airstrip on the estate. They telegraphed him when the task was completed, and Flynn flew down with a friend. They were low on gas when they reached the airstrip. There, to his horror, Flynn found the strip was laid out in an *L*, with a large tree at the angle. The plane nearly crashed trying to avoid the tree. It turned out that Flynn's mother liked to watch the livestock capering under the tree and refused to allow it to be cut down.

Film historian George Frazier recorded a revealing incident about Flynn. One day, while sitting in a screenwriter's office, Flynn started to relate an anecdote about "when I used to buy slaves in New Guinea." The writer, used to Flynn's wild stories, cut him off, refusing to believe Flynn had ever done any such thing. Flynn protested, "But really, old boy." A year later, after the writer had been drafted into the army during World War II, he found himself in, of all places, New Guinea. He met a crusty sea captain, who, when he discovered the writer knew Flynn, got extremely angry. "I got a loaded rifle waiting for that dirty bastard Flynn," he said. The sea captain told the amazed writer that Flynn had bought slaves from him, adding, "He paid me all right, but after he had sailed away I found the bastard had paid me with tokens from the St. Louis World's Fair!" Flynn later said the story was untrue, protesting that the payment wasn't in St. Louis World's Fair tokens—it was in San Francisco Exposition tokens.

Other Birthdays
1931 Olympia Dukakis
1942 Brian Wilson
1945 Anne Murray
1949 Lionel Richie
1952 John Goodman
1953 Cyndi Lauper

June 21

1905   Paris.

Existentialist philosopher Jean-Paul Sartre was born. He was the son of a French naval officer who died when Sartre was one year old and Anne-Marie (Schweitzer) Sartre, a cousin of the humanitarian Albert Schweitzer. Sartre's indulgent mother raised him in the prosperous Paris home of his stern grandparents. A shy, odd-looking child, Sartre had few friends and found company in his books (he began reading at four). Study became his primary occupation. In the 1920s, he entered the elite École Normale Supérieure, where he spurned his family's middle-class life. After graduation, Sartre became a secondary school teacher in the harbor city of Le Havre and began publishing papers on literature and psychology.

In 1938, Sartre published his first novel, *La Nausée*, a milestone in the development of existentialism, which advanced the notion that existence is accidental and that the best relief from the oppressiveness produced by this realization is through the act of creation. It also assigns responsibility to the individual for his own decisions, since what produces them is the individual's will. As Sartre put it, "Man is condemned to be free."

Sartre returned to Paris and became a contributor to *La Nouvelle revue française*, which publicized the work of such writers as Faulkner, Caldwell, Hemingway, Dos Passos, and Steinbeck. Sartre served in the French Army during World War II. He was captured and spent nine months in a POW camp, where he began writing and producing plays to entertain fellow prisoners. In 1940, he escaped and became active in Paris's anti-Nazi underground. He wrote and produced *Les Mouches*, an anti-Facist play, right in front of Nazi censors. His wartime efforts won him a prominent place in postwar intellectual circles.

Considering his lonely, odd-fellow-out childhood, perhaps it is unsurprising that Sartre is famous for observing, "Hell is other people."

Other Birthdays
1922   Judy Holliday
1947   Meredith Baxter
1973   Juliette Lewis
1982   Prince William

June 22

1949   Summit, New Jersey.

Actress Meryl Streep was born Mary Louise Streep. Friends recall her being an assertive child whose good looks were well hidden behind glasses and perm-frizzed hair. When her parents discovered that she had a pretty singing voice, they arranged voice lessons with one of Beverly Sills's teachers. In high school, Streep dropped her lessons to become the ideal high school girl. She bleached her hair blond, got contact lenses, and became a cheerleader. She was voted Homecoming Queen. Streep attended Vassar, where she became interested in acting. After studying at the Yale School of Drama, she joined Joseph Papp's Public Theater. A turn as Kate in a Shakespeare in the Park production of *The Taming of the Shrew* led to a film role in *Julia* (1977). No one took particular notice of that performance, but Streep's next role, in *The Deer Hunter* (1978), won her an Academy Award nomination. She became the most admired actress of the 1980s, winning two Oscars.

Streep hasn't escaped some of the affectations of modern Hollywood. George Cukor said of her, "But oh, how she suffers. In this interview she was agonizing about having to meet the press. She was moaning that she didn't want a lot of people around. And I wanted to ask her, 'Then why the hell are you an actress?' They're so damned sincere these days."

Other Birthdays
1906   Billy Wilder
1936   Kris Kristofferson
1941   Ed Bradley
1960   Tracy Pollan

June 23

1948   Pin Point, Georgia.

Clarence Thomas was born. Thomas was raised by his grandparents. His grandfather was a truck driver who continually feared the loss of his job because it was illegal to license black truck drivers. Like many Jim Crow laws, its purpose wasn't only to humiliate blacks, but also to destroy black businesses. Thomas's grandparents worked hard to send Thomas to a parochial school where the nuns demanded much from him. Thomas did well. He went to a Catholic college, then to Yale Law School. After Thomas worked as an assistant attorney general in Missouri and as a corporate lawyer for Monsanto, Senator Danforth of Missouri took him into his staff. From there, Thomas became an assistant secretary in the Department of Education, then Chairman of EEOC, then a federal judge in the U.S. Court of Appeals, and, finally, in 1991, George Bush nominated the 43-year-old Thomas to the Supreme Court.

Opponents had promised to "Bork" Thomas, but few could have forseen how nasty the confirmation hearings would become. Despite charges of sexual harassment, Thomas became a Supreme Court Justice.

In 1985, in a commencement speech at Savannah State College, Thomas spoke of his life and the problems young blacks face today. He said: "I had the benefit of people who knew they had to walk a straighter line, climb a taller mountain, and carry a heavier load. You all have a much tougher road to travel. Not only do you have to contend with the ever-present bigotry, you must do so with a recent tradition that almost requires you to wallow in excuses. You now have a popular national rhetoric which says that you can't learn because of racism, you can't raise the babies you make because of racism, you can't get up in the mornings because of racism. You commit crimes because of racism. Unlike me you must not only overcome the repressiveness of racism, you must also overcome the lure of excuses. You have twice the job I had."

At the Supreme Court nomination hearings, Thomas said: "My grandparents always said there would be more opportunities for us. I can still hear my grandfather, 'Y'all goin' have mo' of a chance then me,' and he was right. He felt that if others sacrificed and created opportunities for us we had an obligation to work hard, to be decent citizens, to be fair and good people, and he was right."

Other birthdays
1894   Edward VIII of England, who abdicated to marry Wallis Simpson and became the Duke of Windsor
1927   Bob Fosse

June 24

1895   Manassa, Colorado.

Jack Dempsey (his real name was William Harrison Dempsey) was born. Of Native American, Irish, and Scots ancestry, he preferred sports to books. After finishing the eighth grade, Dempsey worked as a fruit picker, a lumberjack, and a miner. He also frequented pool halls. He admired the sporting life and was determined to become a boxer. He worked out, soaked his hands and face in brine to toughen them, and chewed wads of gum to strengthen his jaw. These efforts proved effective. Beginning in 1915, Dempsey began polishing off opponents with unrelenting regularity. He attracted a professional manager who lined up his first-string opponents. Dempsey knocked these down with such amazing dispatch that he was nicknamed the Manassa Mauler. He finished one off in just eighteen seconds.

In 1919, Dempsey took on Jess Willard, the world heavyweight champion. Willard out-weighed Dempsey by seventy pounds and was six inches taller. Dempsey had to stand on his toes to reach Willard but he beat him nonetheless to become champ. Dempsey kept the title until 1926, when Gene Tunney defeated him. During the seventh round of their 1927 rematch,

Dempsey knocked Tunney down but failed to return to his corner. The count couldn't start until he did so. This produced the famed "long count" that allowed Tunney to recover before being counted out. After three more rounds, Tunney won the decision. Dempsey took the defeat with good grace and remained a celebrity.

Dempsey's boxing advice was simple: "Keep your guard up, you chin down and your seat off the canvas."

Other Birthdays
1813   Henry Ward Beecher
1942   Mick Fleetwood

June 25

1945   New York City.

Singer Carly Simon was born. She came from a talented family. Her father, Richard Simon, was a cofounder of the publishing house Simon and Schuster and often entertained such guests as Albert Einstein. Carly's elder sister was a singer with the New York City Opera. A second sister became a rock singer and her younger brother became a photographer. Carly didn't seem as promising. She stuttered so badly that she avoided talking at all and went into analysis at age nine. Her mother noticed that she didn't stutter when she sang. Soon, Carly Simon was relying on her singing to communicate. She became a proficient singer and, despite severe stage fright, a fine concert performer. Her hits include "Anticipation," "You're So Vain," "You Belong to Me," and "Nobody Does It Better."

Other Birthdays
1925   June Lockhart
1949   Phyllis George
1949   Jimmy Walker
1963   George Michael

June 26

1904   Rosenberg, Hungary.

Laszlo Löwenstein was born. He later became famous as Peter Lorre, playing psychotic villains, after a short, pre–Pearl Harbor interlude as the Japanese detective Mr. Moto. Aptly, Lorre's first career choice had been psychology. He studied under Sigmund Freud and experimented with psychodrama. Lorre learned that he enjoyed appearing on stage, which was fortunate, since he decided he didn't have the correct couch-side manner—he couldn't help finding his patients' problems amusing. When a theatrical producer, who had seen Lorre's psychodramas, offered him an acting job in Poland, Lorre abandoned psychology.

Lorre appeared on stage in Austria, Switzerland, and Germany, then began making films. His breakthrough role came in 1931, when Fritz Lang cast him as a serial child killer in *M*. Lorre was so convincing in the role that, when a Berlin crowd spotted the actor on the street, they tried to stone him to death. Lorre survived and went on to a long film career highlighted by such films as *The Maltese Falcon* (1941) and *Casablanca* (1942).

When Lorre was first in Hollywood, a producer reneged on the promise of a part. Lorre hadn't yet learned enough English to express his dissatisfaction. All he could do was give the producer his trademark intense, bulgy-eyed glare. The producer glared back, but as the seconds ticked by, Lorre's eerie expression unnerved the producer. Lorre got the part.

Other Birthdays
1892   Pearl Buck
1939   Chuck Robb

June 27

1930   Texarkana, Texas.

H. (Henry) Ross Perot was born to G. Ross Perot, a cotton broker, and Margot Birmingham Perot, a schoolteacher. An

Eagle Scout, Perot had many boyhood sales jobs, including peddling newspapers, Christmas cards, seeds, and the *Saturday Evening Post*. He used his sales skills to persuade a U.S. senator to give him an appointment to the U.S. Naval Academy at Annapolis. After graduating in 1953, he was assigned to a destroyer. Perot found the U.S. Navy less promising than he had hoped and left in 1957 to work as a computer salesman for IBM.

Perot did well at IBM. He once exceeded his annual sales quota on January 19th. Perot also had ideas. When he suggested that IBM sell custom computer systems complete with software, however, they rebuffed him. Perot quit; then, using $1000 from his wife, he set up Electronic Data Systems, just in time for the vast demand created by the Great Society. Welfare bureaucrats across the nation needed custom computer systems to write millions of checks. Perot made a fortune. In 1968, when EDS went public, he was worth $350 million.

Perot built his fortune larger and larger. He also became interested in nonbusiness issues. He championed Americans held captive in Vietnam, helped some of his employees escape Iran, became involved in educational reform in Texas, and, in 1992, on *Larry King Live,* offered himself as a presidential candidate. His campaign, full of folksy aphorisms, was quirky to say the least.

Newsweek's Tom Morganthau observed, "Perot became a blank screen on which millions of American voters could project their discontents." Others suggested that Perot attributed his wealth solely to personal genius, forgetting his good luck. They said that safe in a nest of yes-men willing to accept the blame for his mistakes and give him credit for their achievements, Perot allowed himself to believe that his business expertise meant universal expertise. Perhaps Perot said it best himself when he said, long before his political gyrations, "As you become successful, you will need a great deal of self-discipline not to lose your sense of balance, humility and commitment."

Other Birthdays
1880   Helen Keller
1949   Lionel Richie
1951   Julia Duffy

June 28

1926   Brooklyn, New York.

Melvin Kaminsky was born. Under the name Mel Brooks, he became a successful comic, comedy writer, and filmmaker. Brooks said, in a 1975 *Playboy* interview, "My father was a process server and he died when I was two and a half—tuberculosis of the kidney. They didn't know how to knock it out, no antibiotics then.... [My mother] was a true heroine. She was left with four boys and no income, so she got a job in the Garment District. Worked the normal ten-hour day and then brought work home. Turned out bathingsuit sashes until daylight, grabbed a few hours of sleep, got us up and off to school and then went to work again."

Of his father, Brooks says, "I can't tell you what sadness, what pain it is to me never to have known my own father.... All I know is what they've told me. He was lively, peppy, sang well. Isn't it sad that that's all a son should know about his father?"

Despite his father's death and his mother's heavy workload, Brooks didn't feel neglected. He said, "I was adored. I was always in the air, hurled up and kissed and thrown in the air again. Until I was six, my feet didn't touch the ground.... My mother was the best cook in the world. 'I make a matzoh ball,' she used to say, 'that will sweep you off your feet.'" Brooks attributes his sense of humor to his grandmother, who used to joke with him in a crazy blend of English and Yiddish. He credits his Uncle Joe with such sage advice as: "Don't buy a cardboard belt," "Marry a fat goil. They strong. Woik f'ya. Don't marry a face. Put ya under," and, when Brooks was five, "Don't invest. Put da money in da bank. Even the land could sink."

In school, Brooks did well at his more theatrical studies. "When I had to read a composition, I would turn into a wild-eyed maniac, fling out my arms and announce in a ringing soprano: 'MY DAY AT CAMP!'" Brooks didn't take his religious training seriously. "We faked it, nodded like we were praying. Learned enough Hebrew to get through a *bar mitzvah*. Hebrew is a very hard language for Jews." Brooks preferred going to the movies, although *Frankenstein*, which he would later parody in *Young Frankenstein*, gave him nightmares.

Brooks's success at entertaining his classmates encouraged him to break into show business via New York's Catskill circuit. He performed in a hotel band and as a comic. World War II delayed his career. Brooks served in the U.S. Army, seeing action in the Battle of the Bulge right off the troop transport. Brooks returned to show business after being discharged and became a comedy writer for Sid Caesar's *Show of Shows*.

Brooks didn't start on equal footing with other Caesar writers. The talented staff, which included Joe Stein (author of *Fiddler on the Roof*), Larry Gelbart (writer-producer of *M*A*S*H*), Mike Stewart (author of *Hello, Dolly!*), Neil Simon, and, later, Woody Allen, was very competitive. Brooks wasn't even allowed in the workroom. He had to stand outside in the hall. The door would open, he'd be requested to come up with three or four gags, then the door would close. One of his bosses used to throw his lit cigar in Brooks's face when irritated. Brooks eventually became a full participant, but the anxiety of the job would cause him to throw up on the way to work and, occasionally, to start him running blindly through the streets of New York. Despite these difficulties, the show gave Brooks his show biz entrance. His career since then has been a long string of comedic successes with only a few stumbles.

Other Birthdays
1491   Henry VIII

1712   Jean-Jacques Rousseau
1946   Gilda Radner

June 29

1900   Lyons, France.

Antoine de Saint-Exupéry was born. His father was an ordinary villager but his mother came from an impoverished line of aristocrats. Saint-Exupéry had an adventurous nature. He spent hours watching flyers at a nearby airport. When he was older, he trained to be a pilot. At the time, air routes were connecting distant parts of the world, and Saint-Exupéry helped in this dangerous effort. He flew the Toulouse-Casablanca run for a year, ran an airfield in West Africa, established a route between Brazil and the southern tip of Argentina, and flew the mail across the Sahara desert. In 1935, while attempting to set a Paris to Saigon record, Saint-Exupéry crashed in the desert, where he nearly died of thirst before being rescued by passing Arabs.

Saint-Exupéry wrote lyrical accounts of his adventures, but is best remembered for his 1943 book *The Little Prince*. He served as a reconnaissance pilot during World War II. It was dangerous flying and, in 1944, he disappeared while flying over the Mediterranean Sea.

Saint Exupéry wrote, "It is only with the heart that one can see rightly; what is essential is invisible to the eye."

Other Birthdays
1901   Nelson Eddy
1915   Ruth Warrick
1919   Slim Pickens
1944   Gary Busey

June 30

1917   Brooklyn, New York.

Lena Horne was born the great-granddaughter of a slave woman and her white master. Horne's parents divorced when she was 13, and she was sent to the South to stay with relatives. A few years later, Horne dropped out of high school and returned to New York to become a chorus girl at the famous Cotton Club in Harlem. With her beautiful voice, she moved up to female vocalist for Charlie Barnet's band. Hollywood was so impressed that Horne became the first black woman offered a film contract. She appeared in such classics as *Cabin in the Sky* (1943) and *Stormy Weather* (1943). Despite her talented performances, Horne was often edited out of films shown to white Southern audiences.

Horne sagely advised,"Always be smarter than the people who hire you."

Other Birthdays
1918   Susan Hayward
1966   Mike Tyson

July 1

1961 Sandringham, England.

Princess Diana was delivered at home by a midwife. She was the fourth child of Viscount Johnny Spencer Althorp and his wife, Frances Roche, who had married Althorp at 18. The couple wanted a male child to carry on the family name but had four children before achieving their goal. The children were Sarah, Jane, John (who died hours later), Diana, and, finally, Charles. They enjoyed a luxurious childhood on a beautiful 20,000-acre estate at Sandringham. Their father was a wealthy, gentleman farmer so they had lots of pets, including horses.

All was not perfect, however. Frances grew tired of her husband. While Johnny enjoyed the country, she loved the social whirl of London. She became enamored of wallpaper millionaire Peter Shand Kydd, a married man. In 1967, Frances took an apartment in London and announced to the press, "I am living apart from my husband now. It is very unfortunate." She sued for divorce on the grounds of cruelty. After a bitter battle, during which Frances's mother sided with her son-in-law, Frances got her divorce and Johnny got the children. Diana didn't see her mother for two years.

Nannies might have filled the role of female authority in the home, but the children rejected discipline from anyone but their father. Diana's first two years of education were at home. A teacher was hired, and a half-a-dozen blue-blood children from surrounding estates were invited to attend with Diana. Diana was next sent to the posh Silfield School. Aside from school assignments, she was never encouraged to read books, or to learn music, or to develop athletic interests. Diana didn't acquire "country" skills, such as fishing, hiking, shooting, or even bird-watching. A broken arm at 10 when she fell from her pony left her with a fear of horses. She never went to a zoo or a circus. She had no idea how to play cricket or soccer. Nor was she encouraged to develop self-discipline.

Diana's lack of ordinary experience might be linked to a quality one of her nannies noted—stubbornness. She wouldn't do anything she didn't want to do. One thing Diana did learn was how to manipulate her father, who spoiled his children out of guilt over his failed marriage. One trick Diana practiced before a mirror was a shy look. She would tilt her head down and then peep upward timidly. It was a pose she would often use later.

At nine, Diana finished Silfield School. Her instructors later remembered little of her, other than that she was "average." She won just one school prize, an unnamed prize reserved for students who "tried hard." Diana soon had something new to try hard to deal with: Her father had found a new romance, Raine, Countess of Dartmouth. Johnny's children resented her attempts to discipline them, styling her Acid Raine and chanting "Raine, Raine, go away..."

After Silfield, Diana attended the exclusive boarding school Riddlesworth Hall. When she graduated at 14, she won two prizes, one for pet care, the other for helpfulness. A more important distinction came in that year, when Johnny inherited the title of Earl Spencer and Diana became Lady Diana. She next entered West Heath School in Kent, where her sisters had preceded her.

Jane had been expelled for drinking. Sarah did better, excelling academically and at sports. Diana split the difference. She pulled a few schoolgirl pranks and was an average student. Meanwhile, Johnny married Raine. The children weren't invited to the wedding. Tensions worsened when Raine sold a number of family treasures to finance the restoration of the family home. The children resented that they weren't consulted. When Raine fired many of the staff, for the first time the children had to do their own laundry. While at home on school holidays, Diana hid in her room to avoid Raine. Diana's school days soon ended when she twice failed her O-level exams, which are administered to all British children to determine who will get advanced education. Those who attend aristocratic schools seldom fail. To make matters worse, Diana refused to try again.

Diana, now 17, left for London, where she babysat and cleaned houses. With an inheritance, she bought an expensive apartment. She found roommates to share costs. After unsuccessfully trying to teach dance, she secured a job as a helper at a kindergarten. Her sister Sarah was dating Prince Charles. When Sarah broke off her romance with Charles, he turned his attentions to Diana.

Charles invited her to royal get-togethers at Balmoral, at Highgrove, and aboard the royal yacht. Diana seemed to fit in. She professed to love the outdoorsy activities that Charles enjoyed. In January 1979, over a bottle of champagne at Highgrove, Charles proposed. Diana accepted. They were married on July 21, 1982. Two children and a decade and a half later, they were living separately and Diana was battling a scandal over childish crank calls.

Other Birthdays
1804   George Sand
1899   Charles Laughton

1916   Olivia de Havilland
1931   Tab Hunter
1942   Genevieve Bujold
1946   Debbie Harry
1952   Dan Aykroyd
1961   Carl Lewis

July 2

1932   Atlantic City, New Jersey.

Dave Thomas was born. He was adopted by Rex and Avleva Thomas, who raised him in Kalamazoo, Michigan. His mother died when he was five and his father became an itinerant handyman. Thomas's father often took him to hamburger joints to eat and, at eight, Thomas determined to own his own hamburger place. At 12, he lied about his age to get a twelve-hour-a-day job in a restaurant. At 15, he became a busboy in Phil Clauss's Hobby House restaurant in Fort Wayne, Indiana. When his father decided to move on, Thomas stayed behind, dropping out of high school to work full-time.

After a term in the U.S. Army managing an enlisted men's club, Thomas returned to the Hobby House restaurant. It became one of the first Kentucky Fried Chicken franchises and Colonel Harland Sanders became Thomas's mentor. In 1962, Thomas was offered the chance to manage four failing chicken restaurants in return for part ownership if he could make them profitable. He took the offer against Sanders's advice. By keeping the restaurants spotless, buying radio commercial time with buckets of chicken, and working long hours, he made a success of the restaurants. He rolled over his profits into four more places. In 1968, he sold his interest in them to Kentucky Fried Chicken for $1.5 million.

Thomas didn't rest on his laurels. He opened the Arthur Treacher's Fish and Chips chain, then, in 1969, founded the Wendy's Old Fashioned Hamburgers chain, named after his daughter. In nine years, he had 1000 Wendy's franchises. It became the third largest restaurant chain in the world. Thomas attributes much of his success to employees who have what he calls an MBA—a "Mop Bucket Attitude." That is, they work hard and keep their restaurants clean.

Thomas has used part of his fortune to set up the Dave Thomas Foundation for Adoption.

Other Birthdays
1904   Johnny Weissmuller
1922   Dan Rowan
1937   Richard Petty
1951   Cheryl Ladd

July 3

1962   Syracuse, New York.
Thomas Cruise Mapother IV was born. Under the simpler name Tom Cruise, he became a movie star while still a teenager. His father is Thomas Cruise Mapother III, an electrical engineer, whose job kept the family moving so often that Cruise attended eight elementary schools and three high schools. Cruise's mother is Mary Lee Mapother, a teacher who specialized in dyslexic students. Her interest in that learning disorder was personal as well as professional. She, Cruise, and his three sisters suffer from dyslexia. Despite her attentions, her son still found school troubling. His problems were compounded when his parents divorced when he was 11 and his mother, who had custody of the children, struggled to make ends meet.

Cruise sought stability in a seminary when he was 14. He had planned to become a priest, but by the time he was 15, he realized that he didn't want a celibate life. He returned to his high school where he discovered that he could win friends through sports. A talented athlete, he played football, baseball, hockey, tennis, and lacrosse. He also skied and wrestled. Cruise lost the social device sports provided when, while training for a wrestling match, he injured himself and had to find less physical school activities. The school glee club coach suggested that he audition for the role of Nathan Detroit in the school's production of the musical *Guys and Dolls*. Cruise won the role and found that he felt "at home" on the stage. He dropped out of school to become an actor.

Cruise tried dinner theater, then left for New York City, where he soon won a part in the 1981 Franco Zeffirelli film *Endless Love*. The movie bombed but the part helped him get a juicy role in *Taps* (1981). The critics liked his performance and Cruise went on to many starring roles in such films as *Risky Business* (1983), *Top Gun* (1986), *Rain Man* (1988), and *A Few Good Men* (1992).

Other Birthdays
1883   Franz Kafka

July 4

1900   Back O' Town section, New Orleans.

Jazz trumpeter Louis "Satchmo" Armstrong was born to Willie Armstrong, a worker in a turpentine factory, and Mayann Armstrong. He was raised in a one-room shack off an alley. Although Mayann was a religious woman who insisted young Louis attend church, she was lively and loved a good time. This led to quarrels with her husband, and, after having a second child, she spent most of her time away from home. It has been suggested that she supported herself through prostitution. Armstrong later said, "Whether my mother did any hustling I cannot say. If she did, she kept it out of sight." Armstrong's grandmother, who had been born in slavery, raised the children.

For the most part, the young Armstrong behaved himself. There were many temptations in his tough neighborhood, however, and he was sentenced to reform school for firing a pistol into the air. While there, he learned to play the trumpet.

Since his family was too poor to pay for a trumpet or lessons, he would never have learned the skill had he not been sent to reform school. Armstrong worked his way up through the many twists and turns of the jazz world to become internationally famous.

Armstrong was once asked, "What's jazz?" He replied, "Man, if you got to ask you'll never know."

1918   Sioux City, Iowa.

Twins Esther "Eppie" Pauline Friedman and Pauline "Popo" Esther Friedman were born. Throughout their childhood the pair dressed alike and happily shared activities. After attending Morningside College, they both went into journalism and wound up in exactly the same newspaper niche as fierce competitors. Esther became "Ann Landers," and Pauline became "Abigail Van Buren," of "Dear Abby" fame.

Other Birthdays
1826   Stephen Foster
1872   Calvin Coolidge
1920   Leona Helmsley
1924   Eva Marie Saint
1927   Neil Simon
1928   Gina Lollobrigida

July 5

1810   Bethel, Connecticut.

Showman Phineas Taylor Barnum was born. Barnum had to become self-sufficient early—his father died when Barnum was 15, leaving him to support his mother and five siblings. He scraped by with odd jobs, then began publishing an antislavery newspaper. After a number of suits for libel, Barnum moved on to less literary pursuits.

Barnum traveled to New York City in 1835, where he took advantage of the rubes by exhibiting a black woman he advertised as the 161-year-old nurse of George Washington. She was actually half that age, but the crowds swarmed to see her, giving Barnum $1,500 a week. He went on to many other ventures, including a phony mermaid, the original bearded lady, the midget General Tom Thumb, the Swedish Nightingale Jenny Lind, Jumbo the elephant, and his renowned circus.

Barnum called himself the Prince of Humbugs, but saw his career as a worthwhile endeavor. He said, "This is a trading world and men, women and children, who cannot live on gravity alone, need something to satisfy their gayer, lighter moods and hours, and he who ministers to this want is in a business established by the Author of our nature."

Other Birthdays
1853   Cecil Rhodes
1904   Milburn Stone
1948   Julie Nixon Eisenhower

July 6

1946   Hell's Kitchen, New York City.

Sylvester Stallone was born. His father ran a chain of beauty parlors, and his mother was a former chorus girl. Stallone was raised in Philadelphia after his parents divorced. He was a difficult kid who got kicked out of several schools. He became interested in acting when he was cast in a school production of Arthur Miller's *Death of a Salesman*. For a time, he studied hairdressing, but following a stint as a gym instructor at a Swiss girls' school, he enrolled in the University of Miami to obtain formal dramatic training.

Stallone had a hard time getting started in films. He supported himself with odd jobs, including demonstrating food, sweeping lion cages, and ushering in a movie house. He met his first wife while ushering. They married and she supported his interest in acting. He needed reassurance.

Stallone considered quitting acting after a director told him that he had a New York accent so thick that it constituted a speech impediment. Stallone later said, "I wanted to go to Australia and work with cattle. Now that's kind of an extreme rejection, you know. It's not like saying let's go home and be, you know, a phys. ed. instructor. I didn't know anything about cattle or Australia."

Stallone's first role on Broadway was in a musical featuring nudity. His first film was a tame adult movie called *A Party at Kitty and Stud's*. Stallone got his first break with the film *The Lords of Flatbush* (1974), which costarred Henry Winkler. Stallone had written a screenplay after watching little-known boxer Chuck Wepner nearly go fifteen rounds with Muhammed Ali. Despite an offer of $300,000, Stallone refused to sell it if he couldn't star in it. After *Flatbush*, he succeeded in getting his terms accepted. The film was *Rocky* (1976). It was a hit, winning three Oscars. It had taken Stallone just eighty-six hours to put together the screenplay.

In a *Rolling Stone* interview, Stallone described the drive to become an actor: "It's like walking around with a present that no one wants. That's the way I felt as a child. A lot of actors felt that way, I think, and now, luckily, there's an outlet for it."

Other Birthdays
1747   John Paul Jones
1921   Bill Haley
1923   Nancy Reagan
1925   Merv Griffin
1932   Della Reese

July 7

1940   Liverpool, England.

Ringo Starr was born. His real name was Richard Starkey, but he got the nickname Ringo from his habit of wearing numerous rings. He chose Starr because of its connotations of success and because it appealed to his fanciful interest in the American West.

Starr was raised by his grandmother in a tough Liverpool slum while his mother worked as a barmaid. His housepainter father had abandoned the family when Starr was three. Starr was sickly, constantly in and out of hospitals suffering from pleurisy, peritonitis, and even a broken pelvis. After leaving school at 14, he worked as an engineer's apprentice until the "Skiffle" craze hit England in the 1950s. Starr's mother got him a set of drums, and he began hammering away. He worked with a number of bands with growing success, but with little thought of making music a career. He hoped to earn enough money to open a hairdressing salon.

In 1962, Starr was performing with Rory Storme and the Hurricanes. That group's principal rival in Liverpool's small clubs was a band called the Beatles. It was amiable rivalry, and Starr sometimes substituted for the Beatles' drummer, Pete Best. When the Beatles decided to dump Best, they tapped Starr as his replacement. Starr played the drums for the group's first British recording, "Love Me Do." Within a year, the Beatles were on the top of the charts, entertaining royalty and touring the world.

Other Birthdays
1906   Satchel Paige
1922   Pierre Cardin
1927   Doc Severinsen
1950   Shelley Duvall

July 8

1839   Richford, New York.

Elizabeth Davison was a pious Baptist woman who married a less-than-pious man. In fact, her husband was a con man who styled himself Doctor and peddled elixirs supposedly capable of curing everything from colic in cattle to cancer in human beings. He traded horses, sold real estate, and made loans at high rates. He also had a secret second wife in a different town. He cheerfully said, "I cheat my boys every chance I get. Makes 'em sharp." He spent much of his time on the road, leaving Elizabeth and their four children on their own.

Elizabeth parceled out chores to her children, reserving the heaviest for her eldest son, John, who was born on this date. Elizabeth was strict. One time, when she was whipping John, he protested his innocence. She replied, "Never mind, we have started in on this whipping and it will do for next time." This might suggest that she had a low opinion of John, but she said, "I don't know what John is going to be when he grows to be a man, but I'm sure of one thing—he won't starve."

Elizabeth proved correct. John, a sober-minded fellow, was nicknamed the Deacon by his friends. When his mother suggested he attend college, he chose to go to trade school and learn more practical skills. He kept meticulous account books detailing his every expense and, when he was asked what career he was going to pursue, he simply replied, "I'm going to make $100,000."

John started out as a clerk in a coal company during the Civil War. He saved his pay but was willing to take chances speculating with his savings. When a method for extracting petroleum from the ground was developed, John was ready. Drilling was speculative but refining was required of all oil. John built a huge refinery. He began forming secret arrangements for transporting his oil at rates lower than his competitors, forcing them to sell out to him or go broke. He saw nothing wrong with this, because he fully expected others to take every advantage they could take against him. One tactic John used was to name his oil company Standard Oil, thereby suggesting it was the standard against which all others were judged. Before the federal government forced its break-up, it was, indeed, the world standard. And even after its break-up, its creator, the son of "Doctor William Avery Rockefeller, The Celebrated Cancer Specialist," John D. Rockefeller, was the wealthiest man in the world.

John D. Rockefeller claimed, "The good Lord gave me my money." If He did, He got a kickback. Rockefeller always tithed to his church and donated to many charities.

Other Birthdays
1838   Ferdinand von Zeppelin
1951   Angelica Huston

July 9

1901   Ebgbaston, Birmingham, England.

Romance super-power Barbara Cartland was born into an aristocratic family. Her parents were Bertram and Polly Scobell Cartland, and Barbara was a direct descendant of the Dukes of Hamilton and the Scobells, an ancient Saxon family. She received a posh education, which prepared her for little other than the social whirl. During World War I, her father was killed at Flanders, leaving his family in poor circumstances. Cartland's mother hoped she would find work to help out the family. Instead, as Cartland says, she "was dancing all night with beautiful men" and "didn't wish to have a job at all." But finances forced her to become pragmatic. As a teenager, she had read as many as three novels a day. Now, she decided to become a writer.

In 1922, Cartland began contributing columns and articles to London's *Daily Express*. The newspaper tycoon Lord Beaverbrook became her mentor. She published her first novel, *Jigsaw*, in 1925. Cartland says, "It wasn't very good but it was a huge success because I was a debutant—a girl who was supposed to be a lady and had soiled her lily-white hands with work." She wrote more novels, earning herself a larger and larger audience. She is now the all-time best-selling romance writer, having published over 400 books.

Cartland's novels usually depict a virginal heroine who wins the love of a glamorously romantic man. She doesn't include much sex. Cartland says, "I never specifically describe the sex act because it's such a bore laid bare." Of her readers, she says, "I'm their escape, their fairy tale. I give them the glamour and the beautiful clothes and the marvelous attentive men they are starved of." She has also said of her happily ending works, "Why shouldn't people be happy? It's ridiculous to say you must be unhappy and write about the kitchen sink."

Cartland retained her connections to Britain's aristocracy. Her daughter, Raine, became the Countess Spencer and the stepmother of Princess Diana.

Other Birthdays
1928   Vince Edwards
1956   Tom Hanks
1976   Fred Savage

July 10

1943   Richmond, Virginia.

Arthur Ashe was born. His father was a city park caretaker-guard. His mother died of heart disease when Ashe was six. A sickly child, Ashe later excelled in sports. He went from a segregated tennis court to international tennis stardom, but his own heart disease led to double-bypass surgery in 1983. When he complained of his slow recovery, his doctor offered him the choice of waiting out the discomfort or taking a couple of units of blood to boost his energy. Ashe later wrote, "I would like the blood, I replied. I don't think I hesitated for a moment. Surely there was nothing to be feared from the blood bank of a major American hospital." Unfortunately, he was wrong. The blood gave him AIDS, which killed him in 1993.

Other birthdays
1871   Marcel Proust
1920   David Brinkley
1926   Fred Gwynne
1947   Arlo Guthrie

July 11

1767   Braintree [now Quincy], Massachusetts.

John Quincy Adams was born to Abigail Adams and John Adams, the second president of the United States. John Adams was a respected, but unpopular, patriot. He stubbornly pushed his ideas forward, despite danger to himself and objections from others. Abigail Adams was the product of a prominent Puritan line stretching back a century. Her parents had been very reluctant to let John Adams marry their daughter. His family wasn't as notable as theirs, and he was considered cantankerous. Reluctantly, they consented, but Abigail's minister father got in one humorous dig at his son-in-law. He chose the text for the wedding. It was Luke 7:33, which reads: "For John came neither eating bread nor drinking wine, and ye say, He hath a devil."

John and Abigail Adams had high hopes for the four children their marriage produced. John Quincy proved the most promising. At 11, he accompanied his father to Paris. Shortly after graduating from Harvard, he was named Minister to the Netherlands by George Washington. He went on to become the sixth President of the United States. He wasn't entirely the dignified statesman, however. As president, John Quincy Adams had the boyish habit of strolling down to a private spot on the Potomac on summer mornings and taking a nude swim. One day, a female reporter, anxious to interview Adams, followed him to the river and sat on his clothes until he answered all her questions.

Adams didn't abandon politics after leaving the White House. He became a congressman, diligently fighting for the anti-slavery cause.

Other Birthdays
1899   E. B. White
1959   Richie Sambora
1959   Suzanne Vega

July 12

1908   New York City.

Milton Berle was born. His show business career started at age four, when he began winning Charlie Chaplin impersonation contests. He became a child model and acted in vaudeville under the guidance of his mother, Sarah. Berle made his film debut at six in the Charlie Chaplin film *Tillie's Punctured Romance*, the first full-length comedy film. At 12, Berle was appearing on Broadway in the hit *Flora Dora*. He went on to perform in the Ziegfeld *Follies*. In 1937, Berle and his mother went to Hollywood where he made over thirty films. In the late 1940s, Berle became America's first television superstar. His *Texaco Star Theater* sold millions of television sets.

Berle credited his mother with much of his success. In the early days of his career, she served as a one-woman *claque*. Sitting in the theater, she primed the audience by laughing loudly at his jokes and wildly applauding his performances. When Berle became a success, his mother was proud of him and enjoyed calling attention to her role as a star's mother. When he once paged her at a New York hotel, she answered the lobby phone with a loud, "Is this my son, Milton Berle?"

Other Birthdays
1915   Yul Brynner
1937   Bill Cosby
1948   Richard Simmons
1951   Cheryl Ladd
1971   Kristi Yamaguchi

July 13

1940   England.

Shakespearean actor and *Star Trek* captain Patrick Stewart was born into a lower-middle class family. He struggled to transcend his background and become an actor. He said, "Life was scary when I was growing up. I wasn't beaten, but there was violence in the house. My father would get very angry. He would lose control. But recently, I came across a photograph. I'm sitting on a beach, in a deck chair, and my father is tickling me. And I am squirming with laughter. I must have been about six years old. If anybody would have asked me, 'Did your father ever make you laugh?' I'd have said, absolutely, not. He made me feel a lot of things, but he never made me laugh. And yet there it was. And I looked at the photograph and I could remember it. I knew what his fingers felt like in my ribs. I'd forgotten that my father made me laugh. And that's as important a memory to record as that he occasionally lost control of himself."

1942   Chicago.

Harrison Ford was born to parents of Russian-Jewish and Irish-Catholic ancestry. Ford was raised in suburban Des Plaines, Illinois, where he was a favorite victim of school bullies. A *Vanity Fair* article by David Halberstam quotes Ford as saying, "I was a real class wimp. And I was very angry, but I did not show it." Internalized anger turned Ford into a troublesome adolescent. When he attended Wisconsin's Ripon College, he rebelled by performing poorly, and his degree was withheld. Still, Ford's headstrong attitude caused him to confront a fear of public speaking by taking roles in school plays. He came to enjoy acting. After a summer of stock theater, he moved to Hollywood to become a professional actor.

Success took longer than Ford had hoped. His contrariness got him ejected from studio talent programs at Columbia and Universal. He got a few small parts but had to rely on working as a carpenter, building kitchen cabinets and hot tubs, to support himself and his new wife and two children. His first job was for Brazilian composer Sergio Mendes, who employed Ford to build a recording studio. Ford says, "Luckily, Sergio forgot to ask if I had ever built anything before, and I got the job. So there I was up on the roof with a library book on how to be a carpenter." Ford had a talent for the work and it gave him enough security to turn down roles he thought would hurt his career. In 1973, he accepted a role in George Lucas's *American Graffiti*. This lead to his starring role in 1976's mega-hit *Star Wars*. Ford went on to star in half of the top ten money-making films of all time.

Ford's son Malcolm once told his preschool pals, "My daddy is a movie actor, and sometimes he plays the good guy, and sometimes he plays the lawyer."

Other Birthdays
1886   Father Edward Joseph Flanagan
1935   Jack Kemp

July 14

1913   Omaha, Nebraska.

Leslie Lynch King Jr. was born to Dorothy and Leslie King. The couple divorced in two years. Dorothy moved to Grand Rapids, Michigan and remarried. Her new husband, paint salesman Gerald Rudolph Ford, adopted her son, who was renamed after his stepfather. Gerald Ford Jr. wasn't told about his adoption. He found out when King approached him while he was at work at a high school job at a diner. Ford's mother finally told him the truth. He only saw King one more time.

After high school, Ford worked his way through the University of Michigan as a busboy. He still led Michigan's football team to Big Ten championships. Ford next attended Yale Law School, graduating in the top third of his class. The athletic ex-football star spent some time as a male model. In 1948, Ford ran as a Republican for Congress. Pausing to marry Betty Bloomer, a divorced ex-dancer, Ford won handily. His goal was to become speaker of the house, but, when Vice President Spiro Agnew resigned, President Richard Nixon chose Ford to replace Agnew. When Nixon resigned, Ford became the thirty-eighth U.S. president.

Ford hoped to revive faith in government following the Watergate scandal and pardoned Nixon to avoid a controversial trial. This decision was widely criticized and Ford lost by just 1 percent of the vote to Jimmy Carter.

1918   Uppsala, Sweden.

Filmmaker Ingmar Bergman was born. His father was Lutheran minister, and Bergman was born in his father's parsonage. Bergman is famous for his gloomy, soul-probing movies. Of him, Liv Ullman said, "Living with Ingmar Bergman is not like living with Bob Hope. Other couples meet for breakfast and have coffee and English muffins and cuddle. Do you know what Ingmar Bergman did at breakfast? He told his nightmares and then told me I had to act in them!"

Other Birthdays
1911   Terry-Thomas
1932   Roosevelt "Rosey" Grier

July 15

1779   New York City.

Clement Moore was born. A prominent clergyman, Moore is remembered for a poem he wrote to entertain his children. Despite Moore's resistance, the poem was published. Moore thought the poem would lessen his reputation as a theologian. For twenty-two years, the preacher refused to have his name associated with the work and never received any payment for its publication. The poem Moore was reluctant to publish was "A Visit from Saint Nicholas," more popularly known as "The Night Before Christmas."

Other Birthdays
1606   Rembrandt van Rijn
1946   Linda Ronstadt

July 16

1911   Independence, Missouri.

Lela Owens McMath, 20, (a distant relative of George Washington's) was about to have her second child when her marriage to William Eddins McMath fell apart. Their marriage had been strained by the death of their first child during childbirth. William had given the doctor permission to use foreceps to hasten Lela's difficult labor and the forceps broke the infant's neck. Lela blamed William and the couple eventually parted, leaving Lela to look for work while nine months pregnant. She got a job as a secretary by promising to come to work on the 1st of August. On her way home from the interview, Lela went into labor and, on this date, gave birth to Virginia Katherine McMath. On August 1st, Lela reported for work with Virginia in a basket.

Lela's employers allowed her to keep the infant with her on the job. Friends would sometimes ask Lela if they could take the baby for a stroll or for ice cream. Shortly after Virginia turned a year old, someone took her without asking. Police could turn up no leads, but, when newspapers carried an account of the kidnapping, a train passenger reported sighting the crying little girl with a man on the train. Lela remembered that her husband had spoken of moving to Ennis, Texas. To get there, one had to take the train that the man had reportedly taken. Lela was convinced that her husband had stolen the child when she discovered that her mother-in-law had departed for Texas. Lela got a gun and took the next train to Ennis.

In Ennis, a Native American taxi driver told Lela that he had seen William and Virginia. When Lela explained the situation, the taxi driver offered to help and drove her to William's house. Lela burst in, grabbed the baby out of a high chair, and, with her mother-in-law scrabbling after her, hopped in the cab. Her mother-in-law latched onto the cab and was dragged fifty yards before letting go. The cab driver hid Lela and Virginia in his mother's teepee until the next train out of town arrived. He also arranged to have the stationmaster, who was his relative, lock William in the train station's cellar when William came looking for Lela. Thanks to the driver's kindness, Lela made her getaway. When William tried to kidnap Virginia again, Lela had him prosecuted. The judge threatened William with Leavenworth if he didn't leave Lela alone. Virginia never saw her father again, although, after Lela remarried, she did wind up living in Texas.

Virginia and her mother settled in Dallas, where Lela became a reviewer for the *Fort Worth Record* and entertained famous vaudevillians. Eddie Foy Jr. taught Virginia how to Charleston. One night one of the Foy children became ill and Virginia successfully filled in. The pleasure she got from this led her to participate in amateur productions. She was offered a scholarship to train as a ballerina, but when her mother discovered that the instructor planned to adopt Virginia if she turned out to be any good, she refused. Foy's Charleston lessons proved more valuable. Virginia won a Charleston contest. This led to a career as a dancer in vaudeville and film. Performing under her stepfather's last name and her nickname, Ginger, she became Ginger Rogers.

Other Birthdays
1821 Mary Baker Eddy
1907 Barbara Stanwyck
1971 Corey Feldman

July 17

1899 The Lower East Side, New York City.

Irish-American Carolyn Nelson had to leave school at 12 to help support her family by working at a pencil factory. Hardship, however, didn't prevent her from growing into an attractive woman with curly, waist-length red hair. James Francis Cagney was a handsome ladies' man and a talented amateur athlete, whose fast ball earned him the nickname Jimmy Steam. Not long after he met Carolyn, they were married. On this date, the couple had their second child, whom they named James, after his father.

The Cagney family had many problems. They lost two of their seven children to disease. James Francis Cagney gambled, drank too much and, to make matters worse, owned a saloon, so he could get booze wholesale. Nevertheless, he had great charm and was loved by his family, who never blamed him for their struggles. He died in the 1918 flu epidemic at 41, leaving his family in poverty. Young Jimmy Cagney had to leave college to help support his family.

Cagney worked as a waiter, a shipping clerk, a poolroom cue boy, and a newspaper vendor before he decided to try show business. By 1920, he was simultaneously dancing in drag in the chorus of a show called *Pitter-Patter*, dressing the show's star, understudying the principal, and serving ice cream as a soda jerk in a Walgreen's drugstore. He eventually found a dance partner and entered vaudeville. Soon, a studio spotted his genuine, Lower East Side manner and gave him a film contract. In 1931, he starred in *The Public Enemy*. His convincing gangsterism made him a success.

Many of Cagney's neighborhood chums died from poverty, labored their lives away in drudgery, or turned to real-world gangsterism, but the Cagney children were all successful. Cagney explained: "We had a mother to answer to. If any of us got out of line, she just belted us, and belted us emphatically. We loved her profoundly, and our driving force was to do what she wanted because we knew how much it meant to her. . . . We loved the great staunchness of her, and at times we four brothers together would impulsively put our arms around her, hold her, and hug her. She'd look at us, her nose would get red, and she'd start to cry. She just couldn't take all that love."

1917   Lima, Ohio.

Phyllis Diller was born to Frances and Perry Driver, an insurance sales manager. While studying to become a music teacher at Bluffton College in Ohio, she worked as the humor editor on her college paper and met Sherwood Anderson

Diller. They fell in love and eloped in 1939. They settled in California, where Sherwood held a variety of jobs, including as a refrigerator salesman for Sears Roebuck. He and Phyllis had five children. In addition to her heavy homemaking duties, Phyllis wrote a shopping column for a newspaper. She moved on to writing ad copy, then worked for KSFO radio in San Francisco handling merchandising and press relations. Phyllis's real talent, however, was displayed at the laundromat, where she entertained housewife friends with her jokes. They encouraged her to try stand-up comedy. Her first job, at San Francisco's "Purple Onion" nightclub, was a success. Diller worked in small clubs, then was booked into Miami Beach's Fontainebleau Hotel, which hired only the best stars.

Of the Fontainebleau engagement, Diller says, "After my first show the manager fired me. I came back to New York to live in a fleabag hotel. My defeat paralyzed my agency. They thought, 'My God, we've picked a loser.' However, my being fired turned out to be a really important break. *Tonight Show* host Jack Paar believed in me. Because I was out of work in New York (where the show was then produced), I was available whenever Jack wanted me. He used me on the show often, and the exposure was tremendous. There is no doubt I owe a disastrous firing and Jack Paar's friendly exposure for my success "

Other Birthdays
1934   Donald Sutherland
1935   Diahann Carroll
1956   Bryan Trottier

July 18

1921   Cambridge, Ohio.

Astronaut John Glenn was born. An honor student and varsity letterman in three sports, Glenn was a Marine combat pilot in World War II and Korea, then became a test pilot. He won a spot in the first batch of astronauts, and in 1959, became the first American to orbit the Earth. His poise in his space capsule was matched by his poise in front of television cameras. It wasn't at all surprising when his Ohio neighbors elected him senator in 1976.

Glenn's orbital predecessor in the American space program was the chimpanzee Enos, who orbited the Earth three times. The chimp had been trained to operate a series of levers in response to light signals so that scientists could learn whether astronauts could function in the same circumstances. An electric charge was administered if Enos pulled the wrong lever. Unfortunately, a wiring error had been made. After Enos was blasted into orbit, he discovered that no matter which lever he pulled he always got a shock. It wasn't long before Enos was angrily tearing apart everything in the space capsule. Flight controllers hurriedly brought the furious chimp back to Earth. It was with great difficulty that handlers pulled the irate Enos into a cage for the trip back to Cape Canaveral.

There, reporters insisted that Enos be brought forth for pictures. NASA officials, anxious for good publicity, nervously did so. Two airmen firmly held Enos's arms as wide as possible to stay clear of his gnashing, snarling teeth. They barely kept him from bounding into the reporters and chewing them up. Luckily for NASA, the reporters were unfamiliar with chimp behavior. The next day newspapers carried pictures of Enos, teeth ferociously bared, captioned: "Space Hero Enos—Happy After Space Flight." They'd thought he'd been grinning. Later, after Glenn's orbital flight, Glenn was brought to the White House to meet President Kennedy. Kennedy brought out his three-year-old daughter, Caroline, to meet the space traveler that had been in all the newspapers. Caroline looked around curiously and asked her dad, "Where's the monkey?"

Other Birthdays
1913   Red Skelton
1918   Nelson Mandela
1939   Hunter Thompson

July 19

1814   Hartford, Connecticut.

Samuel Colt was born. He ran away to sea at 16 to make a voyage to India. During the long trip, he discovered that being a seaman involved extended periods of time with nothing to do but stare at the ocean. He filled this time whittling and imagining inventions. He carved himself a model of a pistol with a revolving cylinder. When he returned to Connecticut, he made a metal copy of his "revolver." It took him four years to perfect it and patent it. In 1836, he set up a company to manufacture his new weapon. The company quickly failed. Colt worked with electrically triggered underwater mines and the telegraph, until 1846, when war with Mexico broke out.

Suddenly, the army needed weapons and they were eager for any technological advantage they could get. Colt and Eli Whitney were contracted to produce 1,000 revolvers. The weapons were so well received that, in 1847, Colt opened a factory. By 1855, it was the largest private armory in the world. Colt "six-shooters" were used during the Civil War and in the winning of the West, earning the gun a reputation for reliability and efficiency. It was said, "God created Man, but Sam Colt made them equal."

Other Birthdays
1922   George McGovern

July 20

1947   Autlán de Navarro, Mexico.

Carlos Santana was born. He began studying the violin at five, but, by the time he was 14, he was playing guitar in Tijuana bars for spare change. In 1967, he headed for San Francisco and Haight-Ashbury. With organist Gregg Rolie and bass guitarist Dave Brown, Santana formed the Santana Blues Band, which mixed African, Mexican, and Cuban sounds with California rock and modern blues. The group became local favorites in San Francisco. After adding Jose Areas on drums and trumpet, the group crossed over into national success under the name Santana, with two successful albums, *Santana* and *Abraxas*. Their hits included "Evil Ways," "Oye Como Va," and "Black Magic Woman."

Other Birthdays
1890   Theda Bara
1928   Diana Riggs
1938   Natalie Wood

July 21

1899   Oak Park, Illinois.

Ernest Hemingway was born the second of six children. His father, a doctor, enjoyed fishing and hunting. Ernest loved him and shared his father's interests. Ernest's mother, however, made him dress like a girl and kept him out of school for two years so that she could dispatch him and his sister Marcelline to school together as "twins." In part to escape the domination of his mother, Hemingway left town as soon as he finished high school to serve as an ambulance driver in World War I. After the war, he lived in Paris as a journalist. With the help of F. Scott Fitzgerald, Ezra Pound, and Gertrude Stein, Hemingway became a successful novelist. His books included *The Sun Also Rises*, *A Farewell to Arms*, *For Whom the Bell Tolls*, and *The Old Man and the Sea*. He won both the Pulitzer and Nobel Prizes for literature.

Hemingway once wrote, "Always do sober what you said you'd do drunk. That will teach you to keep your mouth shut."

Other Birthdays
1938   Janet Reno
1952   Robin Williams

July 22

1923   Russell, Kansas.

Senator Robert Dole was born into a hard-working family. His father, Doran Dole, ran an egg and cream station, and Robert's mother, Bina Dole, sold sewing machines door-to-door. The family once rented their house to oil workers and slept in the cellar. Young Robert sold Cloverine salve, delivered newspapers, and worked as a soda jerk.

Dole was a star athlete in high school, winning an athletic scholarship to the University of Kansas. He hoped to become a doctor, but World War II changed his plans. He served as a second lieutenant in the U.S. Army's 10th Mountain Division in Italy. In 1945, just three weeks before the war ended in Europe, Dole was badly wounded by machine-gun fire while trying to rescue his radioman. He lost most of his right shoulder, his arm dangled from what was left, and injuries to his spinal column paralyzed him from the neck down. He spent three years in military hospitals.

Dole's doctors thought he might never walk again. While in the hospital, mirrors were kept away from him, lest he see how injured he was. One day, a nurse accidentally left a bathroom door open and Dole saw himself in the bathroom mirror. He was horrified. In 1993, during a television interview, he said he still avoids mirrors, not even shaving until he puts on his shirt. He also recalled how his father had made the long train trip from Kansas to Battle Creek, Michigan, to visit him in the hospital on Christmas Day. At the time, trains were jammed with soldiers going home, so his father had to stand for the entire trip. Dole's eyes filled as he recalled his aging father's badly swollen legs.

When Dole was released from the hospital, he was still an invalid. He envisioned himself selling pencils on a street corner. His family and friends encouraged him to lay his former ambitions aside and find new interests. He slowly came to accept this, telling himself, "Maybe Bob Dole can do something else." He was further inspired by the citizens of his hometown, who collected money to help him get special treatment that improved his condition. Dole still suffers pain and never regained complete use of his right arm. He carries a pen in his injured hand to signal to others that he can't use the hand, thereby saving them the embarrassment of reaching for a handshake from his wrong side. Dole lived up to the faith of his family, friends, and neighbors put in him. In time, he became a lawyer, and eventually, the most prominent Republican in Washington, D.C.

Dole has a sense of humor. After the existence of the Watergate tapes was revealed and several prominent politicians had to explain their sometimes-embarrassing comments, Dole quipped, "Thank goodness whenever I was in the Oval Office, I only nodded."

Other Birthdays
1890   Rose Kennedy
1940   Alex Trebek
1947   Albert Brooks
1955   Willem Dafoe

July 23

1888   Chicago, Illinois.

Raymond Chandler was born. His parents, Maurice and Florence Chandler, were Quakers. They divorced when Raymond was nine and Florence, who was Anglo-Irish, brought him to England. He was educated there and in France and Germany. He spent a short time working as a teacher, then tried journalism, which was not his forté—he later said that he "always got lost" while tracking down stories. He switched to feature writing and criticism. During World War I he served in the Canadian Army and was training to be a pilot when the war ended. After his discharge, Chandler went back to the United States.

In America, Chandler first worked as an accountant. He

moved on to become a tax expert, then an oil company executive, before settling into a job writing for the Los Angeles *Daily Express* while working on his own fiction on the side. In 1933, he published his first detective story, "Blackmailers Don't Shoot," in the pulp magazine *Black Mask*. In 1939, he introduced detective Philip Marlowe in his classic mystery novel *The Big Sleep*. Chandler went on to write several hard-boiled yet well-written mystery novels featuring Marlowe.

Chandler's prose was full of evocative images. He described Los Angeles as "A big hard-boiled city with no more personality than a paper cup." Hollywood recognized the film potential of his novels and snatched them up, also hiring Chandler as a screenwriter. He said, "If my books had been any worse, I should not have been invited to Hollywood, and if they had been any better, I should not have come."

While Chandler advised mystery writers "When the plot flags, bring in a man with a gun," for his own recreational reading, he chose English "cozy" mysteries.

Other Birthdays
1913　Michael Foot
1961　Woody Harrelson

July 24

1897　Atchison, Kansas.

Aviatrix Amelia Mary Earhart was born to Edwin and Amy Otis Earhart. Earhart saw her first plane in 1908 at the Iowa State Fair in Des Moines, just five years after the Wright brothers made their first flight. She was unimpressed: "It was a thing of rusty wire and wood and looked not at all interesting." During World War I, Earhart worked as a nurse's aid in a Toronto military hospital. In 1918, she went to an air show put on by returning military pilots. This time, she was impressed by the aircraft she saw. In 1920, she took her first plane ride with the famed barnstormer Frank Hawks. "By the time I had got two or three hundred feet off the ground," she later said, "I knew I had to fly."

Earhart's father had reservations about her wish to become a pilot, but her mother enthusiastically approved when Earhart purchased her own Kinner Canary airplane as her twenty-fifth birthday present. Just six years, in 1928, she became the first woman to cross the Atlantic Ocean in an airplane and, in 1932, she became the first woman to fly the Atlantic solo. She went on to other aviation records, but, in 1937, during an attempt to fly around the world, she disappeared in the South Pacific.

Earhart said of her childhood, "As a little girl...I had explored the fearsome caves in the cliffs overlooking the Missouri; I had invented a trap and caught a chicken; I had jumped over a fence that no boy my age had dared to jump; and I knew there was more fun and excitement in life than I could have time to enjoy."

Other Birthdays
1783   Simón Bolívar
1802   Alexandre Dumas, père
1920   Bella Abzug
1936   Ruth Buzzi

July 25

1978   Oldham General Hospital in Oldham, England.

Louise Brown, the world's first "test-tube baby," was born to Lesley Brown and van driver Gilbert John Brown. They had had trouble conceiving a child in the more customary way because of a blockage in Lesley's fallopian tubes. Doctors took an ovary from Lesley, fertilized it with her husband's sperm in a laboratory dish, and placed the resulting embryo in Lesley. The product of this extraordinary effort was the perfectly ordinary and charming baby girl, Louise. The Browns set aside a nice nest egg for Louise by selling rights to interviews and photographs to a British newspaper for over half a million dollars.

Other Birthdays
1894   Walter Brennan

July 26

1856   Dublin.

George Bernard Shaw was born, the fourth of four children his parents had within three years. The family lived in shabby gentility on Synge Street in Dublin. Shaw later said, "The adult who has been poor as a child will never get the chill of poverty out of his bones." The family's poverty was not improved by his parents' lack of affection for each other. His mother had married Shaw's father, who was the cousin of a banker-baronet, hoping to find security. She soon discovered that her husband had little money and an affection for alcohol. For his part, Shaw's father discovered that his wife was a poor housekeeper, spent money too easily, and was an inept mother. Shaw said of her, "Technically speaking, I should say she was the worst mother conceivable, always, however, within the limits of the fact that she was incapable of unkindness to any child, animal or flower, or, indeed, to any person or thing whatsoever." Despite their deficiencies, Shaw's parents raised an intelligent, self-confident son who became a leading intellectual of his age.

Shaw had a healthy ego and often boasted of his talents. Once, he bragged that he had the recipe for the perfect cup of coffee. A curious parson wrote Shaw, asking for the recipe. Shaw sent it with a note that read: "I hope that this is a genuine request, and not a surreptitious mode of securing my autograph." The parson wrote back: "Accept my thanks for the recipe for making coffee. I wrote in good faith and, in order to convince you of that fact, allow me to return what it is obvious you infinitely prize, but which is of no value to me—your autograph."

Other Birthdays
1875   Carl Gustav Jung
1927   Janet Leigh
1928   Stanley Kubrick
1943   Mick Jagger
1956   Dorothy Hamill

July 27

1940   Hollywood, California.

Bugs Bunny was born when Warner Brothers Studios released the cartoon *A Wild Hare*. The plot of the cartoon became the standard Bugs Bunny adventure—Elmer Fudd unsuccessfully pursues a "wascally wabbit" dinner. Many artists contributed to the creation of Bugs. Warner's animation director, Tex Avery, came up with the idea of a wise-cracking rabbit. He got the tag line "What's up, Doc?" from an irreverent childhood friend. Mel Blanc produced the "part Brooklyn, part Bronx" voice. Animator Chuck Jones contributed plots and says, "Bugs IS what I would like to be: debonair, quick-witted, very fast on the comeback. I'd like to have the ability to be a sort of a male Dorothy Parker, and to have the quip ready every time. I think of beautiful quips, but they're always late. You go home and think, 'I should have said THAT.' Wouldn't it be wonderful to be able to think that fast? And Bugs can, you see."

Other Birthdays
1912   Norman Lear
1948   Peggy Fleming

July 28

1929   Long Island, New York.

Jacqueline Bouvier Kennedy Onassis was born to stockbroker John "Black Jack" Vernou Bouvier III and Janet Lee Bouvier. Their marriage ended in divorce, and Jacqueline and her sister, Lee, were raised by her mother and her wealthy stepfather, Hugh Auchincloss. The family divided its time between Newport, Washington, D.C., and Virginia. Jacqueline attended Vassar and became a newspaper photographer following graduation. She later said, "I always wanted to be some kind of writer or newspaper reporter. But after college—I did other things." The "other things" happened after she met John Kennedy, a young U.S. senator. They married in 1953 and, by the time Jacqueline was 31, she was first lady.

Jacqueline once observed, "There are two kinds of women; those who want power in the world, and those who want power in bed."

Other Birthdays
1901   Rudy Vallee
1948   Sally Struthers

July 29

1892   Pittsburgh, Pennsylvania.
William Horatio Powell was born. When a performance in a school Christmas pageant won him the admiration of his family and friends, Powell decided to become an actor. After high school, a legacy from a wealthy aunt allowed him to attend the American Academy of Dramatic Arts. His stage career, however, was interrupted by World War I. Powell served in the U.S. Army. When discharged, he decided to try Hollywood.

Powell's first film roles were as heavies in Westerns. His break came when he was cast in *Sherlock Holmes* (1922) oppposite John Barrymore as Holmes. This led to a string of successes. When talking movies came along, Powell's stage-trained voice made him a valuable commodity. He appeared in a series of successful Philo Vance films and became so associated with the role that, when he married Carole Lombard, she always called him Philo (they later amicably divorced). MGM next cast Powell in *The Thin Man* (1934) as Nick Charles with Myrna Loy as his film wife. Their blend of screwball comedy and murder mystery broke the common movie mold, in which hero and heroine are unmarried. Sixty years later, they are still audience favorites.

Other Birthdays
1938   Peter Jennings

July 30

1947   Graz, Austria.

Arnold Schwarzenegger was born. His poor family lived in a small upstairs apartment without a telephone or indoor plumbing. Schwarzenegger was a small and sickly child. His father took six-year-old Arnold to see Olympic athlete and Tarzan star Johnny Weissmuller, who was touring Austria. The boy was so impressed that he decided to become a bodybuilder. At 18, while serving in the Austrian Army, he went AWOL to compete in a Mr. Europe Jr. contest. At 20, he won the Mr. Universe title. In 1968, he emigrated to the bodybuilding center of the universe, Venice, California. He continued to win muscle competitions, snaring the Mr. Universe title four more times and winning the Mr. Olympia title six times. In 1975, he left competitive body-building to write the bestseller *Arnold: The Education of a Body Builder*. Schwarzenegger's appearances in *Stay Hungry* (1976) and the documentary *Pumping Iron* (1977) garned good reviews. (He had also appeared in a clumsy Hercules flick when he first reached America.) Despite, or perhaps because of, a thick Austrian accent that made him seem more exotic than other actors, Schwarzenegger starred in a string of hit adventure films, including *Conan the Barbarian* (1982), *The Terminator* (1984), *Total Recall* (1990), and *Terminator 2: Judgment Day* (1991).

Schwarzenegger has parlayed his earnings into a real estate

fortune. In 1977, he met Kennedy family member Maria Shriver and married her in 1986. Despite this connection to Democratic royalty, Schwarzenegger campaigned for George Bush, who styled him Conan the Republican.

John Milius said of Schwarzenegger, "Of course, if Arnold hadn't existed we would have had to build him."

Other Birthdays
1863 Henry Ford
1933 Edd "Kookie" Byrnes
1939 Peter Bogdanovich
1941 Paul Anka
1946 Linda Ronstadt
1956 Delta Burke

July 31

1962 Orlando, Florida.

Wesley Snipes was born. His father, an aircraft engineer, and his mother, a teacher's aide, divorced when Snipes was an infant. His mother moved him and his two siblings to the South Bronx, where Snipes became a favorite of his Aunt Della Saunders, who entered him in talent shows. He got a small role in an off-Broadway play at 12. Snipes later entered New York's High School of the Performing Arts. He also began associating with rowdy types. His mother, fearful for his future, moved back to Orlando.

Snipes was bitter about leaving New York, but he soon discovered advantages to the move. His theatrical background made him stand out in his new high school and he got the best roles in school plays. This led to work in a city-sponsored drama troupe. He performed in puppet shows, did a one-man rendition of Shakespeare's Puck, and played Felix Unger in a production of *The Odd Couple*. Snipes says, "Moving to Florida was the best thing that could happen to me. A lot of cats I grew up with in the South Bronx found themselves in sticky situations."

With his background, Snipes easily secured entry into the theater arts program at SUNY at Purchase. He went on to starring roles in such films as *New Jack City* (1991) and *White Men Can't Jump* (1992). They were a long way from puppet shows in the park, but they were also not the kind of work he had hoped for when he first went into show business. He had dreamed of being a song-and-dance man.

Other Birthdays
1912 Milton Friedman
1919 Curt Gowdy
1944 Geraldine Chaplin

August 1

1942   San Francisco.

Jerry Garcia was born. His father was a Spanish bartender and musician, and his mother was Swedish-Irish. Because Garcia was a troublesome boy, his worried mother bought him an accordion for his 15th birthday to give him a hobby. Garcia traded it in for an electric guitar. After a short hitch in the U.S. Army, he began playing in San Francisco coffeehouses, scraping together a meager living. Friendly associates during this period included then-unknowns Jimi Hendrix and Janis Joplin. Garcia hooked up with drummer Ken McKernan and guitarist Bob Weir to form Mother McGree's Jug Band. Upon adding bassist Phil Lesh and drummer Bill Kreutzman, they renamed themselves the Warlocks. Discovering that this name had been taken, they passed through several identities, including the very-1960s The Mythical Ethical, Icicle Tricycle. This confusion ended when Garcia flipped open the *Oxford English*

Dictionary and found the name Grateful Dead. The band went on to success, with multitudes of "Deadhead" fans.

Other Birthdays
1933   Dom DeLuise
1936   Yves Saint-Laurent
1973   Tempestt Bledsoe

August 2

1933   County Galway, Ireland.

Peter O'Toole was born to a bookmaker father and an aristocratic Anglo-Irish mother. The couple met at the 1929 Epson Derby. O'Toole's father had trouble providing for his family. Hoping to do better, they moved to London, but their finances didn't improve and they lived in a slum neighborhood. O'Toole was placed in a Catholic school, where the nuns beat him for being left-handed. Not surprisingly, his academic life ended early—at 13, he left school to work in a warehouse. He next became a copyboy for the *Yorkshire Evening News*, then enlisted in the Royal Navy. Upon his discharge, he was passing the Royal Academy of Dramatic Arts in London and decided to drop in. The brash seaman charmed the instructors, and he was given admission. His training earned him membership in Bristol's Old Vic, where he played for several years before winning his breakout role as T. E. Lawrence in David Lean's epic *Lawrence of Arabia* (1962). The hard-drinking O'Toole got the part despite having a bottle of liquor tumble from his pocket during his interview.

O'Toole spent many years abusing alcohol before swearing it off. In 1983, he ruefully observed "Sobriety's a real turn-on for me. You can see what you're doing."

Other Birthdays
1905   Myrna Loy
1924   Carroll O'Connor

August 3

1926   Astoria, Queens, New York.

Antonio Dominick Benedetto was born. His father was a tailor and grocer who died when Benedetto was just nine. His mother raised him while working as a seamstress. By the time he was 15, he was working as a singing waiter earning $15 a week and tips. He enjoyed it, saying, "If I never make it, I want to do this the rest of my life." Benedetto's uncle, vaudevillian Dick Gordon, became his mentor, giving him advice on how to get into show business. World War II postponed Benedetto's plans. He served as an infantryman with the U.S. Army in Europe and with the occupation forces following the war. After a racist officer spotted him going into a bar with a black soldier, Benedetto was assigned the gruesome duty of digging up Allied soldiers who had been hastily buried during the fighting and preparing them for shipment back to the United States.

When Benedetto was discharged, he tried show business again. Under the name Tony Bennett, he was singing at a small nightclub in Greenwich Village when Bob Hope discovered him. Bennett became known as the Singer's Singer, with such hits as "I Left My Heart in San Francisco." Bennett's career took a nose dive, however, with the advent of rock and roll. He lost his record contract. After a ten-year hiatus, he attempted to record under his own label but failed. Then Bennett's son Danny became his manager. Danny aggressively pushed his father into the modern music scene, confident that his father's talent and solid songs would win over young audiences. They did. Bennett now performs at rock concerts alongside the newest bands and has a video on MTV. Bennett says, "It's the best I've ever felt in my life."

Other Birthdays
1900   Ernie Pyle
1924   Leon Uris
1940   Martin Sheen

August 4

1901   Russia.

Clara Peller was born. She came to America with her parents when she was a child and settled in Chicago, where she later worked for thirty-five years as a beautician. In 1970, an ad-man trying to fill a manicurist role in a television commercial took the unusual step of actually going to a real beauty shop. One of the shops he visited was Peller's. When the four-foot-ten, 69-year-old grandma greeted him with a gruff "How ya doing, honey?" he knew he'd found a memorable actress. She appeared in several commercials, then made a 1984 Wendy's hamburger spot. In response to being served a small burger in a huge bun Peller bellowed, "Where's the beef?" and became a national sensation. Walter Mondale used the phrase to torpedo Gary Hart in a television debate. Wendy's sales increased by 31 percent and Mondale won the nomination. Peller earned about $500,000. She died shortly after her 86th birthday in 1987, but is remembered fondly by millions.

Other Birthdays
1962   Roger Clemens

August 5

1930   Near Wapakoneta, Ohio.

Neil Alden Armstrong, the first man to set foot on the moon, was born. Raised on his family's farm, he dreamed of becoming a pilot after taking his first airplane ride at age six. By the time he was 14, he was taking flying lessons for $9 an hour, which he earned by working at a pharmacy. He secured his pilot's license at 16 before getting his driver's license. Armstrong didn't immediately wing off to become a professional pilot. Instead, he worked in a bakery while finishing high school, where he played a horn in a jazz band called the Mississippi Moonshiners. He was a good, but unprepossessing student. His mother was so surprised when he won a U.S. Navy scholarship to attend Purdue University that she dropped a quart of preserves on her right big toe, breaking both.

After college, Armstrong became a U.S. Navy pilot. He flew Panther jets off the carrier *Essex* during the Korean War. During his seventy-eight combat missions, Armstrong was shot down behind enemy lines. A quick rescue saved him from a Communist prison camp. Armstrong earned three Air Medals for his Korean service. His skills helped him become a test pilot and, later, an astronaut.

Armstrong's famous line upon stepping onto the Moon, "This is one small step for a man, one giant leap for mankind," was mangled by his spacesuit radio. The "a" wasn't heard. Consequently, millions of puzzled people all around the Earth spent the next few minutes trying to make sense out of what he had said. The Japanese, in particular, were confused. In Japanese, the words for "man" and "mankind" are the same, giving the line a delightful Zen-ish air.

Following his return to Earth, Armstrong went on a goodwill tour around the world. When he visited Scotland, where his family had originated, he was delighted to discover that the sixteenth-century Armstrong clan were noted thieves. The bandit Johnnie Armstrong was the terror of the Highlands before being hanged.

Other Birthdays
1850   Guy de Maupassant
1911   Robert Taylor

August 6

1911   Jamestown, New York.

Diane Belmont, who would later become Lucille Ball, was born. Her parents were working class and they hoped Lucille would do better. They placed her in a drama school, but she soon dropped out. Still, she made it into movies because of her spectacular red hair, which earned her the nickname Technicolor Tessie. Small parts led to bigger ones. In 1951, when more notable actresses scorned television, Lucille and her husband, Desi Arnaz, jumped at the opportunity to star in their own television series. They became a phenomenal success and eventually bought RKO, the film studio that had given Ball her first Hollywood job.

Ball once said, "I have an everyday religion that works for me. Love yourself first and everything else falls into line. You really have to love yourself to get anything done in this world."

Other Birthdays
1809   Alfred Tennyson
1905   Clara Bow
1917   Robert Mitchum

August 7

1942   Anoka, Minnesota, a suburb of Minneapolis.

Garrison Keillor was born to railway mail clerk John P. Keillor and Grace R. (Denham) Keillor. Keillor was raised in a strict, fundamentalist Scots sect called the Plymouth Brethren. They proscribed dancing, drinking, and card-playing, but had a tradition of telling parables during their Sunday meetings. Keillor's great-uncle Lou Powell was also a gifted storyteller, and Keillor grew up with a love of stories. He was slow to learn to read, but, when he did learn, wanted to do nothing else. He says, "I hid in closets and in the basement, locked myself in the bathroom, reading right up to the final moment when Mother pried the book from my fingers and shoved me outdoors into the land of living persons."

Keillor's favorite reading material was the *New Yorker*. He later compared its arrival in the mail to glamorous luxury liner crammed with exotic people magically appearing in the middle of Minnesota. Keillor also enjoyed listening to the radio country music show, *The Grand Ole Opry*, and to the folksy, radio announcer Cedric Adams on WCCO radio. He especially enjoyed Adams's laid-back commentary. Keillor decided to become a writer, ambitiously setting a goal for himself of writing for the *New Yorker*.

Keillor attended the University of Minnesota, where he wrote for the student literary magazine and was an announcer for the student radio station. He married and, to pay his bills, worked parking cars. When he graduated in 1965, he headed east to get a job with a literary magazine. Of the unsuccessful attempt, he says, "I think that during the interview they could tell that I was somebody who had just changed in a public restroom. I had a kind of hangdog look about me." Keillor went back to the University of Minnesota, where he pursued a master's degree in literature and returned to student radio. In 1968, he got a classical radio show during morning drive time on Minesota Public Radio. Keillor kept sending stories to the *New Yorker* and, in 1969, he succeeded.

Keillor became a regular contributor to the *New Yorker* and, in 1974, they assigned him a piece on *The Grand Ole Opry*. Keillor enjoyed seeing his old favorite show up close and was inspired to produce his own folksy, variety show, *A Prairie Home Companion*, set in the mythical Minnesota town of Lake Wobegon. He says, "Lake Wobegon sounded sort of vague, and had an Indian sound to it, as so many towns in Minnesota do." The show, filled with snappy music and tales of "bachelor farmers," was a success, going national in 1980.

Keillor has also become a bestselling author, noted for his mellow observations. He once said, "Cats are intended to teach us that not everything in nature has a purpose."

Other Birthdays
1876   Mata Hari
1885   Billie Burke

August 8

1937   Los Angeles, California.

Dustin Hoffman was born. His father was an assistant set decorator at Columbia Pictures, and his mother was a great movie fan who got the name Dustin from her favorite movie cowboy, Dustin Farnum. His mother's love of movies was transmitted to her son. Despite acne, braces, and a large nose, Hoffman wanted a film career. After studying drama at Santa Monica City College, he directed plays in community theaters from North Dakota, New Jersey, and Connecticut to the Lower East Side of New York City. He secured entry into Lee Strasberg's Actors Studio, supporting himself with odd jobs, such as waiting tables, selling toys in Macy's, working in a psychiatric ward as an attendant, and typing entries for the phone book. For a time, he was so broke that he had to sleep on his friend Gene Hackman's kitchen floor. Then director Mike Nichols cast Hoffman as the lead in *The Graduate* (1967), making him a star.

Hoffman is an advocate of method acting. Robert Mitchum tells a story about Hoffman: "I remember Laurence Olivier asking Dustin Hoffman why he stayed up all night. Dustin, looking really beat, really bad, said it was to get into the scene being filmed that day, in which he was supposed to have been up all night. Olivier said, 'My boy, if you'd learn how to act you wouldn't have to stay up all night.'"

Other Birthdays
1922   Rudi Gernreich
1923   Esther Williams
1938   Connie Stevens
1964   Brett Hull

August 9

1957   New York City.

Melanie Griffith was born to ad exec and real estate developer Peter Griffith and actress Tippi Hedren, best known for her starring role as a reverse scarecrow in Alfred Hitchcock's *The Birds* (1963). After Griffith and Hedren divorced, Hedren married television director Noel Marshall. They raised Melanie, as well as lions, tigers, leopards, and pumas, on a ranch near Los Angeles, applying similar parenting methods to both animals and children. Marshall said, "We give them living room. We only want them to be themselves and play and have a wonderful time." Perhaps the techniques suitable for rearing exotic animals weren't quite appropriate for a young girl. Melanie soon proved a problem child.

At 14, Griffith met Don Johnson (see 12/15/1949), who was in Los Angeles to film *The Harrad Experiment* (1973). Hedren had a starring role in that movie, which was about a progressive college that promotes sexual freedom. Griffith had a role as an extra. A Griffith-Johnson romance ensued. Griffith dropped out of high school and left home at 16. She later said, "It was sex that took me out of the house. I wanted to be a woman. Simple as that. I lived a certain kind of life, and I don't live that life now. You grow up. You get tired of coming in stoned."

In 1976, Griffith married Johnson, but the marriage lasted only one year. By then, Griffith had begun an acting career. She had decided to become a model, but, misreading an ad, she thought she was going to audition for a modeling job when she was actually auditioning for a movie, *Night Moves* (1975). The film and Griffith's performance were well-received. She went on to other successful roles and, in 1989, remarried Johnson. In 1994, the couple split again.

When Hedren was working for Alfred Hitchcock, the director gave six-year-old Griffith a small doll. It was a likeness of Hedren in a miniature casket. The gift was in keeping with Hitchcock's morbid humor but, understandably, Griffith never played with the strange toy.

Other Birthdays
1928   Bob Cousy
1963   Whitney Houston

August 10

1874   West Branch, Iowa.

Blacksmith Jesse Clark Hoover and schoolteacher Hulda Minthorn Hoover had the second of their three children,

Herbert Clark Hoover. Hulda was a Quaker minister who campaigned for Prohibition. Hoover later remembered spending a day as a toddler with his mother, electioneering at the polls against liquor. Hoover lost both of his parents to disease and was raised by relatives. He attended Stanford University, becoming a mining engineer.

Working in Australia, China, Africa, and Central and South America, Hoover made himself a millionaire. During and after World War I, he headed three major relief agencies, saving hundreds of thousands of war refugees from starvation. The Harding and Coolidge administrations employed Hoover as secretary of commerce. In 1928, he won the presidency. Unfortunately for him and America, the Great Depression occurred during his term. When he failed to convince the public that the disaster wasn't his fault and that he was taking corrective action, he was voted out of office.

Hoover had been widely admired for his humanitarian work. One fan said, "He is certainly a wonder and I wish we could make him President of the United States. There couldn't be a better one." That admirer was Franklin D. Roosevelt, who later beat Hoover in the 1934 presidential election.

Other Birthdays
1900   Norma Shearer
1923   Rhonda Fleming
1928   Jimmy Dean

August 11

1921   Ithaca, New York.

Alex Haley was born. His father taught at Alabama A&M, and his mother taught grammar school. His grandmother lived with the family and told him stories about his ancestors. Haley disappointed his parents by not sharing their academic interests. He left college to join the Coast Guard, where he spent twenty years working his way up from steward to cook. His shipmates turned to him for help in writing love letters. His success at this encouraged him to begin writing short stories. In 1948, he sold one to a Sunday supplement. When he retired from the service, in 1958, he settled in New York City, where he freelanced articles for *Playboy* and *Reader's Digest*. In 1965, he wrote the bestseller *The Autobiography of Malcolm X*, but this wasn't his greatest success. That was *Roots*, which sold millions and was made into a popular television miniseries. Despite serious challenges regarding its veracity and originality, it became a significant statement about the history of black Americans.

Other Birthdays
1902 Lloyd Nolan

August 12

1939 Memphis, Tennessee.

George Hamilton was born. His father was George "Spike" Hamilton, an Ivy League band leader. George's mother, Anne Hamilton, claimed that when her doctor held her son up, he urinated in the doctor's eye. It wasn't quite what might be expected of a descendant of a First Family of Virginia, but then, Anne wasn't exactly staid herself. One of the mildest things to happen to this Southern belle was being thrown out of boarding school for wearing rouge. She went on to four divorces in nine years (she caught Spike with a singer). Her upbringing hadn't prepared her to support herself. For a time, Anne and her three sons lived in a Mexican hotel, subsisting on popcorn and avocados.

Anne never lost any of her airs and managed to pass them on to her son George. Despite their poverty, they always employed a maid. Anne Hamilton said, "We just had a hell of a struggle. When George was very little he used to say to me, 'I can't bother picking up my clothes. I can make money while those clothes are being picked up. I'll pay somebody to pick them up.' And he was so right."

Hamilton attended twenty-five prep schools across the country without graduating from any of them, but the confidence his mother gave him proved more than enough education when he decided to become a movie star. His films include *Love at First Bite* (1979) and *Zorro, the Gay Blade* (1981).

Other Birthdays
1881   Cecil B. DeMille
1927   Porter Wagoner
1929   Buck Owens

August 13

1899   London.
Prosperous grocer William Hitchcock and his wife had their third and last child, Alfred Joseph Hitchcock. A shy, chubby child, he spent most of his time alone. He was also well-behaved, perhaps because his father, wishing to give him a lesson, punished a five-year-old misbehaving Alfred by having the police put him in a jail cell. The terrified boy never got over his phobia of policeman.

After attending Catholic boys' school, Hitchcock studied drafting at a trade school. His first job was with a cable manufacturer. Hitchcock wasn't conscripted during World War I because of physical problems, but he patriotically enlisted in a volunteer corps of the Royal Engineers, where his duties consisted only of attending a few lectures. Perhaps to escape his mundane employment and unexciting service, Hitchcock spent much of his time in movie houses. He also broadened his drawing skills by studying art at London University. In 1919, when he heard that Famous Players-Lasky British was opening a film studio nearby, he decided to go into the movies.

Since films were silent in those days, it was necessary to supply dialogue through title cards. Hitchcock read that Famous Players-Lasky British were about to film *The Sorrows of Satan* by Marie Corelli. He bought the book, read it, then prepared a group of title cards liberally adorned with devils and flames. He brought these to the studio, only to be informed that they had dropped *Satan* for a film called *The Great Day*. Undaunted, Hitchcock showed up the next day with suitably decorated title cards. He got the job. In time, his duties grew to include set design and, finally, directing.

Hitchcock once remarked, "The cinema is not a slice of life but a piece of cake." Of directing his specialty, the suspense film, Hitchcock advised, "Always make an audience suffer as much as possible."

Other Birthdays
1895 Bert Lahr
1912 Ben Hogan
1930 Don Ho

August 14

1945 Waco, Texas.

Steve Martin was born. He grew up in Garden Grove, California, the son of a realtor. Martin spent his summers selling souvenirs at Disneyland. He also picked up some magic skills while working at a theme park magic shop and used them to entertain at parties. For a time, Martin took a stab at a more serious way of life by studying philosophy at UCLA. When he found philosophy unfulfilling, he switched to theater, concocted a stand-up comedy act, and began performing at nightclubs. His first break came as a writer for the Smothers Brothers' television show. He went on to write for John Denver, Glen Campbell, Dick Van Dyke, and Sonny and Cher.

In the 1970s, Martin quit comedy writing to return to performing. After appearing on Johnny Carson's *Tonight Show*, he became a comedy sensation, known for his trademark white suit and banjo. Martin made many appearances on *Saturday Night Live* and starred in numerous successful movies, including *The Jerk* (1979), *Dead Men Don't Wear Plaid* (1982), and *All of Me* (1984). Beginning with *Roxanne* (1987), Martin expanded into more serious roles.

Martin once observed, "A celebrity is any well-known TV or movie star who looks like he spends more than two hours working on his hair."

Other Birthdays
1925   Russell Baker
1941   David Crosby
1959   Earvin "Magic" Johnson

August 15

1912   Pasadena, California.

Food expert Julia Child, neé McWilliams, was born. After graduating from Smith College, Child worked as an ad writer for a furniture store. During World War II, she joined the Office of Strategic Services, the precursor of the Central Intelligence Agency. She was posted as a cables clerk to Ceylon, where she met and married fellow OSS member Paul Child. They were later sent to Kunming, China, and then to Paris. Julia, who was a poor cook, took advantage of their Paris stay to study cooking at the Cordon Bleu. She took similar advantage of their transfers to Bonn, Oslo, Marseilles, and Washington to learn more of the culinary arts. In 1961, Child and Simone Beck wrote the bestselling *Mastering the Art of French Cooking*. It led to a series of successful books and a popular television series.

Child observes of *nouvelle cuisine*, "It's so beautifully arranged on the plate—you know someone's fingers have been all over it."

Other Birthdays
1769   Napoleon Bonaparte
1888   T. E. Lawrence, "Lawrence of Arabia"
1944   Linda Ellerbee

August 16

1958 Pontiac, Michigan.

Tony Ciccone, an engineer with General Dynamics, and his wife, Madonna Ciccone, had their third child, Madonna Louise Ciccone. The younger Madonna says of her mother, "She was beautiful and very loving and devoted to her children." Madonna's father emphasized the importance of hard work and pride. The Ciccones had three more children, but then Madonna's mother suddenly died of breast cancer, at 30, in 1963. Madonna, just seven years old, took on some of her mother's responsibilities. She also became more self-reliant. She has said that she thought, "If I can't have my mother, I'm going to take care of myself." This self-reliance was heightened when her father remarried. Madonna didn't like her stepmother and was eager to rebel.

The Catholic school Madonna attended provided much to rebel against. Madonna was known as a good student but also as a thrill-seeker. She peeked into the nuns' quarters, hoping to catch a glimpse of them out of their habits. She wanted to know what their hair looked like and what kind of underwear they wore. She also shocked the nuns by hanging upside down on the monkey bars so the boys could catch a glimpse of her underwear as her skirt hung around her head.

In high school, Madonna continued to seek attention. She was a cheerleader and appeared in student plays. She studied jazz dance, training at a ballet school run by Christopher Flynn. Flynn, a frequenter of gay nightclubs, introduced Madonna to club life. When he became an instructor at the University of Michigan, he persuaded Madonna to follow him there. After three years of study, Flynn encouraged her to drop out and go to New York City. Arriving in Times Square with just $37, Madonna was forced to make friends fast. She found people to stay with and worked odd jobs that barely kept her fed. She often relied on popcorn as the main component of her diet. She says, "I still love it. Popcorn is cheap and it fills you up."

Madonna had no success getting work as a dancer. One night, at a party, would-be rock star Norris Burroughs spotted her dancing by herself in the center of the room. He was intrigued, and soon she was living with him and performing in his rock group, the Breakfast Club. She tried guitar, then organ, then drums before discovering a talent for singing. She still had little money. A part in a low-budget film earned her nothing but screen credit. She scraped by, posing nude for artists for $7 an hour. In 1980, she left the band because the other performers weren't willing to let her sing as often as she wanted.

Madonna went from group to group. Though one critic called her voice, "Minnie Mouse on helium," she built up a following. Finally, a friend got a recording of one of her songs to a record executive who was stuck in a hospital bed, recovering from heart surgery. He wasn't so sick that he couldn't recognize talent. He signed Madonna. The song "Everybody" was soon number one on the dance charts. In 1983, Madonna recorded "Lucky Star." The music video of the song was made just in time to cash in on the rise of MTV. Soon, Madonna was a superstar. She was also a good business woman, who learned as much as she could about the record business. This, combined with a talent for self-promotion through shock, has earned her millions.

Madonna once said of herself, "I'm just a midwestern girl in a bustier."

Other Birthdays
1930   Robert Culp
1935   Julie Newmar
1946   Lesley Warren
1960   Timothy Hutton

August 17

1888 or 1892 or 1893 or 1900   Brooklyn, New York.

Mae West was born. The year Mae West reported varied. While West claimed her ancestors included James I of England

and Alfred the Great, her mother and father were actually the less aristocratic Mathilda Dilker, a native of Bavaria (or Alsace-Lorraine or Paris), who went by the nickname of Champagne Til, and the more simply named John Patrick West, an Irish-American who was called "Battlin' Jack" because of his earlier boxing career (he also claimed to have worked as a detective, a stable manager, a chiropractor, and a doctor). The Wests named their daughter Mary Jane, but called her Mae. They spoiled her outrageously. She had the best toys, the finest clothes, and as many boyfriends as she liked. She claimed to have lost her virginity at 13 to a 21-year-old music teacher.

Mathilda West, a corset model and a frustrated actress, was a true stage mother. She got Mae training, arranged performances, and was always in the wings, encouraging her daughter. Matilda also encouraged Mae in her romantic adventures. Rather than having a single beau, who might become a rival to her influence, Matilda thought Mae should have multiple boyfriends. Whenever Mae seemed interested in a boy, Mathilda would point out his defects, thereby deflating him in Mae's vain eyes. Mae remained devoted to her mother and never successfully married.

Mae West was noted for her many risque aphorisms. For example, "He who hesitates is last," "It's better to be looked over than overlooked," and "To err is human—but it feels divine."

Other Birthdays
1786   Davy Crockett
1931   Robert De Niro

August 18

1937   Santa Monica, California.

Robert Redford was born to Charles and Martha Redford. Redford's father worked two jobs, milkman and accountant, so that he could raise his family in the suburbs. Redford, with a crewcut and a face full of freckles, was hardly a matinee idol in high school. His female classmates later described him as "a nice guy, but a wimp—an average-looking nerd." He developed into a star athlete but wasn't happy and indulged in petty vandalism.

Redford won a baseball scholarship to the University of Colorado but dropped out to travel in Europe as an art student. When he came home, he met and married a Mormon girl. Redford wanted to pursue his artistic ambitions, but needed money to support his wife. A friend suggested acting and Redford reluctantly tried it. A 1963 appearance on Broadway in Neil Simon's *Barefoot in the Park* led to stardom.

Redford remains skeptical of the movie industry. He says, "If you stay in Beverly Hills too long you become a Mercedes."

Other Birthdays
1924   Shelley Winters
1927   Rosalynn Carter
1943   Martin Mull

August 19

1921   El Paso, Texas.

Gene (Eugene Wesley) Roddenberry was born. His father, Eugene Edward Roddenberry, was a sergeant in the U.S. Cavalry, who had served in France during World War I and was stationed at Fort Bliss in Texas after the war. His mother, Caroline Goldman Roddenberry, was 16 when she married Roddenberry's father. Ten months later, Roddenberry was born. Less than a year later, the family moved to Southern California, where Roddenberry's father became a Los Angeles police officer.

Roddenberry was a good student and a science fiction fan. At Los Angeles' City College, he studied pre-law and police studies. He also became a pilot at age 19 through the Civilian Pilot Training Program. When World War II broke out,

Roddenberry became a second Lieutenant in the U.S. Army Air Corps. Too tall to be a fighter pilot, he became a B-17 bomber pilot, flying eighty missions in the South Pacific. He was shot down during one, and although his navigator and bombadier were killed, Roddenberry survived. He earned a Distinguished Flying Cross for his wartime service.

After the war, Roddenberry became a Pan Am pilot. A second crash in the Syrian desert that killed fourteen persuaded him to leave flying. He followed his father into the Los Angeles Police Department. He did his duty in that city's streets, but had other ambitions. Using his police experience, he began selling scripts to television. He could earn $700 a week writing and only $440 a month as a police officer. It wasn't long before he was writing full-time for such shows as *Dragnet, Naked City, Have Gun Will Travel,* and *Highway Patrol.* He next produced his own series, *The Lieutenant.* It was successful and established Roddenberry as contender in the television industry.

In the early 1960s, Roddenberry came up with an idea for a science fiction series. At the time CBS was eager to keep their biggest star, Lucille Ball, happy. In addition to paying her for her show, they gave her half a million dollars to develop new programs through her studio, Desilu. Roddenberry persuaded Ball to bankroll a pilot. The first one didn't sell, but a second, with a different cast, was purchased by NBC. On September 8, 1966, Roddenberry's series, *Star Trek,* aired for the first time. Although it was canceled in three years, it refused to die out. It became a successful series of movies, pulling in over $500 million, launched the bestselling line of books in publishing history, earned over $650 million in merchandizing, and returned to television twenty years later, spawning two spin-offs and another movie.

When it premiered, *Star Trek* seemed very strange to its audience, who had little experience with science fiction. Roddenberry's own father, after seeing the first show, apologized to his neighbors, telling them not to worry because his son would soon be back writing "real television...westerns."

1946   Hope, Arkansas.

Bill Clinton was born to Virginia Cassidy Blythe and traveling salesman William Jefferson Blythe III, who died in a car accident weeks before Clinton was born. Arkansas records and Clinton's mother say that the Blythes were married in 1943. In 1993, the *Kansas City Star* and the *New York Daily News* ran stories revealing that, in 1941, William Blythe was married to Kansas City resident Wanetta Ellen Alexander, who Blythe eventually divorced. Jackson County records indicate that this divorce wasn't granted until April 13, 1944, seven months after Blythe married Clinton's mother. Wanetta Alexander, now living in Tucson, has a daughter, born in 1941, she claims is Clinton's half sister. Blythe apparently had other romantic entanglements: A California man, also born in 1941, claims Blythe as his father, and his birth certificate backs his claim.

Following the death of Blythe, Clinton's mother married Roger Clinton Sr., a car dealer in Hot Springs, Arkansas. Hot Springs had once been a racy resort town, a favorite vacation spot of 1930s gangsters. Bill Blythe became Bill Clinton and, in a few years, half brother to Roger Clinton Jr. Clinton's half brother says their father was abusive and alcoholic. The elder Roger died of cancer in 1967. Clinton's mother supported her family by working as a nurse, earning a good enough income to employ a housekeeper to care for her children. She died in 1994 of cancer.

From an early age, Bill Clinton wanted a political career. A high school meeting with John Kennedy fueled his ambition. He won a Rhodes Scholarship, dodged the draft during the Vietnam War, didn't inhale, went to law school, got himself elected governor of Arkansas, ran for the 1988 Democratic presidential nomination, dropped out after Gary Hart's infidelities became a national joke, then won the White House in 1992.

Other Birthdays
1871   Orville Wright (see 4/16/1867)

1940   Jill St. John
1947   Gerald McRaney

August 20

1946   Washington, D.C.

Connie Yu-hwa Chung was born. Her father, William Ling Chung, was an officer in the Nationalist Chinese intelligence service who lived according to many old Chinese traditions. His marriage to Chung's mother, Margaret, was an arranged one. He saw his wife for the first time when he lifted her veil at the wedding ceremony. Connie's father also followed another custom once common in China—he kept concubines. In a *People* magazine interview, Chung said, "My mother would tell us these horrible stories where she would walk into a restaurant and say, 'I'm here to meet with Mr. Chung,' and they would say, 'Oh, Mrs. Chung is already back there.' She would be livid." Mr. Chung left his concubines behind when the family moved to the United States in 1945. In 1946, Connie became the tenth and last of the Chungs' children (five died in China).

As a child, Chung felt driven to succeed. She says, "I wanted to be my father's son and perpetuate the family name." After earning a journalism degree from the University of Maryland in 1969, she went to work as a reporter for the Washington, D.C., CBS new affiliate. By the 1970s, she was a network correspondent. Chung says she literally elbowed her way through crowds of reporters to get her questions in. Her elbows proved productive. In 1993, she became Dan Rather's coanchor on the *CBS Evening news,* with a salary of $2 million a year. In 1996, Chung put off having children and now wishes she had a child. She and talk show host husband, Maury Povich, have admitted to "aggressively" pursuing parenthood.

Other Birthdays
1833   Benjamin Harrison

1890   H. P. Lovecraft
1926   Jacqueline Susann

August 21

1936   Philadelphia.

Basketball star Wilt "the Stilt" Chamberlain was born. His parents were both five-foot-eight, but Chamberlain reached seven-foot-one. Chamberlain displayed his talents in high school and was offered 140 different basketball scholarships. He chose the University of Kansas, where he distinguished himself. A spectacular professional career followed. He set record after record during his fourteen years as a pro, but his most spectacular professional achievements came in his last year of play, when he led the Los Angeles Lakers to a thirty-three-game winning streak and an NBA championship. Off court, Chamberlain achieved similar records in his romantic life.

Other Birthdays
1938   Kenny Rogers

August 22

1940   Suffern, New York.

Valerie Harper was born. Her father was a traveling sales-man who moved the family all over the United States. After high school, Harper tried acting and, in 1958, won a role in the chorus of *Li'l Abner*. When she found herself underweight after a bout of hepatitis, she followed her doctor's prescription to eat sweets. The five-foot-four-inch actress topped 155 pounds before she got a handle on her sugar cravings. This experience added veracity to her role as Mary Tyler Moore's ditzy, ever-dieting neighbor on *The Mary Tyler Moore Show*, which led to her own successful television programs, *Rhoda* and *Valerie*.

Other Birthdays
1925   Honor Blackman
1934   Norman Schwarzkopf
1948   Cindy Williams

August 23

1912   Pittsburgh, Pennsylvania.

Eugene "Gene" Kelly was born. He had set out to get a degree in economics from Pennsylvania State University, taking odd jobs to pay his own way, but the Depression provided few opportunities. Kelly dug ditches before finding easier work teaching dancing in his basement. He later admitted that it also helped him meet girls. He decided to become a professional dancer and, after a few years of struggle, made it to Broadway in the musical *The Time of Your Life*. This led to more Broadway parts and a film career.

Later in life, Kelly remarked, "Musicals are my real love. I didn't want to make pictures with messages. I just wanted to make people happy and bring joy."

Other Birthdays
1933   Pete Wilson
1934   Barbara Eden
1949   Shelley Long
1970   River Phoenix

August 24

1965   Morton's Grove, Illinois.

Used car dealer Don Matlin and his wife, Libby, had a daughter, Marlee Matlin. When Marlee was eighteen months old, she contracted the measles. Her parents, unaware of the danger, took her by plane to visit her grandmother in California. When they returned home, they discovered that pressure changes during the flight had destroyed Marlee's hearing. Her parents did everything they could to help her cope with her deafness. Still, Marlee had trouble dealing with her handicap. She later said, "I wanted to be perfect and I couldn't accept my deafness. I was so angry and frightened."

Marlee Matlin found a means of venting her emotions at seven when she played Dorothy in a production of *The Wizard of Oz* by Chicago's Children's Theater. During her summers, she studied acting at camp. By the time she was ready for college, she had decided on a career in police work or acting. She soon discovered that her opportunities in law enforcement were limited, so, when she heard of a casting call for a Chicago production of *Children of a Lesser God*, a play featuring deaf players, she auditioned and won a supporting role. When the film version of the play was cast, the casting director reviewed video tapes of the theatrical productions. He spotted Matlin and gave her the female lead. Matlin won the Best Actress Academy Award for her performance.

Other Birthdays
1899   Jorge Luis Borges
1958   Steve Guttenberg

August 25

1930   Edinburgh, Scotland.
Sean Connery was born, the son of a Scottish lorry driver. He left school at 15 and enlisted in the British Navy. After leaving the service, he worked as a coffin-polisher and bricklayer. Interested in weight training, he became a champion body-builder and male model, and it was through his muscles that he got into acting. A London production of *South Pacific* needed a bunch of muscular guys to play American sailors, so they went to the body-building halls to recruit.

Connery got a role and decided acting beat bricklaying. After several small parts, he made his screen debut in *Let's Make Up* (1954). He won stardom with his role as James Bond in *Dr. No* (1962), which led to a series of successful 007 films. Despite his wealth and fame, Connery was stung by criticism that suggested he could play no other role. He branched out in the 1970s to more demanding parts, insisting that he would never play Bond again. Nevertheless, he was lured back in 1983 to appear as Bond in *Never Say Never Again*. By then, critics were well aware that he was a capable actor. They, like the general public, missed his unique version of Bond.

Other Birthdays
1910   Ruby Keeler
1916   Van Johnson
1923   Monty Hall
1947   Anne Archer
1954   Elvis Costello

August 26

1980   New York City.

Child star Macaulay Culkin was born to Patricia Culkin, a receptionist, and Kit Culkin, a cab driver and sacristan at Manhattan's St. Joseph's Catholic Church. Kit had been a child star, dancing in New York City Ballet's *The Nutcracker* with his sister, actress Bonnie Bedelia. Kit also had appeared with Laurence Olivier on Broadway in *Becket*, with Richard Burton in *Hamlet*, and in the movie *West Side Story* (1961). However, by the 1980s, Kit Culkin's career had been reduced to occasional small roles in off-Broadway productions. The large Culkin family was getting by on a modest income. Kit Culkin's part-time job as sacristan helped by providing a tuition cut for his children, but the family needed more money. Family friend Susan Selig, a stage manager, suggested that the Culkin children had acting potential. In 1987, Macaulay, six, was cast in an off-Broadway play called *Afternoon Special*. Critics responded well and he won more off-Broadway parts and movie roles. His break-out role came in 1990, with the surprise holiday hit *Home Alone*, which became the fourth-highest-grossing film ever, earning half-a-billion dollars.

Kit Culkin keeps his children down-to-earth. Macaulay has household chores to do, just like his siblings. Kit is also considered a sharp manager. Reportedly, on Macaulay's first film after *Home Alone*, when Kit arrived on the set, there wasn't even a chair for him to sit in. Now, he chooses directors and has been accused of postponing production to extract concessions. Considering Hollywood's past treatment of child stars, perhaps father and son Culkin know what they're doing.

Other Birthdays
1935   Geraldine Ferraro

August 27

1908   Near Stonewall, Gillespie County, Texas.

Lyndon Baines Johnson was born to Rebekah Baines Johnson, the daughter of a lawyer who had been a Confederate soldier, and Sam Ealy Johnson Jr., a politician and cattle rancher whose family had grown prosperous driving longhorn cattle up the Chisholm Trail. Rebekah hoped that Sam would become a prominent politician, but when he failed to live up to her ambitions, she shifted them to her son.

Rebekah started teaching Lyndon early: At two, he knew his alphabet; at three, he could recite Longfellow; and at four, he was attending school. Lyndon's Grandpa Johnson boasted that Lyndon would be a U.S. senator before he was 40. The Johnsons had another son and three daughters, but Lyndon was his mother's favorite. She praised him for taking care of his younger siblings. One of his sisters later disagreed with this praise, saying, "He was always bossy. I think he thought he was papa." Lyndon grew wild as a teenager and, after high school, ran off to California, where he bummed around, picking fruit to support himself, before meekly returning to his mother. Though he graduated Southwest State Teachers College in San Marcos, he spent little time teaching. Instead, he ran for Congress in 1937 and won. He was elected to the Senate in 1949, one year behind his grandfather's schedule. Johnson went on to become senate majority leader and U.S. president.

Johnson's political victories were tainted by shady politicking. For example, when he realized that military service in World War II would be a political asset, he swung a cushy service job, then arranged to go along on a routine bombing mission. Somehow, he got a medal for this endeavor. During his next political campaign, he had the medal awarded to himself at rally after rally.

Johnson's son-in-law, Patrick Nugent, once remarked that Johnson was a compulsive gift-giver. Nugent said, "Whether it was a pocketknife or a cigarette lighter, and it always had his name on it...he'd pull something out of his pocket and say, 'Here, I want you to keep this as a memento of your visit to the Ranch; but for God's sake don't embarrass me by leaving it in a whorehouse someplace.'"

Other Birthdays
1910   Mother Teresa
1916   Martha Raye
1943   Tuesday Weld
1952   Peewee Herman

August 28

1749   Franfurt on Main, German.

Johann Wolfgang von Goethe was born to Katherina Elisabeth and lawyer Johann Kaspar von Goethe, who had eight children. Only two survived childhood. The Goethe family was well-to-do, having inherited money, but Goethe's father also wanted professional prominence. Despite diligent study, he had little success in his legal career. He turned his diligence on his family, giving his children their early education. By the time he sent his son to law school at 15, Goethe knew six languages and had studied art and music. He had also learned to be indifferent to his parents and saw little of them as an adult.

Goethe's first major success came when he published his novel *The Sorrows of Young Werther* during the *Sturm und Drang* period of German literature. The novel's theme of suicide over love made self-destruction fashionable. Fortunately, the fad passed quickly. Goethe didn't take his own theme to heart. He had many romances, but never became suicidal when they failed. He eventually married a woman after living with her for fifteen years. He lived a long, productive life and became one of Germany's great literary figures.

Goethe once gloomily remarked, "We are own devils, we drive ourselves out of our own Edens."

Other Birthdays
1930   Ben Gazzara
1943   Lou Piniella
1950   Ron Guidry

August 29

1958   Gary, Indiana.

Michael Jackson was born, the son of Catherine and Joe Jackson, a crane operator and occasional jazz musician, who had dreams of success for his musically talented children. Michael used to dance to the rhythmic squeaking of his mother's washing machine when he was eighteen months old. Joe formed his sons into the Jackson Five, featuring the tiny Michael, and drilled them relentlessly. According to Jackson biographer Lois P. Nicholson, neighborhood children teased the Jackson boys about their continual rehearsing. Michael loved his teachers, who treated him kindly, and gave them jewelry he had snitched from his mother's jewelry box.

Joe's instruction paid off when he managed to get singer Diana Ross to see his sons perform. Impressed, she arranged an impromptu audition for record executive Berry Gordy Jr. beside a swimming pool. He, too, recognized talent, and the group shortly released their first album. It was a hit.

By 1993, Jackson was the foremost entertainer in the world. He had not only recorded dozens of hit songs, but he had also demonstrated great savvy in managing his fortune, which reached into the billions. Charges of child molestation, however, threatened Jackson's fame. Perhaps the pressures of his childhood, performing concert after concert and never being allowed to have friends his own age, left Jackson with a craving to play like a child. He even transformed his home into an amusement park. Jackson has entertained countless children, some ill with serious diseases, but this has left him wide open to unsavory speculation and charges of child abuse. His marriage in 1994 to Elvis Presley's daughter, Lisa, surprised the world. David Letterman observed of the wedding, "If Elvis Presley were dead, he'd be rolling over in his grave."

Other Birthdays
1915   Ingrid Bergman
1938   Elliott Gould
1962   Rebecca DeMornay

August 30

1908   Kankakee, Illinois.

Fred MacMurray was born. His father, Frederick MacMurray, was a concert violinist. When his mother, Maleta, and father separated, MacMurray was deposited in a military school. In his teens, MacMurray lived with his mother in Beaver Dam, Wisconsin. He was an impressive high school athlete, winning ten varsity letters in three sports. He was also a talented artist and solid saxophonist, recognized by the local

American Legion Post when they awarded him a scholarship to Carroll College in Waukesha, Wisconsin. He studied music, forming his own band, Mac's Melody Boys. After graduation, he enrolled in the Chicago Art Institute to study art, supporting himself by playing saxophone in a band. In 1928, his mother decided she wanted to live in Los Angeles, and MacMurray offered to drive her there.

In Los Angeles, MacMurray worked as a movie extra until he found a spot in a vaudeville band, the California Collegians. The band appeared in the Broadway comedy *Three's a Crowd*. Tall, dark, and talented, MacMurray stood out and won the job of understudy to Bob Hope in the Broadway musical *Roberta*. That job got him a film debut in *Friends of Mr. Sweeney* (1934). He played polished rich boys, then branched out into comedic roles. He also made one of the best *film noire* productions of the 1940s, *Double Indemity* (1944). MacMurray was also admired for his Disney films *The Absent Minded Professor* (1961) and *Son of Flubber* (1963), and his television sitcom *My Three Sons*. That sitcom, which had reportedly been planned with a different gender in mind as a vehicle for the Lennon Sisters, ran for twelve years—so long that the show had to add a fourth son to keep a youthful slant.

MacMurray was always modest about his talents. At a 1986 tribute dinner, he said, "Well, I've done pretty good for a guy who plays the saxophone."

Other Birthdays
1918 Ted Williams
1947 Peggy Lipton
1951 Timothy Bottoms

August 31

1928 Laurel, Nebraska.

Actor James Coburn was born, the son of a car salesman who took his family to California during the Depression. After a stretch in the U.S. Army, Coburn attended Los Angeles City

College, where he studied acting. Further work with famed acting teacher Stella Adler helped Coburn get a role in a Remington shaver commercial. Coburn must have marveled at the amount of training it took to obtain this one modest part. However, this minor job led to a role in a Randolph Scott Western, *Ride Lonesome* (1959). Coburn was still starring in films like *The Great Escape* (1965) and *The Magnificent Seven* (1960). Coburn still works in commercials. For one Schlitz Light beer commercial, he was paid $850,000.

Other Birthdays
1897   Fredric March
1924   Buddy Hackett
1945   Van Morrison
1948   Richard Gere
1955   Edwin Moses
1970   Debbie Gibson

BASIC
AERODYNAMICS

EM

September 1

1939   Detroit, Michigan.

Lily Tomlin was born. The daughter of a factory worker, she studied English at Wayne State University. After graduation, she got a job as a casting director's secretary in New York City. She saw many performers chasing parts and decided she should try show business, too. Tomlin tried out her first comedy routines at the famed Upstairs at the Downstairs club, which paid little but helped comics get started. She got parts in off-Broadway productions, then secured a spot on *The Merv Griffin Show*. A slot on television's *Rowan & Martin's Laugh-In* made her a national favorite through such characterizations as Edith Ann, a child in a rocking chair, and Ernestine, the phone operator from Hell. The last was so successful that Bell Telephone offered her $500,000 for the rights to the character. Following *Laugh-In*, Tomlin appeared in several films and a one-woman Broadway show.

Tomlin quips, "Why is it we are always hearing about the

tragic cases of too much, too soon? What about the rest of us? Too little, too late."

Other Birthdays
1875   Edgar Rice Burroughs
1922   Yvone DeCarlo
1923   Rocky Marciano
1933   Conway Twitty
1957   Gloria Estefan

September 2

1917   Nahant, Massachusetts.

Critic and animal rights activist Cleveland Amory was born. His father was a wealthy textile manufacturer who spurred Amory's interest in animals. Amory later said, "I shot a bird with a BB gun, and my father looked at me with disgust as this little bird flopped around on our porch. He said: 'You shot it, you kill it.' I had to stomp on that bird until it was dead." The horrible incident helped turn Amory into a crusader against animal cruelty.

Amory also wrote social commentary. "Relations between the sexes are so complicated that the only way you can tell if two members of the set are 'going together' is if they are married. Then, almost certainly, they are not."

Other Birthdays
1948   Terry Bradshaw
1951   Mark Harmon
1952   Jimmy Connors

September 3

1811   Brattleboro, Vermont.

John Humphrey Noyes was born. His father was a business-man and politician who was seldom at home. His mother, who was devoutly religious, prayed that her son would become a minister. Noyes decided to live up to his mother's hopes and enrolled in the Yale Theological Seminary in New Haven. His studies, however, led him to some unusual conclusions. He decided that the Second Coming had already happened back in 70 A.D. and that therefore, a perfect, sinless existence was possible just by accepting Christ. Noyes made a public "confession of salvation from sin" and was promptly booted out of school. Back in Vermont, he began setting up his own "Perfectionist" Church. His empassioned sermons got him followers. The first of these was Abigail Merwin. Noyes fell in love with her and proposed, but her parents thought he was insane. Noyes married a schoolteacher, but this didn't stop him from following Merwin around, hoping she would change her mind. She didn't, and he grew bitter with the institution of marriage. He decided to change it.

Noyes and his Perfectionists adopted a form of communal marriage in which promiscuity was vigorously enforced. They established the successful Oneida Community; however, when Noyes began monopolizing the community's females, male followers threatened to have him arrested for statutory rape. He had reportedly slept with girls as young as 10. Noyes fled to Canada, where he ended his days peacefully in the company of his favorite wife.

Other Birthdays
1913   Alan Ladd
1915   Kitty Carlisle
1944   Valerie Perrine
1965   Charlie Sheen

September 4

1923   Fort Wayne, Indiana.

Actor Dick York was born. He was raised in Chicago, where his poor family had to keep a family member in their apartment at all times, lest their landlord padlock them out for missing their rent payments. During York's turns on watch, he listened to radio soap operas and serials and became fascinated with radio drama. The nuns at his parochial school encouraged him. York got a job at a children's theater that paid in acting lessons. Soon, he was playing in radio programs. He moved on to Broadway and films, making his better appearances in *They Came to Cordura* (1959) and *Inherit the Wind* (1960). While filming the former, York injured his back and was placed on prescription pain killers. In 1965, York got the role of Darrin Stephens, the ad exec who finds himself married to a witch in the television sitcom *Bewitched*. It was a success but, unfortunately, York had become addicted to the pain killers, and his back condition worsened. He left *Bewitched* in 1972, unable to continue acting.

York and his wife, Joan, cleaned apartments to support their five children. When this work became too difficult for York, who had developed emphysema, they were reduced to living on a meager Actor's Guild pension. Many in similar circumstances might give up. York did quite the opposite. Despite constant pain, he broke his addiction to pain killers. Although confined to his bed with oxygen tubes up his nose, he took up the cause of the homeless and impoverished. Via telephone he participated in a series of fundraising efforts, raising many thousands of dollars before he died in 1992. York's son said of his father, "He was not only my father, he was my hero."

Other Birthdays
1918   Paul Harvey
1930   Mitzi Gaynor

September 5

1929   Chicago.
    Comic Bob Newhart was born. Educated at Loyola University, Newhart spent two years in the U.S. Army. After a stab at becoming a lawyer, he worked as a copywriter, clerk, and

accountant while assembling a comedy routine. Newhart says, "I was a lousy accountant. I always figured that if you came within eight bucks of what you needed you were doing okay. I made up the difference out of my own pocket."

Fortunately, Newhart's comedy skills were better than his accounting skills. A disc jockey friend played some recordings of Newhart on his show. These got the attention of Warner Brothers Records, who signed him to make a comedy album. They wanted to record his nightclub act, but Newhart had to admit that he had never performed in a nightclub. Warner Brothers booked him into a Houston, Texas, club in 1960. Newhart prepared just enough material to fill a thirty-minute record. The show went well, and he got heavy applause as he exited the stage. The maître d' insisted Newhart go back out and do some more jokes. Newhart returned to the stage and asked, "Which one would you like to hear again?"

The recording, *The Button-Down Mind of Bob Newhart*, made Newhart an overnight success. He went on to become a television star and appeared in several films. His first, *Hell is for Heroes* (1962), was a World War II story starring Steve McQueen, Bobby Darin, Fess Parker, and James Coburn. During the shooting in Europe, as Newhart became more popular back home, his agent quadrupled Newhart's performance price. Newhart was actually losing money as he performed in the film. He begged the film's makers to write him out of the movie by having the Germans kill his character, but to no avail.

Other Birthdays
1847   Jesse James
1940   Raquel Welch

September 6

1944   Omaha, Nebraska.

Actress Swoosie Kurtz was born to Colonel Frank Kurtz and his wife, Margo. Kurtz, the most decorated American pilot of

World War II, flew a B-17 bomber nicknamed The Swoose because it was half graceful swan and half un-graceful goose. When his daughter was born, a newspaper ran a picture of the infant with the caption "A little Swoosie." A nurse in the maternity ward read the article and entered the name "Swoosie" on the child's birth certificate. Kurtz's parents liked the odd name. Kurtz endured more than a little teasing in school, but has learned to like being named after the aircraft that brought her father home safely.

Kurtz was raised on military bases. She says, "I think what made me a good actress is the fact that as an army officer's daughter, I was always on the move. I attended 17 different grammar schools and was constantly assaulted with traumas. I had to keep adjusting. Thank God for my wonderful parents. If it hadn't been for them, I might be deeply disturbed instead of only mildly disturbed."

Other Birthdays
1937   Jo Anne Worley
1947   Jane Curtin

September 7

1533   Greenwich Palace.

Elizabeth I of England was born to Henry VIII and the ill-fated Anne Boleyn. Henry beheaded not only Elizabeth's mother but her stepmother, Catherine Howard, as well. Elizabeth was further traumatized when, at 14, she discovered that Lord Admiral Thomas Seymour, the object of a girlish crush, was hoping to marry her and seize control of England. It was rumored that young Elizabeth miscarried a child by Seymour, who wound up on the executioner's block.

When Elizabeth became queen in 1558 (she ruled forty-four years), she continued to be intrigued by men similar to Seymour—youthful, adventurous, dashing—but she never married. It would be romantic to think that this was because of her affection for Seymour, but it is more probable that she simply didn't want to share power with a husband. She once said, "I am already married to a husband, which is the people of England." This had the positive result of keeping England free from the international entanglements that a foreign consort could have created.

Elizabeth once said, "Anger makes dull men witty, but it keeps them poor."

Other Birthdays
1860   Grandma Moses
1936   Buddy Holly
1942   Richard Roundtree

September 8

1922   Yonkers, New York.

Max and Ida Caesar had a son, Sidney Caesar. They called Sid a "makeup child" because he was the product of a reconciliation following an argument. They had three other sons—which suggests they had at least three other arguments.

Of Polish heritage, the Caesar family name had been given to Max by an Ellis Island clerk. One of Max's first jobs in America had been a rather odd one. Someone with new, tight shoes would pay him to wear them until they were comfortably stretched.

When Sid's father opened a luncheonette Sid's older brother Dave was delegated babysitting duty. Dave amused himself by tying a rope to Sid's baby carriage, then launching the carriage down a steep hill to the length of the rope. Dave would then haul it back up and repeat the procedure again and again.

Sid's father rented rooms over the luncheonette. One day, a tenant skipped without paying his bill. He did, however, leave a saxophone behind, and Sid was soon toodling away. When Max went bankrupt in 1935, Sid played in a Catskills band to help support the family. While World War II service interrupted the careers of other entertainers, Sid's service in the Coast Guard actually helped his career. Assigned to guard a pier in Brooklyn, he also performed in a service comedy show that was turned into a film. After the war, Sid appeared on Broadway and then was cast as the host of *Your Show of Shows*, which became a television smash. Caesar was making over a million dollars a year before he was 30.

Unfortunately, the pressures of success and the demands of producing a show each week affected Caesar badly. He took a twenty-year plunge into alcohol and drug abuse. In 1982, Caesar chronicled his troubles and recovery in his autobiography, *Where Have I Been?*

Caesar says of comedy, "The best thing about humor is that it shows people that they're not alone."

Other Birthdays
1932   Patsy Cline
1946   Freddie Mercury

September 9

1828   Tula, Russia.

Count Leo Tolstoy was born. Following the death of his aristocratic parents, he was raised by relatives. When he finished his education, he was supposed to manage his family's estate but he preferred the social life of Moscow and St. Petersburg. Tolstoy acquired a wild set of friends who threw parties and provided plenty of distractions. Eventually, he grew annoyed with himself and joined his brother in the Russian army to get away from his friends' bad influence. He served in the Caucasus, where he filled his off hours writing his first novel, *Childhood*. Transferred to the Danube front, he saw combat during the Crimean War. He left the service after the war. By then, his novel was a success, and Tolstoy became one of the most renowned of Russia's writers, with works such as *Anna Karenina* and *War and Peace*.

As a boy, Tolstoy and his brother formed a club whose initiation required the prospective member to stand in a corner for thirty minutes and not think of a polar bear.

Other Birthdays
1925   Cliff Robertson
1941   Otis Redding
1962   Kristy McNichol

September 10

1934   Wilmington, North Carolina.

Journalist Charles Kuralt was born. Kuralt had his first brush with the powerful in high school when he won an American Legion essay contest, earning him a trip to Washington, D.C. and an introduction to President Truman. After studying journalism at the University of North Carolina, CBS News hired him. He was eventually given the assignment of traveling cross-country reporting on folksy, small-town stories. He journeyed over a million miles while making his "On the Road" reports. Kuralt observes, "Reporters flying from one city to another on assignment never have time to learn anything about those little clusters of lights in between."

Other Birthdays
1929   Arnold Palmer
1945   Jose Feliciano
1953   Amy Irving

September 11

1885   Nottinghamshire, England.

David Herbert Lawrence was born to coal miner Arthur Lawrence, who was energetic and charming but had a weakness for drink, and Lydia Beardsall Lawrence, a teacher whose family had been prosperous lace manufacturers. David was the fourth of the couple's five children. His mother had to resort to selling lace in her front parlor to feed them because Lawrence's father routinely drank away his pay. Lawrence's mother grew to despise her husband, concentrating all her affection upon her children. She had great hopes for them and tutored them carefully. Lawrence, a sickly, bronchitic child, was her favorite. His brother later said, "We all petted and spoiled him from the time that he was born—my mother poured her very soul into him." Lawrence said, "My mother has been passionately fond of me and fiercely jealous. She hated Jessie [his first sweetheart] and would have risen from the grave to prevent my marrying her."

Lydia Lawrence's efforts helped Lawrence become a schoolteacher and fueled his desire to become a literary figure. His works promoted sex, nature, and the primitive subconscious as palliative to the problems of modern life. The sex part made his work controversial. *Lady Chatterley's Lover*, for example, was banned for years in many nations. Lawrence spent much of his life traveling around the world seeking a hospitable artistic environment. He ultimately returned to England and, in his last years, was surrounded by a gaggle of devoted women who thought of themselves as his disciples.

Lawrence once said, "Sex and beauty are inseparable, like life and consciousness."

Other Birthdays
1862   O. Henry (William Sydney Porter)
1924   Tom Landry
1932   Bob Packwood

September 12

1902   Cleveland, Ohio.
Margaret Hamilton, best known for playing the Wicked Witch of the West in *The Wizard of Oz* (1939), was born. Hamilton, the terror of generations of children, was actually

an ex-kindergarten teacher who loved children (she had tea parties with Judy Garland on the *Oz* set). She became interested in acting after appearing in a high school play, but her practical parents insisted she acquire a more reliable profession such as teaching. Hamilton still found time to explore acting and became a character performer at the Cleveland Play House. Their successful production of the play *Another Language* took Hamilton to Broadway and then to Hollywood in 1932 to make the film version. Starring opposite Helen Hayes and Robert Montgomery, Hamilton, 30, played a gossipy old biddy. It was a role she reprised in seventy-five films over the next fifty years.

Hollywood offered Hamilton the chance to make a sequel to *The Wizard of Oz* but, while she did perform in a stage version of the story, she refused to make a sequel, saying, "Little children's minds can't cope with seeing a mean witch alive again...they think maybe I'm going back and cause trouble for Dorothy again."

Other Birthdays
1880   H. L. Mencken
1888   Maurice Chevalier
1913   Jesse Owens

September 13

1905   Paris.
   Claudette Colbert was born to Georges and Jeanne Colbert. Her father was a French banker who moved his family to New York City in 1910. Claudette fantasized about becoming a glamorous ballerina but despaired of her short neck, which she considered un-swanlike. After high school, Colbert got a job in a dress shop and gave French lessons at night. One of her students, a theatrical producer, suggested that Colbert was pretty enough to be an actress. He helped her get a three-line part in a Broadway play. This led to better parts, and she was soon starring on Broadway and in Hollywood.

Colbert's relationship with her mother wasn't as successful as her career. She blamed the failure of her first marriage on her mother's overbearing personality. Colbert's mother had actually forced Claudia and her husband to maintain separate domiciles. Clenching her fist, Colbert once told a *New York Times* interviewer, "She had a grip on me like that. She ruined the first marriage, no doubt about that. She even tried the second time. That's when I bought her her own house, and my dear little aunt moved in with her." Ironically, Colbert's best role in *It Happened One Night* (1934) opposite Clark Gable was as a girl defying a parent's interference in her romantic life. The film won all five major Academy Awards, including Best Actress for Colbert.

A less successful effort by Colbert was a 1956 television production of *Blithe Spirit*, in which she starred with Noel Coward. Colbert and Coward argued constantly. They eventually patched things up but Colbert later said, "The thing Noel said that hurt me the most—but funny it was—he said, 'If she had a neck, I'd wring it.'"

Other Birthdays
1925   Mel Torme
1944   Jacqueline Bisset

September 14

1883   Corning, New York.

Birth control campaigner Margaret Sanger was born. Sanger's mother was Irish and a devout Catholic; her father was a freethinking Socialist. They were an incongruous couple, yet they produced eleven children, taking a terrible toll on Margaret's mother, who had also had seven miscarriages. She contracted tuberculosis and died when Margaret was 16.

Sanger became a maternity nurse. One of her patients, who was suffering from complications following a self-induced abortion, asked her doctor for a means of birth control. Her doctor jokingly suggested she tell her husband to sleep on the roof. The woman later died after another self-induced abortion. Outraged, Sanger became involved in the birth control movement. She successfully campaigned to legalize contraceptives, helped set up birth control clinics, and helped develop the birth control pill

Sanger was also an advocate of free love, a cause she personally furthered by running through a long list of lovers. She advised her granddaughter, "Kissing, petting, and even intercourse are all right as long as they are sincere."

Other Birthdays
1914   Clayton Moore
1934   Kate Millett
1944   Joey Heatherton

September 15

1890   Torquay, Devonshire, England.

Agatha Mary Clarissa Miller was born. For a time she considered a career in opera. During World War I, she served as a volunteer pharmacist. A fan of mysteries, she often discussed them with her sister, who suggested Agatha write her own mystery novel. Marriage to the dashing military officer Archie Christie delayed her writing career a bit, but, in 1916, she began her first novel, *The Mysterious Affair at Styles*, which featured a retired Belgian police detective called Hercule Poirot. It took Agatha Christie four years to get it published, but it was a success. Christie went on to become the bestselling fiction author of all time.

Christie said of mystery writing. "The best time for planning a book is when you're doing the dishes."

Other Birthdays
1907   Fay Wray
1946   Oliver "I am not a trendy, Boomer paranoid" Stone

1947   Tommy Lee Jones
1961   Dan Marino
1984   Prince Henry

September 16

1924   New York City.

Natalie Weinstein, an executive secretary, met businessman William Perske at work. They fell in love and married but Natalie soon discovered that William was jealous and demanding. Still, she became pregnant and, after going into labor in a movie theater, she gave birth on this date to a daughter. She named the girl Betty. By the time Betty was six, her parents were divorced. Natalie replaced her married name with Bacal, a fragment cut from her Rumanian family name Weinstein-Bacal. Bacal worked hard to give her daughter a stylish life. Betty attended an expensive private school and, when she decided to be a dancer and actress, she received lessons.

Betty was a sensitive girl. When she and her Grandma Sophie listened together to King Edward abdicating the British throne for Wallis Simpson, they both cried over how romantic it seemed. Betty had a crush on Leslie Howard and idolized Bette Davis, whose scenes she reenacted with friends. High school plays encouraged Betty's dreams of acting, but when her Uncle Charlie arranged for her to meet Bette Davis, she was over the moon. Davis spoke kindly to Betty, encouraging her. Davis also warned, "Be sure it's really what you want to do with your life. It's hard work and it's lonely." Afterwards, Betty wrote Davis a gushing thank-you letter, to which Davis replied, "I hope we meet again sometime."

In 1940, Betty entered the American Academy of Dramatic Arts where she dated aspiring actor Kirk Douglas. After a year at the Academy, she became a model in the garment district, then got a job as an usher to get closer to the theater. She introduced herself to Danny Kaye and Vincent Price when they played in her theater, and they encouraged her. She worked at the USO's Stagedoor Canteen and sold a theatrical newspaper on a street corner, which gave her another pretext to introduce herself to theater people. Gradually, she met more and more important people who gave her advice. In 1942, she won a walk-on role in a Broadway play. To make her last name more easily pronounceable, Betty added an extra *l*. This role led to another role, a *Harper's Bazaar* magazine cover, and to Hollywood, where she changed her first name to Lauren. As Lauren Bacall, she became a star and the wife of Humphrey Bogart, whom she met on her first film, *To Have and Have Not* (1944).

Years later, Bacall wrote of her mother, "her eyes shone when she looked at me. She always made me feel that I could do anything once I made up my mind. . . . I respected her and I loved her. If she but held my hand, I felt safe."

Other Birthdays
1925   B. B. King
1927   Peter Falk
1949   Ed Begley Junior

September 17

1951   Manhattan, Kansas.

Cassandra Peterson, better known as "Elvira, Mistress of the Dark," was born. Raised in Colorado Springs, Colorado, her father was an insurance salesman who also ran a costume shop. Peterson received third degree burns over 35 percent of her body in a childhood accident. Her scars caused other children to label her a "monster," and she became a loner until her rebellious teenage years. She says, "I think what happened is that somewhere along the line I just kind of burst out of this shell and became like, 'I'm going to prove to you, to everybody, that even though I have scars I *can* do anything I want.' And the first thing I wanted to do was become a showgirl in Las Vegas, which is about as far as you could possibly ever go with scars all over your body."

Peterson took the first step towards her goal when her parents stopped in Las Vegas on the way home from a California vacation. She was 17, too young to enter the casino and watch the shows. She persuaded her parents into letting her pretend to be older, then put on a heavy coat of makeup and her most adult clothing. Not only was she allowed in, but the maître d' invited her to a showgirl audition where she was offered a job. As Peterson had grown, her scars had faded enough to be easily hidden with body makeup. After three months of pleading, her parents allowed her to take the job.

For a year, Peterson performed on a Las Vegas stage. She was platonically befriended by Elvis Presley, who encouraged her to become a singer, saying, "Get out of Vegas, you don't want to stay here, you're going to ruin your life, you'll become an old showgirl and marry a dealer and become an alcoholic." Peterson left for Paris, hoping to join the Folies Bergère, but she found the other performers too unpleasant. She went on to Italy, where she met Federico Fellini, who gave her a small part in his film *Roma* (1972) because she reminded him of his wife. Peterson next sang lead for a rock band. Overcome by homesickness, she walked out on the band during a break and returned to America.

Peterson settled in Los Angeles, supporting herself by working as a cocktail waitress and as a temporary secretary while pursuing parts in films and television. She also performed in an improvisational comedy group with Laraine Newman, Paul Reubens, Jon Lovitz, and Phil Hartman. She had little success and decided to quit show business when she turned 30. One week before her 30th birthday, she married. While out of town on her honeymoon, she received the call to play Elvira, a vampirish bombshell hostess for late-night movies. At first she didn't want the job. Eventually, she accepted, becoming a cult heroine.

Other Birthdays
1907   Warren Burger
1928   Roddy McDowell

1931   Anne Bancroft
1939   David Souter
1948   John Ritter
1955   Rita Rudner

September 18

1905   Stockholm.

Greta Louisa Gustafsson was born, the third and last child of Anna and Karl Gustafsson, a laborer. The Gustafssons were poor but hardworking. When Karl became ill, the older children got jobs while young Greta nursed her father. He died in 1919, and Greta left school to work in a barber shop, where she lathered faces for the barber to shave. She became a salesgirl at Stockholm's P.U.B. department store in the early 1920s. The store's public relations man decided to film some ads to run in the local movie houses. To save money, he used Gustafsson and three other salesgirls, as models. She was paid $3 a day. Three of the girls were to illustrate how one ought to dress and use cosmetics, while the fourth was to serve as the example of how not to look. The poor dresser was to wear an oversized, garish dress with a checked skirt and checked scarf. Gustafsson got the oddball role. Perhaps the other girls were happy not to appear foolish on film, but Gustafsson became the star. She enjoyed the attention and appeared in more ad films. Despite her mother's opposition, Gustafsson decided she wanted to be an actress, and, when a Swedish film director visited her store to buy costumes, she cornered him and quizzed him about how to get into the movies. Impressed by her chubby, wholesome good looks, he gave her a screen test and cast her in her first film, the comedy *Peter the Tramp*, when she was 16.

When Gustafsson saw herself in the film, instead of letting success go to her head, she clinically analyzed her performance and realized she needed professional training. She talked her way into the Swedish Royal Dramatic Theatre Academy.

There, director Mauritz Stiller took her under his wing and cast her in *Gosta Berling's Saga*. He also changed her name. He considered Greta Gabor but settled on Greta Garbo. Garbo's mother eventually accepted her career, although she made it clear she didn't care for Greta's kissing strange men on screen.

Other Birthdays
1933   Robert Blake
1939   Frankie Avalon
1964   Holly Robinson

September 19

1940   Omaha, Nebraska.

Composer Paul Williams was born. Despite being five feet tall, Williams went to Hollywood when he turned 21 to become a movie star. It took years for him to get his first part in a major film, *The Loved One* (1965), and then he played a 10-year-old. He got small parts in *The Chase* (1966), *Planet of the Apes* (1968), and *Watermelon Man* (1970), but had to support himself by working as a housepainter. He filled his spare time by noodling on his guitar and writing songs.

Williams the songwriter did much better than Williams the actor. The Carpenters recorded his "Rainy Days and Mondays" and "We've Only Just Begun," a tune that was first used for a bank commercial. Helen Reddy recorded his "You and Me Against the World." Three Dog Night recorded his "Just an Old-Fashioned Love Song." All were hits.

Other Birthdays
1914   Frances Farmer
1923   Jean Stapleton
1941   Cass Elliot
1949   Twiggy

September 20

1934 Rome.

Sofia Scicolone was born in a charity ward. She was the illegitimate daughter of Romilda Vilani and Riccardo Scicolone, a handsome engineer. They also had a second child, Maria. Romilda took her children to live with her in Naples. Her mother helped her care for them after Riccardo abandoned his family to marry another woman. Sofia and Maria were raised in near-poverty, with the streets as their playground. Sofia acquired the nickname Stechetto, or Toothpick, because she was thin from poor diet. Movies became a natural escape. Sofia later recalled, "I would go the first thing in the morning and stay through the last showing at night. There was always something magic to me about movies. I couldn't get over the way it was: on the walls, persons suddenly started to live." Sofia also observed, "Like every little girl in every little Italian town, the movies were our only pleasure. They gave us dreams about a life we didn't have." Those pleasant dreams would help the girl during the nightmare years of World War II. Sofia's family suffered terribly but survived.

Sofia's mother Romilda shared her daughter's love of the movies, having once won a Greta Garbo look-alike contest. After the war, when Sofia was 14, Romilda allowed her to enter a "Queen of the Sea of Naples" beauty contest. Sofia came in second, but won enough money to go to Rome with her mother. Romilda heard that an American film company was there filming *Quo Vadis?* (1951). She got herself and her daughter jobs as extras. In 1950, Sofia entered a Miss Rome contest. Again, she didn't win. However, one of the judges, film producer Carlo Ponti, arranged a film test for Sofia. It went terribly. Her hair was too short, and she was still too thin. Ponti told her to forget acting because she didn't photograph well.

Sofia didn't give up. She tried modeling, which led to tiny movie roles and, finally, to a lead in an opera film. Her singing was done by someone else, but when Ponti saw the movie, he changed his opinion of Sofia. He asked her to sign a film contract, then asked her to marry him. Sofia agreed to both. They were married in 1957 in Mexico. Sofia, who now went by the stage name, Sophia Loren, became a star.

Other Birthdays
1885   Jelly Roll Morton
1917   Fernando Rey

September 21

1947   Portland, Maine.

Nellie Ruth King, wife of merchant seaman Donald King, gave birth to a child who would create great fear around the world: writer Stephen Edwin King, their second son. While Nellie and Donald didn't murder each other, like some of their son's characters, they did break up when Stephen was two years old. Donald King was never seen again by his family. Nellie took on a series of humble jobs to support her sons.

Several incidents during King's childhood in Indiana and Connecticut may have influenced his writing. When King was four, he went to play with a neighbor friend. King came back an hour later in a white-faced state of shock. His friend had been horribly killed by a freight train. King couldn't remember whether he'd been with the boy at the time or not. In 1953, King eavesdropped as his mother listened to a radio version of Ray Bradbury's frightening "Mars is Heaven." It so terrified him that, when his brother refused to let King crawl into bed with him, King slept *under* his brother's bed. After Nellie moved the family to Maine to be near her parents, King discovered a box of fantasy and horror magazines that once belonged to his father. These inspired him to try writing his own fiction. In 1965, while attending the University of Maine, he published his first story, "I Was a Teenage Grave-Robber." He was paid $35.

After college, King wrote a great deal, but with little

success. He married and had two children. The bills piled up. King worked as a janitor and as a gas station attendant while flirting with alcoholism and despair. He got a job teaching English at Hampden Academy in Maine and continued writing, using a child's desk in the academy's boiler room. He finished three novels without selling one. He threw out the third in frustration, but his wife retrieved it and convinced him to mail it to Doubleday. They bought it, and the prom-queen-gone-amok novel, *Carrie*, became a best-seller. He has since turned out one hit book after another and has had three books on the bestseller list simultaneously. Perhaps King is still the little boy who hid under the bed. He keeps a light burning in his bathroom all night long.

King once said, "We make up horrors to help us cope with the real ones."

Other Birthdays
1866   H. G. Wells
1931   Larry Hagman
1950   Bill Murray

September 22

1956   Hackensack, New Jersey.

Singer Debbie Boone was born. The daughter of singer Pat Boone, Debbie Boone's 1977 hit "You Light Up My Life" won an Oscar and is one of the biggest-selling singles ever. According to celebrity biographer Christopher P. Anderson, as a child, Boone didn't always live up to her wholesome father's expectations. He transferred her from one school when he found her reading Eldridge Cleaver's *Soul on Ice*. When he discovered counterculture posters on the walls of her room, he plastered them with Bible stickers. Boone tore them down. Nevertheless, she remained religious and stated on the *Phil Donahue Show* that she and her husband-to-be, Gabriel Ferrer, would be virgins on their wedding night. Donahue reacted with astonishment that such a thing was possible or even desirable.

Other Birthdays
1927   Tommy Lasorda
1954   Shari Belafonte
1960   Joan Jett
1962   Scott Baio

September 23

1920   Brooklyn, New York.

Vaudevillians Joe Yule and Nell Carter had a son, Joe Yule Jr. Joe Jr. first appeared onstage at eleven months in a small tuxedo. He became a part of his parents' act, then branched out to play midgets. He lost four front teeth when he had to appear with a big cigar clamped in his mouth. Joe Jr.'s folks split up and, to make matters worse, his agent told his mother that her son was all washed-up. He was just five. Joe Jr. kept scrambling for parts. In 1935, he auditioned for the role of Puck in a film version of Shakespeare's *A Midsummer Night's Dream*. He got the part and appeared under his new stage name, Mickey Rooney.

Rooney became a star at MGM, earning a fortune playing Andy Hardy. Often cast together, he and Judy Garland grew to be close friends. She later said, "The whole trouble was we met when we were too damned young, so it was all puppy stuff. A few years later, maybe something real could have happened. I was really crazy about that little bastard. Not only him, but his talent, too. Maybe we could have been a real forever team. As it turned out, we seemed to have an Olympic marrying competition. Five for me and seven for him. So far, that is. But he must be slowing down, don't you think so? Who knows, maybe one of these days I'll catch up with him." She never did.

Other Birthdays
1930   Ray Charles

1943   Julio Iglesias
1949   Bruce Springsteen

September 24

1936   Greenville, Mississippi.

Jim Henson was born. He was raised in Hyattsville, Maryland, near Washington, D.C. His father was an agronomist with the U.S. Department of Agriculture, but Henson wanted to work in television. In high school, he discovered that puppets might allow him to do so. He hadn't played with puppets as a child, but now he signed up for the puppetry club. He then studied the art at the University of Maryland, where he met his wife, Jane. They soon got their own five-minute late-night television show on a local station, featuring their combination marionettes-and-puppets, or "muppets." Their show was called *Sam and Friends* and starred a muppet made out of Henson's mother's old green coat and a pair of Ping-Pong balls. Henson christened this creation "Kermit the Frog."

In 1962, the Hensons went to New York, where they became regulars on the *Today* show. In 1970, they signed with *Sesame Street*. Soon, every child in America considered Kermit a personal friend.

According to Bernie Brillstein, CBS turned down the pilot for *The Muppet Show* because their marketing-research department said any show with a frog as the host just wouldn't work.

Other Birthdays
1896   F. Scott Fitzgerald
1942   Linda McCartney
1946   Mean Joe Greene

September 25

1944   New Brunswick, New Jersey.

Michael Douglas was born to Kirk Douglas (see 12/9/1916) and British actress Diana Douglas. Douglas received a good education, attending Choate, then the University of California at Santa Barbara. He intended to become a lawyer, but fell in love with acting when he performed in a student production of Shakespeare's *As You Like It*.

Acting wasn't easy for Douglas, whose stage fright was so severe that he kept a wastebasket just off stage to accommodate his terror-induced vomiting. Douglas overcame his fear and learned his craft on the job in a series of off-Broadway plays and minor movies. His big break came with the part of a rookie cop in the television series, *The Streets of San Francisco*. He left the series to become a producer. His first production, *One Flew Over the Cuckoo's Nest* (1976), became the first film to win all five top Academy Awards since *It Happened One Night* (1934).

1952   Oakland, California.

Mark Hamill was born. Because his father was a navy man, Hamill spent his childhood moving from base to base. He lived in ten cities, both inside and outside the United States, before the family settled in California, where Hamill dropped out of college to try acting. He appeared in almost a hundred television shows, including a run on the soap *General Hospital*, before he signed with ABC to appear in the sitcom *Eight is Enough*. Shortly after signing, he was offered the role of Luke Skywalker in *Star Wars*. ABC didn't want to release him and, to make things worse, Hamill accidentally drove his car over a cliff, badly smashing his face. Three operations restored his good looks, but the discouraged Hamill was considering leaving acting when Diana Hyland, who played the mother on *Eight is Enough*, visited him in the hospital and talked him into sticking it out. She died just three weeks later. Hamill continued acting, ABC released him from his contract, and *Star Wars* made him a millionaire.

Other Birthdays
1897 William Faulkner
1931 Barbara Walters
1952 Christopher Reeve

September 26

1895 New York City.

Actor George Raft was born and raised in Hell's Kitchen. He later described himself as "a layabout" who fiddled around as a boxer before becoming a dancehall taxi dancer. The money he made from dancing encouraged him to audition for stage roles. Raft danced on Broadway, then tried movies. Hollywood was looking for authentic-looking actors to play gangsters and Raft's tough background helped him get parts. His big break came in 1932, when he played opposite Paul Muni in *Scarface*. The film was so violent that its release was delayed by censors. Raft became a star, making numerous gangster films. He also became an associate of real gangsters such as Al Capone.

George Raft mentioned in his autobiography his favorite fan letter. It read:
"Dear George.

You are my favorite movie actor. I like all your pictures. You are a greater actor than John Barrymore. I love you.
(Signed) Your Mother."

Other Birthdays
1898 George Gershwin
1914 Jack La Lanne
1948 Olivia Newton-John
1956 Linda Hamilton

September 27

1840 A military barracks, Landau, Bavaria, Germany.

Thomas Nast was born. His father was a musician in a regimental band. Despite this patriotic occupation, the elder Nast took his family and left his country for the United States in 1846. The younger Nast quickly adapted to his new home. By the time he was 15, he was working for Frank Leslie's *Illustrated Weekly*, one of the most popular magazines of the day. In 1858, he became a freelancer and his work appeared in journals such as *Harper's Weekly* and *The New York Illustrated News*.

During the Civil War, Nast provided eyewitness illustrations of the fighting while befriending Ulysses S. Grant and Abraham Lincoln. Lincoln called his illustrations "our best recruiting sergeant. His...cartoons have never failed to arouse enthusiasm and patriotism, and have always seemed to come just when those articles were getting scarce." Nast's wartime experiences sharpened his idealism. A relative observed, "From a roving lad with a swift pencil for sale, he had become a patriot artist, burning with the enthusiasm of the time."

After the war, Nast became a political cartoonist for the influential *Harper's Weekly*. Nast's drawings, which belittled New York's infamous "Boss" Tweed, helped drive the Tweed machine from power. Nast provided the symbols for both the Democratic and Republican parties when he used donkeys and elephants to represent them. Nast also provided the world with another, even more recognizable symbol. He illustrated some Christmas stories with a portly interpretation of Santa Claus conjured out of his Bavarian childhood. That chubby gentleman is still depicted as Nast drew him.

Other Birthdays
1920 William Conrad
1923 Jayne Meadows
1948 Meat Loaf

September 28

1924   Fontana Liri, south of Rome, Italy.

Actor Marcello Mastroianni was born. The son of a carpenter, he worked as an industrial designer during World War II. When the Italians surrendered, Mastroianni was sent to a labor camp by the Germans. Fortunately, he managed to escape. After the war, Mastroianni supported himself by selling paintings to tourists, until he got a job as an accountant with a British film company. To fill his spare time, he joined a theatrical company, then began getting film parts. Soon, he was an international star. His best-known film was *La Dolce Vita* (1960).

Luchino Visconti said of Matroianni, "He's very human and easily identifies with the man in the street. He's never a hero. Rather, he's an anti-hero, and that's why, in turn, the public adore him. That's his great merit and his appeal."

Other Birthdays
1902   Ed Sullivan
1934   Brigette Bardot
1967   Moon Unit Zappa

September 29

1907   Tioga, Texas.

Gene Autry was born. His ancestors had come to Texas from Tennessee with the first settlers. One family member died at the Alamo. Autry's father was a livestock and horse trader, whose business interests took the family to Oklahoma, where Autry walked five miles to school after his morning chores. A more pleasant duty for Autry was singing in his choir. He started learning country tunes on an $8 guitar he had ordered from the Sears Roebuck Catalog. When the Field's Brothers' Marvelous Medicine Show came to town, Autry earned $15 a week singing for them. In high school, he got a job at the center of town life: the local railroad depot. Autry passed his idler moments on the job by playing his guitar and singing. A stranger passing through told him he ought to sing on the radio. Autry took it as just good-natured pleasantry until he discovered that the stranger was Will Rogers. Autry decided to take a shot.

After finishing high school, Autry used his railroad employee pass to travel to New York City. He literally wore out his shoes trying to get a singing job, but had no luck. He returned to his job at the railroad depot, but didn't give up his dream. He got a fifteen-minute show on a local radio station, becoming a small-time hit as the "Oklahoma Yodeling Cowboy." Autry kept working at the depot, and it was that job, not the radio job, that proved key to his success. Autry and Jimmy Long, the chief night dispatcher at the station, wrote several country songs. One of these was "That Silver-Haired Daddy of Mine," which became the world's first gold record, selling over one million copies.

This success led to Autry's being hired by the Sears Roebuck Company, which then had a large recording branch. They also sponsored the radio show *The National Barn Dance,* the forerunner of Nashville's *Grand Ole Opry.* Autry became a regular on the show and, in 1934, began a long, successful Hollywood career as a singing cowboy. Autry said, "I'm no great actor. I'm no great rider. I'm no great singer. But whatever it is I'm doing, they like it."

Other Birthdays
1758   Lord Horatio Nelson
1942   Madeline Kahn
1943   Lech Walesa
1948   Bryant Gumbel

September 30

1935   San Francisco, California.
     Singer Johnny Mathis was born, the fourth of the seven children of a valet-chauffer and a maid. Mathis was athlet-

ically gifted, breaking track and field records and later starring on his basketball team at San Francisco State College. As a boy, he loved singing, and his father, a frustrated entertainer, provided him with a piano and plenty of Ella Fitzgerald, Peggy Lee, and Lena Horne records. Mathis pragmatically planned to be a physical education instructor. When he was 13, his parents brought him to singer Connie Cox for a professional appraisal of Mathis's voice. Cox was so impressed that, for no fee, she trained Mathis for six years. Mathis began singing in local jazz clubs. His audiences often didn't like his voice. Mathis says, "People told me I sang too high and that I sounded like a girl. I thought it was a horrible thing God had given me, this strange voice."

Professional singers, such as Dizzy Gillespie and Miles Davis, encouraged Mathis to continue. When Mathis was 19, Helen Noga heard him jamming with some friends. Impressed, she became Mathis's manager and got him a recording contract with Columbia Records. Although his first album wasn't a hit, it led to a job singing at New York's Blue Angel Club. The club's emcee, jazz composer Bart Howard, gave Mathis a couple of love songs to record, "Wonderful! Wonderful!" and "It's Not for Me to Say." Mathis was an overnight success. He went on to record dozens of hits, including "All the Way," "Chances Are," and "Misty."

Other Birthdays
1924   Truman Capote
1932   Angie Dickinson
1943   Marilyn McCoo

October 1

1924   Plains, Georgia.

President James Earl Carter Jr. was born to Bessie Lillian Gordy Carter, a nurse, and James Earl Carter, a World War I veteran and small businessman. Carter was the first member of his family to finish high school. He then attended the U.S. Naval Academy at Annapolis and became the captain of a nuclear submarine. Carter might have continued to serve in increasingly responsible naval commands, but, in 1953, his father died, and Carter left the navy to run the family peanut business.

Carter did well in the peanut business, but it didn't hold his attention. He developed an interest in politics. He won a Georgia Senate seat, then, in 1970, became governor of Georgia. In 1974, unable to succeed himself as governor under Georgia's constitution, Carter began a campaign for president. At that time, he was so obscure that he stumped the panel on the television game show *What's My Line?* Nonetheless, public anger at the Watergate scandal carried Carter into the White House in 1976. His performance in office caused him to be voted out by a two-to-one margin. Since then, he has written books, participated in international organizations, promoted housing for the poor, and served as an international negotiator for President Bill Clinton. In this last role, he has found virtues in dictators that were overlooked by the rest of the world.

Carter once said, "Have faith in me. I am a Christian."

Other Birthdays
1920   Walter Matthau
1933   Richard Harris
1933   George Peppard
1935   Julie Andrews
1950   Randy Quaid

October 2

1869   Porbandar, India.

Mohandas Karamchand Gandhi was born into the Vaisya, or merchant caste. For three generations, members of his Hindu family had served as prime ministers in various Indian states. Gandhi's father had been prime minister in four Indian states. His mother was his father's fourth wife. They raised Gandhi in the traditions of their caste, teaching him to be a vegetarian, a nonsmoker, and a nondrinker, and hoped that he, too, would become a government official. To help him realize his adult responsibilities, they arranged a marriage for him when he was just 13.

Gandhi went to England as a young man to study law. He tried to shed his Indian background and become an English gentleman. A pamphlet in an English vegetarian restaurant, however, and English theosophists, who avidly studied Eastern religions, persuaded him to return to his Hinduism.

After becoming a barrister, Gandhi went back to India in 1891 to practice. He failed his first cases and decided to try practicing law in the Indian community of Natal, South Africa. There, he became a successful lawyer but was disturbed by the treatment Indians received at the hands of South Africans. He left his practice to found a nonviolent resistance movement. In time, the movement took him back to India and led to India's independence.

Gandhi, who won the title Mahatma ("great soul") from his followers, once said, "In matters of conscience, the law of the majority has no place."

1895   Asbury Park, New Jersey.

Bud Abbott was born to Rae Abbott, a bareback rider for the Barnum & Bailey Circus, and Harry Abbott, an advance man for that circus. After Bud was born, his family moved to Coney Island, where Harry organized the first burlesque circuit. At 16, Bud became an assistant treasurer for a Brooklyn burlesque theater. It was there that he met his wife, dancer Betty Smith. She encouraged Bud, who was unhappy with his office job, to become a performer. They formed a comedy team, with Bud as straight man. He became so noted for his ability to help put over jokes that many comics tried to woo him into teaming with them. In 1936, Bud met comic Lou Costello and the duo became stars (see 3/6/1906).

Betty wasn't angry at being supplanted and enjoyed her husband's success. She and Bud were married for fifty-five years, until his death in 1974.

Other Birthdays
1890   Groucho Marx (see 3/22/1887)
1938   Rex Reed
1951   Sting

October 3

1925   West Point, New York.

Intellectual grasshopper Gore Vidal was born. He was christened Eugene Vidal but changed his first name to honor his beloved uncle, Senator Thomas Gore of Oklahoma. Gore distinguished himself as a boy by becoming a pilot. After an elite education at Phillips Exeter, he joined the U.S. Army, serving three years before creating a large controversy with the publication of *The City and the Pillar,* which contained homosexual themes. Gore has published a series of well-received historical novels, including *Burr* and *Lincoln.* His essays, which showcase a bitter view of the world, are also popular, unlike Gore, who has, at one time or another, made enemies of Norman Mailer, Truman Capote, William F. Buckley Jr., Lyndon Johnson, Richard Nixon, and the Kennedy clan. Perhaps wisely, Gore spends much of his time in a villa near Rome with an ocean between him and his enemies.

Gore is noted for his aphorisms. He once said, "A narcissist is someone better looking than you are."

Other Birthdays
1900   Thomas Wolfe
1941   Chubby Checker

October 4

1895   Piqua, Kansas.

Buster Keaton was born. His parents, Joseph and Myra Keaton, were vaudevillians, and, at five, Buster became the featured performer in their act, The Three Keatons. Indeed, the name Buster had a show biz origin. When the magician Houdini saw the boy gamely take a tumble without complaining, he remarked "What a buster!" The boy's durability became the cornerstone of the family comedy act—he was comically slapped and tossed around like a dummy, used like a human mop, and even kicked in the face. The violence was so realistic that child protection organizations continually tried to get the boy away from his parents. Sometimes stage managers passed Buster off as a midget just to avoid controversy. In New York City, the mayor was dragged into the debate. Child protection authorities forced him to summon the boy to his office. There, the mayor ordered him to strip to see if the boy had any bruises or marks. Discovering none, he sent Buster on his way.

Buster's years of experience came in handy when he went to Hollywood, where he made some of the funniest movies of all time.

1941   London.
Author Jackie Collins was born. Collins began writing and selling scandalous fiction as a teenager when she sold peeks into her fictionalized diary. After being kicked out of school at 15 for smoking, she accepted an invitation from her actress sister Joan Collins to come live in California. At 18, she married a 30-year-old movie executive. Collins's husband was a drug addict and a manic-depressive who died four years into their marriage. She next married businessman Oscar Lerman. Drawing upon her insight into the Hollywood and business worlds, Collins again began writing. After a British critic labeled her first book, *The World Is Full of Married Men,* "the most disgusting book ever written," it became a bestseller. Every book she has written since has been hugely successful, and many have been made into films. Two, *The Stud* and *The Bitch,* provided theatrical vehicles for her sister.

Other Birthdays
1924   Charlton "More Moses Than Moses" Heston
1945   Clifton Davis
1946   Susan Sarandon

October 5

1830   Fairfield, Vermont.
Chester Alan Arthur, the twenty-first U.S. president, was born to Malvina and William Arthur. Malvina, born in Vermont, had been raised in Quebec, where she met and married William, an Irish schoolteacher who became a Baptist preacher. He took Malvina back to Vermont, conducting

revival meetings while Malvina took care of their children.

The studious Arthur became a lawyer. An active abolitionist and Republican, he served as U.S. President James Garfield's vice president. When Garfield was assassinated, Arthur became president. His administration secured the enactment of the Pendleton Civil Service Act, which did much to remove politics from civil servant appointments. Since he had become president without running, Arthur had little support in his party and didn't win its nomination for president when his term ended.

When Arthur ran for vice president, his Democratic opponents circulated a curious story about him. They claimed that he had been born in Canada and was therefore ineligible for the vice presidency. They admitted that a son had been born to the Arthurs in Vermont but said that this child had died. The Democrats maintained that the corpse of the Vermont-born child—the real Chester A. Arthur—was sold to a medical school and that a second son, born while the Arthurs lived in Canada, was given the name of the dead Chester. Like most conspiracy tales, it required considerable precognition. The Arthurs would have had to predict when their boy was an infant that he would later need American citizenship. Arthur wisely refused to comment on the story. Unfortunately, all official records of his birth had been destroyed, and his parents were dead by the time the charges were made. Only the memories of elderly neighbors verified Arthur's origins.

Other Birthdays
1919   Donald Pleasence
1924   Bill Dana
1952   Clive Barker

October 6

1846   Central Bridge, New York.

George Westinghouse was born. Following service in both the Union Army and Navy during the Civil War, Westinghouse developed inventions for the railroad, most notably the air brake. Previously, each car had its own brake that was activated by a brakeman turning a wheel on the car, a dangerous procedure. Brakemen often fell, and missing limbs were a common badge of ex-brakemen. Westinghouse's system allowed one man to safely do the job. He became wealthy and continued to invent, becoming one of Thomas Edison's rivals.

Edison had developed the DC (direct current) system for delivering electricity. Westinghouse produced the AC (alternating current) system. A fierce debate ensued over which should be adopted as cities began electrifying. Millions of dollars were at stake. Edison claimed AC was dangerous. When New York State decided to execute criminals by electrocution, Edison saw an opportunity to associate this terrible method of punishment with Westinghouse's system and built an AC electric chair. The executioners underestimated how long to leave it on and, although the criminal was rendered unconscious by the device, he wasn't killed. In horror, they gave him a long blast. The criminal died amidst clouds of smoke. Electrocution became very controversial.

Despite the gruesome association, Westinghouse's system was better suited to long-distance power transmission and became the standard.

Other Birthdays
1906   Janet Gaynor
1908   Carole Lombard
1942   Britt Ekland

October 7

1943   San Antonio, Texas.

Oliver Laurence North was born. His parents were Ann North, a teacher, and Oliver Clay North, a World War II veteran who went into the wool business. They raised their four children in the small textile town of Philmont, New York.

North preferred chess to sports and served as an altar boy, but also had an adventurous streak that he demonstrated by jumping off a local railroad bridge. He earned an appointment to the U.S. Naval Academy at Annapolis, but nearly forfeited his military career when he was a passenger in a car wreck, seriously injuring his back and knee. North was afraid he would never walk again. To force his body to regain its strength, he climbed his six-foot garage and jumped to the ground over and over. This nutty therapy seemed to work. He went on to serve eleven months as a marine officer in Vietnam, winning the Silver Star, the Bronze Star, and two Purple Hearts.

After Vietnam, North advanced through the ranks to serve at the Naval War College. A paper he wrote outlining new uses for battleships in the modern navy attracted the attention of Navy Secretary John Lehman. He brought North to Washington, D.C., where he went to work for the National Security Council. North became a key player in the Iran-Contra Affair and has since pursued a career in radio, following a failed bid to become Virginia's U.S. Senator.

Other Birthdays
1951   John Mellencamp
1955   Yo-Yo Ma

October 8

1943   New York City.

Chevy Chase was born (his real name is Cornelius Crane Chase). His father, writer and editor Ned Chase, was a Phi Beta Kappa graduate of Princeton. His mother was a concert pianist. The couple later divorced. Chase says, "I saw my father on special occasions and weekends. But he was very available."

Chase, the grandson of plumbing millionaire Cornelius

Chase, grew up in a privileged and successful family. His brother went to Harvard, and his half-sister was Princeton's first female valedictorian. However, having thousands of toilets carry his grandfather's name may have affected Chase's character. He has said, "My humor has always been different.... Like peeing on the wall when my mother was out. Bringing a cow onto the third floor of a dorm at Haverford College. I was never a perfect, golden child by a long shot. For much of the time I was raising hell."

Chase discovered comedy writing at Bard College, where he and friends filmed parodies of television commercials. The best of these were later released in the cult comedy film *The Groove Tube* (1974), which, in words that might be applied to Chase's entire career, was reviewed by Leonard Matlin as "Sometimes funny, sometimes stupid..." In 1972, Chase went to Los Angeles to write comedy. His clients included Alan King and the Smothers Brothers, but he had limited success. One day, while waiting in line to see *Monty Python and the Holy Grail,* he began chatting with the guy next to him. The stranger turned out to be Lorne Michaels, who was producing a new comedy show, *Saturday Night Live,* for NBC. Impressed with Chase's sense of humor, Michaels hired him to write and act for the show. Chase became a star but, after one year with the program, left to make movies. Some fans thought he had developed a swelled head. Chase's explanation was quite different.

According to Chase, he fell in love with model Jacqueline Carlin, who had hopes of becoming an actress. Chase wanted to marry her, but she refused to leave Los Angeles for New York City. Chase chose her over his *SNL* job. Nine months after their marriage, the couple divorced. Chase dived into alcohol and drug abuse. The drug death of John Belushi spurred Chase's retreat to the Betty Ford Clinic. With the support of his third wife, Jayni, he straightened himself out.

Chase claims that the funniest person he has ever met was his father: "I steal a lot of his stuff."

Other Birthdays
1939 Paul Hogan
1941 Jesse Jackson
1949 Sigourney Weaver

October 9

1940 Liverpool, England.

John Lennon was born. His father was a merchant seaman who abandoned his family when Lennon was six. His mother, Julia, was an eccentric woman who left her son with her sister, Mimi, to raise. Although Julia often visited Lennon, she was more a friend than a parent.

Lennon was a troublesome boy. In school, he was disciplined for insolence, cutting classes, and throwing a blackboard out the window. His Aunt Mimi said, "The main reason he was such a worry to me while he was growing up was because I knew he had *something*. He knew he had it too. But he didn't know where exactly to put this talent he had, or where it might lead him." Lennon tried painting and poetry before settling on music as a means of self-expression. When "Skiffle," a type of rockabilly music, swept England in the 1950s, Mimi bought Lennon a guitar.

Lennon formed his own Skiffle band, the Quarrymen. They played for little or nothing but got valuable experience. In 1957, while playing at a church festival in Woolton, Lennon met 14-year-old Paul McCartney (see 6/18/1942). McCartney impressed Lennon with his guitar skills. Lennon, in turn, impressed McCartney with his confident dreams of stardom, and McCartney joined the band.

Paul's school friend, George Harrison (see 2/25/1943), joined the band after persistently tagging along after them. They played dances, changing names several times: first the Quarrymen, then Johnny and the Moondogs, then the Moonshiners, next the Beatles, then the Silver Beetles, and, finally, the Beatles, again. Their first truly professional engagement was a two-month stint in Hamburg, Germany.

Hamburg was a wild town. The Beatles were booked into a seedy bar where they played up to seven hours a night. When they returned to England, the boyish band had hardened into leather-jacketed, long-haired professionals. Drummer Pete Best, whose mother owned a night club, joined the band. They began attracting a following and played dance halls and cellar bars. A second visit to Hamburg in 1960 led to their first recording. Lennon and McCartney had written over 100 songs, but their first record was a rock version of "My Bonnie Lies Over the Ocean." Upon the Beatles' return from Hamburg, Best was replaced by Ringo Starr (see 7/6/1940) just before the group released their first single, "Love Me Do," which launched the Beatles into superstardom.

Many were unimpressed by the Beatles. For example, the February 24, 1964, *Newsweek* observed: "Visually, they are a nightmare: tight, dandified Edwardian-Beatnik suits and great pudding bowls of hair. Musically they are a near-disaster: Guitars and drums slamming out a merciless beat that does away with secondary rhythms, harmony, and melody. Their lyrics (punctuated by nutty shouts of 'yeah, yeah, yeah!') are a catastrophe, a preposterous farrago of Valentine-card romantic sentiments." In 1963, John Lennon himself said, "We're lucky if we last three months."

Other Birthdays
1900   Alistair Sim
1948   Jackson Browne

October 10

1900   Washington, D.C.

Actress Helen Hayes was born to Frances Van Arnum, a manager for a wholesale butcher, and his wife, Catharine Brown. As a toddler, Hayes was pigeon-toed. Her parents thought dance lessons might correct this, so they sent her to Miss Minnie Hawkes's dancing school. The lessons were effective. By the time Hayes was five, she was a member of a theatrical company. At nine, she was performing in New York. She left the stage to finish her education at a Catholic academy, then went back as soon as she graduated, winning starring roles. In 1928, a young man at a cocktail party offered Hayes a bowl of peanuts with the elegant pick-up line: "I wish these were emeralds." The man was playwright Charles MacArthur and Hayes married him. They had two children, Mary, who died of polio, and James, who became an actor.

Hayes continued her stage career. She played ingenue roles until, as she put it, "I was squeezing cuteness out of my greasepaint tubes and scooping charm out of my cold cream jars." Hayes sought out meatier roles, developing her acting skills. She became one of America's foremost stars on both Broadway and in films.

Hayes said, "Actors cannot choose the manner in which they are born—consequently it is the one gesture in their lives completely devoid of self-consciousness."

Other Birthdays
1946   Ben Vereen
1955   David Lee Roth
1958   Tanya Tucker
1975   Sean Lennon

October 11

1884   New York City.

Eleanor Roosevelt was born. Her father was Elliott Roosevelt, the younger brother of President Theodore Roosevelt and godfather to Franklin Delano Roosevelt. Her mother, Anna Hall Roosevelt, was a descendant of a signer of the Declaration of Independence who had administered the oath of office to

George Washington. Eleanor was the first of their three children. The couple was well off and socially active. Anna, noted for her fine hair and beauty, was also admired for her inner strength. Unfortunately, she had need of it. Preoccupied with business and the sporting life, Elliott paid little attention to his wife. When a broken ankle required Elliott's taking powerful pain-killers, he became addicted and then worsened his condition with alcohol. For a time, Anna considered having him declared insane to prevent his squandering the family fortune. She also contemplated divorce but settled for Elliott's moving out. Young Eleanor missed her father and felt neglected by her mother.

Eleanor later recalled watching her mother dress for parties. "She looked so beautiful, I was grateful to be allowed to touch her dress or her jewels or anything that was part of the vision which I admired inordinately." Eleanor's mother, however, didn't conceal her less-flattering opinion of her daughter's looks. She considered Eleanor plain, at best, and nicknamed her Granny, purportedly because Eleanor had old-fashioned notions. Eleanor tried to get attention by telling fibs, which only increased her mother's disdain.

Anna became ill and underwent surgery in 1892. When she contracted diphtheria shortly afterwards, it proved fatal. She had forbidden her husband to visit her during her illness, and the rest of the Roosevelt family also scorned him, insisting that Eleanor be raised by her grandmother, Mary Livingston Ludlow Hall. Elliott died alone in 1894.

Eleanor received a Victorian upbringing. In 1905, when she was 19, her distant cousin, Franklin Delano Roosevelt, who had known her since childhood, began courting her. He admired her intelligence and temperament. He wrote her poetry and proposed while taking a walk. Eleanor accepted and went on to become first lady.

Other Birthdays
1844   Henry J. Heinz

October 12

1935   Modena, Italy.

Singer Luciano Pavarotti was born. His grandmother had high hopes for him. "You're going to be great, you'll see," she would say, bouncing his then-diminutive bottom on her knee. His mother also had dreams of success for her son. She wanted him to become a banker. Pavarotti didn't oblige, becoming an elemetary schoolteacher instead. He also developed an interest in opera. Unlike some parents, who might insist their son stay with a stable career, Pavarotti's baker father realized his son had a great talent and insisted he use it. Somewhat reluctantly, Pavarotti complied with his father's wishes. At 22, he quit teaching to become an insurance salesman, which allowed him enough time to study voice. His lessons led to one of the most successful opera careers of all time.

Pavarotti later said, "It's a mistake to take the safe path in life. If I hadn't listened to my father and dropped teaching, I would never be here. And, yes, my teacher groomed me. But no teacher ever told me I would become famous. Just my grandmother."

Other Birthdays
1932   Dick Gregory
1950   Susan Anton

October 13

1941   Newark, New Jersey.

Songwriter Paul Simon was born. His father was a bass player and bandleader who didn't approve of rock music. Simon grew up in Queens, New York, where he teamed up with Art Garfunkel when they were both in the sixth grade. Their first stage appearance together was in a school play, a version of *Alice in Wonderland*. Art played the Cheshire Cat, and Paul played the White Rabbit. At 15, as Tom and Jerry, they recorded a song called "Hey, Schoolgirl." Its mild success was enough to allow them to record "Sounds of Silence" under their own names after they finished high school and college. They followed this with such hits as "Feelin' Groovy," "At the Zoo," "Cecilia," "Parsley, Sage, Rosemary and Thyme," "Mrs. Robinson," and "Bridge Over Troubled Water." Garfunkel did the musical arrangements, while Simon composed. They won six Grammys before Garfunkel left the duo, in 1970, to try acting.

Simon scored many more hits on his own, including "Love Me Like a Rock," "Kodachrome," and "Slipsliding Away." His recent work often incorporates African music, which has led some black critics to claim he is exploiting African artists. Simon angrily denies this, saying he has enlarged the audience for African performers.

Other Birthdays
1925   Nipsey Russell
1925   Margaret Thatcher
1959   Marie Osmond

October 14

1890   Denison, Texas.

David Eisenhower and his wife Ida Stover Eisenhower, had Dwight Eisenhower, the third of their six sons. The couple had married while attending Lane College in Lecompton, Kansas. Ida's family had moved west after their farm in the Shenandoah Valley was destroyed by the Union Army during the Civil War. The smell of burning haystacks was one of her earliest memories. David's family had come to America in 1741 and moved west with the frontier. David's father, a well-to-do farmer, gave him a farm. David sold it, and with a partner, bought a shop in Hope, Kansas. Unfortunately, David's partner proved nefarious. He stole all the partnership's money and left town, leaving David with the shop's debts. David struggled, but paid them off. The family then moved to Texas, then Abilene, Kansas, where David wound up working as the director of a savings group. The Eisenhowers had little money, and the boys all helped out. Ida taught them to be self-reliant and religious. She was a member of the pacifist sect later called the Jehovah's Witness but didn't force her son to follow her beliefs, and Dwight chose a military career.

Dwight Eisenhower was turned down by the U.S. Naval Academy in Annapolis; West Point, however, accepted him. His first posting was to San Antonio, Texas, where he met and married Mamie Geneva Doud, in 1916. Despite slow advancement and poor pay, Eisenhower became a career officer. His skills were key to the Allied victory during World War II.

Ida Eisenhower was a good mother to all her sons. When Ike returned to Abilene from the war, the entire town was decked out to welcome him. A reporter asked Ida if she was proud of her son. Ida replied, "Which one?"

Other Birthdays
1896   Lillian Gish
1928   Roger Moore
1939   Ralph Lauren

October 15

1942   New York City.

Actress-director Penny Marshall was born. She grew up in the Bronx, where her father made industrial films. Her mother was a dance teacher who turned Marshall into her best pupil. As a child, Marshall appeared on the *Ted Mack Amateur Hour* and *The Jackie Gleason Show*. She attended the University of New Mexico and was briefly married before following her producer brother, Garry, to Hollywood. Marshall joined a repertory group, where she met fellow Bronxite Rob Reiner. They moved in together, and Marshall auditioned for the role of his wife,

Gloria, in *All in the Family.* She lost that fictional role to Sally Struthers but won the real role as Reiner's wife in 1971.

Marshall's career started gaining momentum when she was cast in several television commercials, including as the "before" in a shampoo commercial featuring Farah Fawcett as the "after." Marshall appeared on *The Paul Lynde Show* and *The Mary Tyler Moore Show,* and became a regular on *The Odd Couple.* Then, she and Cindy Williams were cast as easy, low-class dates for Henry Winkler and Ron Howard on *Happy Days.* Their performances were so entertaining that they were given their own show, *Laverne and Shirley.* For three years, it was at the top of the ratings. Success had some unhappy effects on Marshall. She began taking drugs, and her marriage failed in 1979. Eventually, she cleaned up and began directing films. *Big* (1988) established her as a first-string director.

Other Birthdays
1844   Friedrich Nietzsche
1881   P. G. Wodehouse
1921   Mario Puzo
1924   Lee Iacocca

October 16

1925   London.

Angela Brigid Lansbury was born. Her father, a lumber merchant, died when she was nine. Her mother, Moyna, was a stage actress and Lansbury loved to watch her from the wings. In 1940, her family was evacuated from England to America to escape German bombing. Lansbury was soon pursuing a career in show business. She began by singing in nightclubs, supplementing her income by wrapping gifts at a department store, then headed for Hollywood. She visited every film studio before winning the role of the Cockney maid in *Gaslight* (1944). She got an Academy Award nomination for best supporting actress for that film and also for her next one, *The Picture of Dorian Gray* (1945).

Lansbury went on to a long acting career, usually playing nasty women who were older than she actually was. For example, she played Laurence Harvey's mother in *The Manchurian Candidate* (1962): Harvey was 34, and Lansbury was 37. The film wasn't given wide release until 1987 because President Kennedy was killed shortly after the film was finished. Studio executives decided that it was an inappropriate time for a film depicting an attempted presidential assassination. Many critics say Lansbury should have gotten an Oscar for her performance.

In the mid-1960s, Lansbury decided to change her image. She says, "I just stopped playing bitches on wheels and people's mothers. I have only a few more years to kick up my heels!" Kick up her heels she did, when she got the lead in the Broadway smash *Mame*. She won a Tony for it and, again, two years later for *Dear World*. Her success soured when, within a few months, her mother died of cancer, her Malibu home burned, and her two children began flirting with drug addiction. Lansbury and her husband, Peter Shaw, packed up their kids and left for rural Ireland, far from the drug culture. After her children recovered, Lansbury returned to Broadway. In 1974, she won another Tony for *Gypsy*. She won a fourth for *Sweeney Todd*.

In 1984, Lansbury began her most successful role as Jessica Fletcher of television's *Murder, She Wrote,* the woman who has had over two hundred close associates murdered when she was nearby, yet still gets invited to house parties.

Other Birthdays
1854   Oscar Wilde
1888   Eugene O'Neill
1946   Suzanne Somers

October 17

1920   Omaha, Nebraska.

Montgomery Clift was born. His parents were Bill and Ethel Clift, who raised him in New York City. After Montgomery, the couple had twins, but Montgomery remained his mother's favorite. Bill, a stockbroker, often traveled on business, leaving Ethel alone with the children. She conjured up imaginary intruders so often that Bill paid his office boys to stay with her while he was out of town. Once, Ethel woke a neighbor woman staying with her in the middle of the night by pointing a flashlight and revolver in her face, sure that there were burglars or worse inside the house. As usual, there weren't.

Ethel was more stubborn than timid; she was so certain of her imaginings that she refused to accept anyone's assurances. Certainly, a timid woman wouldn't have traveled the world with her children, leaving her husband behind, which is what Ethel did as soon as the children were old enough to travel. She ranged as far as Switzerland in her journeys. Montgomery hated it. He later said, "Traveling is a hobgoblin existence for children. Why weren't roots established? My brother has been married three times now."

Clift was smothered by Ethel's domineering attentions but, oddly, he never rebelled. Instead, he developed an interest in acting. After he became successful, he continued to live with his parents. Ethel planned his activities, including encouraging him to avoid the company of young ladies who might supplant her. She practically staged a friendship for Clift with musician Lehman Engel.

Engel later remarked on another oddity of Ethel's. Although she had no bank account and Clift's father wasn't prosperous, her purse always seemed stuffed with hundred-dollar bills. Ethel told Engel that she was helping a Boston factory owner write his biography, but Engel later claimed that " .... anyone who's talked with Mrs. Clift knows that she doesn't use the King's English; she doesn't know a verb from a pronoun. She couldn't write an English sentence. Both Monty and I wondered if there wasn't something between [Ethel and the factory owner]."

Slowly, Clift gained some independence. He left home to perform in stock theater. Friend Janet Cohn recalled that Ethel tried to intrude upon Clift: "Once she came up from New York with a lot of expensive lilies, and planted them in his garden. As soon as she went back to New York, he tore up every single one of them and threw them in the lake." In 1943, Elia Kazan, a friend and mentor to Clift, talked him into leaving home for good, suggesting that his relationship with his mother was causing gossip. Clift got an apartment over a laundromat just minutes away from his parents. He complained to his friends about Ethel, yet visited her regularly for meals, staying for days. His relationship with Ethel influenced his romantic life as a bisexual. Clift's male lovers were artistic types, but his female associates were usually strong, older women.

One of these women was actress Myrna Loy. She said of Clift, "Everything got to him. He needed a few more layers of skin to cope with this mad world."

Other Birthdays
1905   Jean Arthur
1918   Rita Hayworth
1938   Evel Knievel
1948   Margot Kidder

October 18

1926   San Jose, California.

Charles Edward Anderson "Chuck" Berry was born (some sources list his birthday as January 15). Berry and his five siblings spent much of their childhood in St. Louis. The family lived in a pleasant middle-class neighborhood, but despite a congenial environment, Berry became a delinquent and spent time in a reformatory. A less harsh influence on Berry was his membership in the Antioch Baptist Church choir, where he received his first musical instruction. He also sang in his high school glee club. His music teacher, impressed by his musical talent, inspired him to buy a guitar and teach himself to play.

After high school, Berry went to work in a factory, then became a hairdresser. He married and had two children. Berry might have settled into an ordinary life but for his self-taught guitar skills. To make extra money, he took jobs playing, eventually forming his own combo. In 1955, while on vacation in Chicago, Berry met blues legend Muddy Waters, who, in turn, introduced him to record company executive Leonard Chess. Chess offered Berry an audition.

Berry performed a number called "Wee Wee Hours," and then, almost as an afterthought, added a song that he had written as a parody of country western songs titled "Maybelline." Chess liked it much better than the first song. After Berry gave New York radio disc jockey Alan Freed, inventor of the term "Rock and Roll," a 25 percent writing credit for the song, Freed promoted it on his popular show. Within weeks it became the first song to be a number one hit in three of *Billboard* magazine's categories—pop, rhythm-and-blues, and, despite its satirical intent, country western. Berry went on to record more hits, including "Roll Over Beethoven," "Johnny B. Goode," "Sweet Little Sixteen," and "My Ding-A-Ling."

Of his fame, Berry said, "I never looked for recognition. I was paying for a home and a new car."

Other Birthdays
1927   George C. Scott
1951   Pam Dawber
1956   Martina Navratilova

October 19

1937   Berlin, Germany.
Artist Peter Max was born, the only child of Jacob and Sala Max. Shortly after his birth, his parents fled Germany for Shanghai, China where Max's father became an importer-exporter. It wasn't the end of the family's travels. They lived in

Tibet, Africa, Israel, and France before settling in Brooklyn. Aptly enough, Max recalls his first canvas as his mother's steamer trunk. He covered it with drawings. Max recalled, "She didn't spank me, she just made a big fuss. That was the greatest encouragement. I thought it was all about my work."

Max became a successful commercial artist, and then, in 1967, he became a pop iconographer with his colorful cartoonlike posters. His images wound up on stationery, coffee mugs, bed linens, T-shirts, gift wrap, buses, and even the Manhattan Yellow Pages.

Other Birthdays
1945   John Lithgow
1949   Lynn Dickey
1967   Amy Carter

October 20

1928   New York City.

Psychologist Dr. Joyce Brothers was born. The daughter of two lawyers, she grew up intelligent and ambitious. After earning a Ph.D. in psychology from Columbia University, she taught there and then at New York's Hunter College. Brothers didn't achieve celebrity through her profession, however, but through a TV quiz show. In 1955, she won $134,000 by answering questions on boxing on *The $64,000 Question.* Brothers wasn't a boxing fan—she chose the topic only because she thought it narrow enough for her to memorize every important fact. In just six weeks, Brothers mastered twenty volumes of boxing lore. After her TV victory, Brothers parlayed her fame into a newspaper column, a radio show, several books, and thousands of lectures.

Dr. Brothers once said, "Marriage is not just spiritual communion and passionate embraces; marriage is also three-meals-a-day and remembering to carry out the trash."

Other Birthdays
1882   Bela Lugosi

1931   Mickey Mantle
1946   Lewis Grizzard

October 21

1956   Los Angeles, California.

Actress Carrie Fisher was born. Her parents were singer Eddie Fisher and actress Debbie Reynolds (see 4/1/1932). When Fisher left Reynolds for actress Elizabeth Taylor, Reynolds became a single parent. Debbie Reynolds later said of Fisher, "He had no influence on the children, but they were born with what he was born with—which was great vocal prowess." Carrie and her brother, Todd, later joked about coming from a "broken mansion," and Carrie wrote about the difficulties of having a celebrity mother. Still, she admired her mom and said, "I always wanted to do what my mother did—get all dressed up, shoot people, fall in the mud. I never considered anything else."

Fisher dropped out of Beverly Hills High School to study acting in London. She turned her lessons to practical effect in her movie debut, the Warren Beatty vehicle *Shampoo* (1975). The film got so-so reviews, but it led to her role as Princess Leia in the blockbuster film *Star Wars* (1977). Fisher has also become a highly regarded writer.

Other Birthdays
1833   Alfred Nobel
1943   Brian Piccolo
1948   Bill Russell

October 22

1942   Utica, New York.

Mouseketeer Annette Funicello was born. She was the daughter of an Italian-American auto repair shop owner and his homemaker wife. Over 1,000 children auditioned for the original Mouseketeers; just 24 were chosen. Funicello, one of the last picked, became the most popular Mouseketeer.

After Mouseketeering, Funicello appeared in such Disney films as *The Shaggy Dog* (1959), then costarred with Frankie Avalon in a series of beach movies. The modest Funicello refused to wear revealing bikinis. She said, "I wouldn't even wear them around my own pool." Funicello put her career on hold while marrying twice and raising three children. In the late 1980s, she and Avalon appeared in a new beach movie, *Back to the Beach* (1987). During shooting, she noticed that she was having trouble balancing. She thought little of it until vision problems led her to a neurologist. Funicello was diagnosed as suffering from the degenerative nerve disease multiple sclerosis (MS).

In a 1992 *People* magazine article, Funicello related the story of her illness and said, "For two years I didn't even tell my father, because if I even have the flu he goes to pieces. One day in 1989 I finally said, 'Daddy, I want to talk to you about something before you read it someplace.' So we had our good cry, and he's been wonderful. Still, I watch his eyes when he sees me walking toward him, and I see his pain. It's really hard. I say, 'Daddy, I don't want tears, and I don't want pity. I'm strong and I'm going to be fine.' "

Other Birthdays
1811   Franz Liszt
1943   Catherine Deneuve
1952   Jeff Goldblum
1963   Brian Boitano

October 23

1925   Corning, Iowa.

Johnny Carson was born. He was raised in Norfolk, Nebraska. A mail-order magic course led to a local career as "The Great Carsoni." He entertained at parties and Elks

Clubs. During World War II, Carson served in the U.S. Navy and later used the GI Bill to attend the University of Nebraska. Upon graduation, he worked in radio as an announcer, which led to a job writing for television's *The Red Skelton Show.* When Skelton injured himself once during a rehearsal, the show's directors needed a substitute host quickly and seized Carson, knowing of his radio experience. He did so well that he was offered a job emceeing the game show *Who Do You Trust?* After five successful years, Carson replaced Jack Paar on the *Tonight Show* when Paar abruptly left in 1962. Carson became one of the highest-paid performers in show business during his thirty years on air.

Ironically, Carson was not NBC's first choice for the *Tonight Show* job. Jackie Gleason, Bob Newhart, Groucho Marx, and Joey Bishop all declined the job before it was offered to Carson.

Carson, who has married four times, once said "Married men live longer than single men. But married men are a lot more willing to die."

OtherBirthdays

1956   Dwight Yoakam
1959   "Weird Al" Yankovic

October 24

1632   Delft, Netherlands.

Anton van Leeuwenhoek was born. Apprenticed to a linen draper, he became a haberdasher. In 1660, he won a government post that allowed him to devote his time to his hobby, grinding lenses and looking at tiny objects. Reportedly, when he showed his neighbors close-up views of insects, they thought he was showing them demons.

Leeuwenhoek, credited with inventing the first microscope, was the first to observe bacteria and protozoa, which he called "very little animalcules." By carefully following the life cycle of grain worms, fleas, and flies, he refuted the notion of spontaneous generation, which maintained that such creatures were spontaneously created by noxious substances. When he died at 90, he left his lenses to the Royal Society of England; no one, however, could figure out how he had assembled them. Others developed their own microscopes, but to this day no one has explained exactly how Leeuwenhoek made his microscope work.

Other Birthdays
1947   Kevin Kline

October 25

1881   Málaga, Spain.

Pablo Picasso was born to Maria Picasso Lopez and José Ruiz Blasco, a painter and art teacher. In keeping with Spanish custom, Picasso signed his work with his mother's maiden name. Picasso's father delighted in his son's talent and carefully coached him. According to legend, one day Picasso painted a picture so impressive that Picasso's father gathered his own brushes, gave them to his son, and never painted again.

Picasso's early work was realistic, unlike his later abstract paintings, which marked the forefront of the art world. In 1904, he and Georges Braque launched the Cubist movement. It was a sensation, subject to violent critical attacks and adoring admiration. Picasso spent the rest of his long life pushing the boundaries of modern art. When he died, he left an estate valued at over $1 billion.

The flamboyant Picasso once remarked, "Everything is miraculous. It is miraculous that one does not melt in one's bath." Of his life's work, he said, "Art is lies that tell the truth."

Other Birthdays
1912   Minnie Pearl
1942   Helen Reddy

October 26

1914   Los Angeles, California.

John Leslie "Jackie" Coogan was born to Jack Coogan, a vaudeville dancer, and Lillian Rita Coogan, who had been the child actress "Baby Lillian." Coogan's mother took him to a film studio when he was eighteen months old. She stuck him in a high chair and made him burble and cry, earning him a role in *Skinner's Baby*. In 1919, Coogan's waif appearance got him cast opposite Charlie Chaplin in *The Kid*. By 1923, Coogan was the number-one box office star, beating out Rudolph Valentino and Douglas Fairbanks. Coogan was earning $22,000 a week in the days when $500 could buy an automobile. As he grew older, demand for him decreased, but he should have been set for life. When he turned 21, Coogan found otherwise.

He discovered that his father (who had since died in a car crash) and mother had spent nearly every cent of the $4 million he had earned. Coogan sued his mother and stepfather, but there was little money left. His mother said, "No promises were ever made to give him anything." The scandal caused the California legislature to pass the "Coogan Law," which required that the managers of child actors place a large portion of the child's earnings in trust.

Coogan married and divorced Betty Grable in the late 1930s. During World War II, he served as a glider pilot with the U.S. Army Air Force in Asia, winning the Distinguished Flying Cross and the Air Medal. After the war, Coogan became a character actor. He appeared in many films and television programs, but it wasn't until the 1960s that Coogan got a part that won him national attention. He became Uncle Fester in television's *The Addams Family*.

Other Birthdays
1946   Pat Sajak
1947   Hillary Rodham Clinton
1947   Jaclyn Smith

October 27

1858   New York City.

Theodore Roosevelt was born. His parents were Martha "Mittie" Bulloch Roosevelt, a Georgia belle, and Theodore "Thee" Roosevelt Sr., a prosperous New York businessman who could trace his family line back to the days when New York City was New Amsterdam. The couple lived in a respectable brownstone on Union Square. Mittie had trouble managing the household accounts and was given to hypochondria. Her faults, however, were balanced by a cheerful, humorous nature, which made helping her easy and pleasant. The couple's first child was Anna, nicknamed Bamie.

Bamie's doctors soon discovered that her spine was twisted. Thee refused to accept pessimistic medical opinions. He invented games to help Bamie exercise, and she overcame her affliction. The arrival of Mittie's mother and sister also helped, as both were capable homemakers.

The Civil War could have broken up the Roosevelts. Mittie was pro-South, with three brothers in the Rebel Army; Thee was pro-North and spent his time organizing pay benefits for the Union Army. He often visited troops in the field and was sometimes under fire. Meanwhile, his womenfolk in New York were smuggling supplies and money to the South.

Theodore Jr., nicknamed Teedie, was even more sickly than his sister. He suffered from severe asthma, stomach problems, and colds. Again the Roosevelts responded with loving attention. Mittie spent evenings telling him stories about plantation life and her odd relatives while Teedie lay sick in bed. His father urged exercise and optimism. The boy's health improved and he became as fanatical as his father for the "rigorous life." This led Teedie to pursue a political career that took him to the White House, where energy became his trademark.

When Roosevelt was inaugurated, he swore an oath to uphold the Constitution. A newspaper printing error gave the event an entirely different and unique character. The paper substituted a *b* for an *o* and printed: "For sheer democratic dignity, nothing could exceed the moment when, surrounded by the Cabinet, Mr. Roosevelt took his simple bath as President of the United States."

Other Birthdays
1872　Emily Post
1914　Dylan Thomas
1920　Nanette Fabray
1950　Fran Lebowitz
1963　Tracy Nelson

October 28

1952　Nashville, Tennessee.

Actress Annie Potts, noted for her role on television's *Designing Women,* was born. She was raised on an isolated farm near Franklin, Kentucky. To David Letterman, Potts said: "My mother, she's a great gal, let me tell you. When we were tiny and my Dad would be away on business, we had no neighbors. It wasn't like there was 911 anywhere if you heard a little noise. There were three of us little girls. We'd go down in the middle of the night and go, 'Mama, I heard something.' And she'd go, 'All right.' And she'd reach up on the back of her bed for a Kool cigarette, light that, kick the covers back, get her peignoir, slip it on careful not to burn it, and she'd go out to the front hall closet, get a shotgun, put the cigarette in her mouth, go to the back door, kick it open with her hip, stick the barrel of the gun out, and fire off about five rounds, shut the door, and go, 'Go back to bed.'"

This no-nonsense attitude rubbed off on Potts and helped her become an actress. For example, in her first role, as an extra in a Linda Blair film, she played an inmate locked away in a tiny cell who waves as the lead walks by. Potts was locked in the cell and the scene was shot, then Potts was promptly forgotten. She spent hours in the cell before someone remembered to let her out.

Other Birthdays
1939   Jane Alexander
1949   Bruce Jenner
1955   Bill Gates
1967   Julia Roberts

October 29

1947   Brooklyn, New York.
Richard Dreyfuss was born. Raised in Beverly Hills, he began appearing in bit parts on television as an adolescent. Dreyfuss characterizes these roles as "dinks." He elaborates, "A 'dink' is the guy with owlish glasses who is always asking Sally Field to the school prom and is always being refused." Dreyfuss's film debut was as a more troublesome sort of dink, Baby Face Nelson in *Dillinger* (1973). The movie that made Dreyfuss a star was the hit *American Graffiti* (1973).

1971   Winona, Minnesota.
Actress Winona Laura Ryder was born. Her parents were hippies who raised her on a Northern California commune. Her godfather was Timothy Leary. After attending San Francisco's American Conservancy Theater, Ryder was spotted by a talent scout at 13. Her films include *Heathers* (1989), *Mermaids* (1990), and *The Age of Innocence* (1993).

Other Birthdays
1740   James Boswell
1891   Fanny Brice
1948   Kate Jackson

October 30

1945   New York City.
Actor Henry Winkler was born to Jewish parents who had fled Nazi Germany for the United States. They provided Winkler with a private school education in Manhattan and

Switzerland, hoping he would work for the state department. Instead, Winkler chose to study drama at Boston's Emerson College, then earned a master's degree at the Yale School of Drama. Though he acted in student productions of the classics, Winkler's first jobs were in commercials, peddling toothpaste and pizza. He won a part playing a 1950s juvenile delinquent in the film *The Lords of Flatbush* (1974). (Sylvester Stallone was a costar.) The film became a cult favorite but didn't boost Winkler into stardom, which came with the role of Fonzie, another 1950s juvenile delinquent, in the television sitcom *Happy Days*.

Winkler was largely responsible for making *Happy Days* a success and when that show ended, he had to fight typecasting. He appeared in a few films but was more successful as a producer. Winkler has also involved himself in several charities, including Toys-for-Tots and the Starlight Foundation.

In 1985, Winkler was chairman of an arts festival for handicapped children when he discovered one benefit of celebrity. He says: "I was walking through the crowd when a little girl behind me said: 'FONZ!!' I turned around and her mother nearly passed out. This girl was autistic and she had just spoken her first word."

Other Birthdays
1885   Ezra Pound
1939   Grace Slick
1951   Harry Hamlin

October 31

1936   Forest Hills, New York.

Eugene Orowitz was born to Eli Orowitz, an ex-publicist for Paramount Studios, and Peggy O'Neill, an ex-actress. Raised in the factory town of Collingswood, New Jersey, where his friends nicknamed him Oogie, he had an unhappy childhood.

His parents were usually arguing or not talking at all, using Oogie to relay messages across the dinner table. His mother faked suicides by sticking her head in their gas oven and carefully regulating the gas flow to avoid passing out. Oogie later said, "I was 10 before I knew you put anything but a head into a gas oven."

Oogie won an athletic scholarship to USC with his javelin-throwing skill. Excessive practice, however, spoiled his throwing arm, causing him to drop out after just one year. Oogie felt that he was a failure and passed through a series of odd jobs, including process server, mill worker, blanket salesman, and car washer. His father came to Hollywood, hoping that he could use some of his old connections to get work for himself and his son, but when he visited his old studio, former "friends" claimed they didn't know him. By then Oogie had changed his name by picking a name at random from the Los Angeles phone book. It was as Michael Landon that he got his first break—singing with a Jerry Lee Lewis tour.

The tour helped Landon get the starring role in the film *I Was a Teenage Werewolf* (1957). It was a dog movie in more ways than one, but it led to his first major role—as Little Joe on the television series *Bonanza*. Landon went on to two other successful series, *Little House on the Prairie* and *Highway to Heaven*.

Other Birthdays
1930   Lee Grant
1950   Jane Pauley
1951   John Candy
1967   Vanilla Ice

November 1

1957 Klein, Texas.

Musician Lyle Lovett was born. His father was an Exxon executive and his mother was of an old Texas family. Klein, a small farming town near Houston where his family resided, had been founded by her family. Lovett, an only child, had an ordinary middle-class childhood. He was a shy boy. When asked how his high school classmates might remember him, he remarked, "I think they'd use a lot of interrogative pronouns, like 'Who?' I was pretty forgettable—which in retrospect is most likely a blessing."

Lovett gradually grew to love music. His parents were fans of Nat "King" Cole and Ray Charles. Lovett liked Hank Williams, the Eagles, and Willie Nelson. He had learned to play the guitar by the ninth grade and, when some friends in the Future Farmers of America formed a band, they invited him to join them. Lovett learned that he liked singing and composing. While attending Texas A&M, where he pursued a journalism degree and later a graduate degree in German, Lovett played his own compositions in coffeehouses. In 1983, while studying in Germany, he met a European country western music promoter, who had named himself Buffalo Wayne after his two favorite American cowboys, Buffalo Bill and John Wayne.

Buffalo Wayne persuaded Lovett to perform at a country western festival in Luxembourg. Lovett says, "[I was] background entertainment for people who were drinking beer and pretending they were cowboys. And I was really getting lost in the shuffle, being a solo acoustic act. I was having a tough time. I was actually thinking about going back home because nobody would have noticed if I did. But what happened was these guys from Phoenix called J. David Sloan and The Rogues saw that I was having a tough time. They took pity on me, learned some of my songs, and invited me up to play with them during their set. And that worked out really well. We hit it off good."

The next year, back in America, Lovett hunted up his Luxembourg friends to record a demo tape. It got Lovett an MCA recording contract. Lovett enlisted his friends into his own band, called His Large Band, and recorded a series of hit albums. A recurring theme in his early work was disappointed love.

Lovett, the Texas country western star, admits to being afraid of cows, having been kicked by one as a child. He also never wears western headgear, citing his tall, bristling coiffure. He says, "It's hard to get a cowboy hat over my hair."

Other Birthdays
1871   Stephen Crane

November 2

1913   East Harlem, New York City.

Burt Lancaster was born. The son of Irish immigrants, he was raised in a tough neighborhood. He won a scholarship to New York University. Scholarship, however, didn't appeal to

Lancaster—he ran off with a circus to become a trapeze artist. When he had difficulty becoming a circus star, he left to work in a department store selling ladies' lingerie. It didn't last long. Lancaster was riding an elevator one day when Hollywood agent Harold Hecht noticed the handsome young man and got him a screen test. Lancaster became an overnight star with the 1946 movie *The Killers*. He went on to a series of fine performances, using his circus training in *Trapeze* (1956) and winning an Oscar for *Elmer Gantry* (1960).

Other Birthdays
1755   Marie Antoinette
1795   James Knox Polk
1865   Warren G. Harding
1890   Groucho Marx (see 3/22/1887)
1938   Patrick Buchanan
1942   Stefanie Powers

November 3

1922   Ehrenfeld, Pennsylvania.

Charles Bronson was born (his real name is Charles Buchinsky). Bronson's father was a coal miner. After a stint driving a delivery truck, Bronson went into the mines with his father. He soon grew tired of digging coal and bought a bus ticket to Hollywood to become an actor. He performed at the Pasadena Playhouse and struggled for bit parts in films. In 1953, Bronson got the worst job of his career: He played a wax dummy in the Vincent Price vehicle *The House of Wax*. He had no lines and didn't even move.

Bronson did get to move in later roles, although he usually played villains who got shot out of the saddle. Gradually, his parts improved. *The Magnificent Seven* (1960) and *The Dirty Dozen* (1967) highlighted his talents, but Bronson achieved superstar status in 1974 through his role as a vigilante in *Death Wish*.

Of himself, Bronson says, "I'm not one of my favorite characters."

Other Birthdays
1933 Michael Dukakis
1949 Larry Holmes
1953 Roseanne

November 4

1916 St. Joseph, Missouri.

Walter Cronkite was born. His father was a dentistry professor at the University of Texas. Cronkite says he made his own career choice in junior high school. "I became the happy victim of childhood Walter Mittyism, and it's never really gone away. *The American Boy* magazine ran a series of short stories on careers. They were fictionalized versions of what people did in life. And there were only two that really fascinated me at that point. One was mining engineering and the other was journalism." No mine being available for the teenage Cronkite to work in, he went to work for his school paper. He worked his way through the University of Texas as a newspaper reporter. After graduation, he got a job with United Press.

Cronkite became a foreign correspondent during World War II, covering the battle of the North Atlantic, the African landings, the D-Day landing, and the Battle of the Bulge. He even filed a story from a B-17 over Germany. CBS hired him in 1950 for their news division, and, by the 1960s, he was anchoring the evening news. He became one of America's most popular announcers before retiring in 1981.

Of his war years, Cronkite said: "Personally, I feel I was an overweening coward in the war. Gee, I was scared to death all the time. I did everything possible to avoid getting into combat. Except the ultimate thing of not doing it. I did it. But the truth is that I did everything only once. It didn't take any great courage to do it once. If you go back and do it a second time—knowing how bad it is—that's courage."

Other Birthdays
1879   Will Rogers
1918   Art Carney
1943   Loretta Swit

November 5

1913   Darjeeling, India.

Screen legend Vivien Leigh was born Vivien Mary Hartley. Leigh's French-Irish mother wasn't the most devoted of parents. She planted Leigh in a convent when she was six and left her there for eighteen months without visiting her. Later in life, Leigh's mother provided a constant stream of criticism of nearly every decision Leigh made, all the while claiming to be a perfect mother. She once said of her daughter, who suffered severe emotional problems, "There's nothing the matter with Vivien. She doesn't need all those psychiatrists. Why, as a little child at the convent the nuns told me she loved me so much she used to cover up my photograph with her blankets at night so my picture wouldn't get cold."

Leigh hoped for an acting career, but when she turned 17, she postponed her plans and married Herbert Leigh Holman. Following the birth of their daughter, Leigh renewed her interest in acting. After a few minor parts, she scored a solid stage success with *Mask of Virtue.* Alexander Korda gave her a quarter-million-dollar film contract. During her appearance in *Mask of Virtue,* Leigh met actor Laurence Olivier. Both were married, but fell in love. They appeared in two films together, then Olivier left for New York to appear in a stage play. Leigh followed to be with him but also to try out for the part of Scarlet in *Gone With the Wind.*

Every actress from Katharine Hepburn to Lucille Ball was courting producer David O. Selznick to grab the role of

Scarlett. Leigh didn't think she could beat them out—she was British, and her relationship with Olivier could prove scandalous. Nevertheless, agent Myron Selznick thought Leigh perfect for the role. In December 1938, David Selznick staged the burning of Atlanta. He and select executives were watching doubles of Rhett Butler and Scarlett O'Hara escape the towering flames when Myron yelled, "Hey, genius. I'd like you to meet your Scarlett O'Hara," and introduced Leigh. She got the part.

Other Birthdays
1912   Roy Rogers
1941   Art Garfunkel
1941   Elke Sommer
1963   Tatum O'Neal

November 6

1946   Pasadena, California.

Actress Sally Field was born to character actress Maggie Field. Sally pursued an acting career from childhood, easily outshining her classmates in her high school drama classes. At 17, she won the starring role in the television series *Gidget,* which led to a second starring role in the oddball television series *The Flying Nun.* She went on to better roles. In 1980, she won an Academy Award for the film *Norma Rae.*

At 20, Field developed bulimia. She says, "Everybody then was Twiggy, except me. I felt immensely unattractive." It took her three years to overcome the problem.

Other Birthdays
1948   Glenn Frey
1955   Maria Shriver

November 7

1918   Charlotte, North Carolina.

Billy Graham was born. A Presbyterian, he converted to the Southern Baptist Church when he was 16. After graduating from Wheaton College, he became a radio preacher in Chicago, spending a lot of time preaching at tent meetings before newspaper tycoon William Randolph Hearst discovered him and used his newspapers to popularize Graham. Graham became the first preacher to fully exploit television.

Graham once said, "I'm an optimist. I've read the last page in the Bible. It's all going to turn out all right."

Other Birthdays
1867   Madame Curie
1943   Roberta Joni Anderson
1943   Joni Mitchell

November 8

1907   Hartford, Connecticut.

Dr. Thomas Norval Hepburn and his wife, Katharine, had their second child, a girl, whom they named Katharine after her mother. Katharine's parents insisted that their children begin each day with a cold shower and finish it with spirited dinner table discussion. Her father encouraged his children to be athletic, running a cable across their backyard with a trapeze hung from it. Her mother taught them to be considerate of others. As Hepburn wrote, in her autobiography *Me,* "We felt that our parents were the best two people in the world—that we were wildly lucky to be their children. And we still feel that way."

Hepburn started acting in college and went directly to the New York stage following graduation. In 1932, she was signed to RKO. Her first film role was in *A Bill of Divorcement* (1932), in which she uttered the line most often associated with her: "The calla lilies are in bloom again." It was a successful appearance and, despite being labeled "box office poison" following the failure of her next five films, Katharine Hepburn became one of Hollywood's all-time superstars.

Hepburn has said, "The secret of life is how you survive failure."

Other Birthdays
1847   Bram Stoker
1900   Margaret Mitchell
1933   Esther Rolle
1951   Mary Hart
1954   Rickie Lee Jones

November 9

1841   Buckingham Palace, London.

Edward VII was born to Queen Victoria and Prince Consort Albert. To insure that Edward would grow up to be a virtuous king, Victoria had him raised in near isolation. She hoped he would approach the perfection she saw in Albert, who sent his son memoranda on how to lead an upright life.

Victoria must have been disappointed, for Edward grew up to be a connoisseur of the good life. He loved fine cigars and gourmet meals. He dressed in the latest fashions, gambled with celebrities, and romanced the most beautiful women of his time. Victoria heartily disapproved. Indeed, she blamed Edward for the death of her beloved Albert. When Edward was 19 and serving with the British Army in Ireland, his buddies decided to help him lose his virginity and smuggled a willing young actress into his quarters. Word got back to his father, who was greatly upset. Albert became ill during his trip to confront Edward and died upon his return home. Victoria could barely disguise her anger with Edward, saying to an associate, "It quite irritates me to see him in the room."

To discourage Edward's sexual adventuring, Victoria chose a

wife for him, the Danish Princess Alexandra. They obligingly fell in love. Still, Edward didn't let his marriage interfere with his romances. Alexandra shrugged them off, confident that he loved her most.

Some of Edward's favorite adventures occurred in France. At a dinner given for him by some Parisian pals, for example, a very large covered serving dish was placed before him. When the cover was lifted, a beautiful woman wearing just a sprig of parsley was revealed. Perhaps because of these associations, Edward was a staunch friend of the French and helped popularize the diplomatic alignment of England with France, ending centuries of contention. This alignment positioned England on the side of France in World War I, which, in turn, placed England on France's side during World War II.

Victoria grimly held onto the crown till her death in 1901. By then, Edward was 60. He reigned for just nine years, dying in 1910. Upon his death, Edward's wife, Queen Alexandra, wryly remarked of her errant husband: "Now at least I know where he is!"

Other Birthdays
1869   Marie Dressler
1913   Hedy Lamarr
1934   Carl Sagan

November 10

1925   Pontrhydyfen, South Wales.

Richard and Edith Jenkins had their twelfth child, a boy, whom they named Richard Jr. but called Richie. The Jenkins were a hard-drinking family. The boy's grandfather was confined to a wheelchair following a mining accident that paralyzed his legs. One day, he won a wager on a horse called Black Sambo and happily spent his winnings at the local pub. On the way home, playfully pretending his chair was the horse, he let it roll free down a steep hill. Yelling "Coom on, Black

Sambo!" he crashed into a wall, killing himself. Richard Sr. was also a drinker. When drunk, he spun elaborate, wild stories that delighted Richie.

After Edith died in childbirth, Richie, then two years old, went to live with his sister and her husband, but he preferred his hometown, which he visited regularly, enjoying the antics of his father. One time, Richard Sr. disappeared for three weeks. The family grew desperate. Finally, he showed up. His eyes were red. His balance was precarious. His voice was slurred. He also held a rope to which was attached the most decrepit greyhound possible. He proudly announced, indicating the nearly dead dog, "Boys, our troubles are over!"

Richie liked to fight and enjoyed silent cowboy films, but he also liked singing. His singing ended, however, when his voice changed. His drama teacher, Philip Burton, who accompanied the boy on the piano, couldn't help but laugh when Richie's voice yo-yoed up and down during a lesson. The boy stormed out, shouting, "Someday, I'll show you." Still, the drama teacher had enough faith in his student that, when Richie was forced to leave his sister's home, he took the boy into his own home and made him his ward. In gratitude, Richie took his teacher's surname.

Richie finished school and went onto the stage. Two decades later, his drama teacher, Philip Burton, attended the Broadway opening of *Camelot*. After the show, Richard Burton quipped to his benefactor, "Well, I showed you, didn't I?"

Other Birthdays
1483   Martin Luther
1889   Claude Rains
1899   Pat O'Brien

November 11

1925   Dayton, Ohio.
Jonathan Winters was born after his parents divorced, and he was raised by his radio actress mother. Winters was a

classroom cutup with a talent for drawing that led him to enter the Dayton Art Institute. He married in 1949. According to his wife, Eileen, he lost his wristwatch six or seven months later. She suggested he enter a talent contest offering a wristwatch as first prize. Winters won the watch with a comedy routine and realized that others like his humor. He dropped out of school and went to New York to become a comic. He was soon entertaining at the New York club Blue Angel and making appearances on both Steve Allen's and Jack Paar's incarnations of the *Tonight Show*.

Winters had trouble dealing with the pressures of show business. He suffered a nervous breakdown and spent eight months in a sanitorium. He later observed, "People ask 'How do you feel?' I always say, 'Well, I'm out.' A very normal person says, 'But I don't understand.' Well, you'd have to have been in to understand that."

Winters developed an alcohol problem after leaving the sanitorium. Membership in Alcoholics Anonymous helped him return to sobriety. He renewed his celebrity in Stanley Kramer's *It's a Mad Mad Mad Mad World* (1963), *The Loved One* (1965), and numerous television appearances.

Other Birthdays
1885   George S. Patton
1963   Demi Moore

November 12

1929   Philadelphia.
John Brendan Kelly, a prosperous business contractor who had started out as a bricklayer, and his wife, Margaret Majer Kelly, a former model, had the third of their four children, Grace Kelly. Grace was a shy, sickly girl. Her mother said, "She never minded being kept in bed and would sit there with her dolls for hours on end...making up plays."

Kelly's family had show business connections. Her Uncle Walter C. Kelly, was a vaudevillian, and her Uncle George

Kelly was a Pulitzer Prize–winning playwright. Kelly first appeared on stage at 12 in an amateur production. Following a private education, she studied at the American Academy of Dramatic Arts in New York City, supporting herself by working as a model and appearing in television commercials. After her studies at the Academy, Kelly worked with a Pennsylvania theater company and in such television shows as *Studio One* and *The Philco Television Playhouse.* She made a film in New York, but it wasn't until she moved to Hollywood and made her second film, *High Noon* (1952), that she became a star. Kelly went on to make several fine films, including *Mogambo* (1953), *Dial M for Murder* (1954), *Rear Window* (1954), *Country Girl* (1954), and *To Catch a Thief* (1955). She received an Oscar for *Country Girl*, but *Rear Window*, directed by Alfred Hitchcock, was probably her best film.

While performing in *To Catch a Thief,* which was set in Monaco, Kelly met Prince Ranier, that country's ruler. She was not impressed at first, but a series of letters, beginning with a thank-you note, led to romance. In 1956, Kelly left acting to marry him. They had three children, and Princess Grace became an elegant spokesperson for her husband's small country. She died unexpectedly in a car accident in 1982.

Princess Grace, despite being a successful, independent woman, had some traditional views. She once said, "Women's natural role is to be the pillar of the family. . . . Emancipation of women has made them lose their mystery."

Other Birthdays
1866   Sun Yat-sen
1961   Nadia Comaneci

November 13

1949   New York City.
   Whoopi Goldberg was born Caryn Johnson to Robert and Emma Johnson. After Goldberg's father left the family, her mother worked as a nurse and Head Start teacher while raising

Goldberg in a public housing project in Manhattan's Chelsea section. Goldberg says her mother encouraged her to become cultured: "She would say, 'Get on the bus, go to hear the Leonard Bernstein concert, go see the children's ballet, go to the museum.'" Goldberg did just that, learning early to love the arts.

Goldberg performed in children's theater between the ages of eight and ten. She enjoyed the work, but school proved less fun. She suffered from dyslexia, which her teachers misdiagnosed as retardation. Shunted into inappropriate classes, she dropped out of school in her teens and became a heroin addict. She now tells kids who use drugs, "Save the money and just kill yourself, because that's what you're doing." Goldberg kicked the habit with the help of a counselor, whom she married.

Goldberg returned to acting, snagging parts in the chorus lines of Broadway shows such as *Hair, Jesus Christ Superstar,* and *Pippin.* She also had a daughter. Her marriage, however, fell apart. When a friend offered her a ticket to California, Goldberg, eager for a change, accepted and settled in San Diego. For six years, she worked at a variety of jobs, including bricklayer, bank teller, and, after attending a beauty school, hairdresser and makeup artist at a funeral parlor. Between jobs she was sometimes on welfare.

Beauty school classmate Lucille Carretta says, "She had all the odds against her. She was young and had her daughter, was poor and lived in the projects with her mom. She wasn't what you would call a beauty queen, she was on welfare and it took her two years to graduate from a nine-month beauty program. But Caryn was naturally funny and she could always make people laugh. Caryn was so good-hearted she would gather up the junkies in the street and do their hair for nothing just to get them off the street for a day."

Goldberg joined an improv group and was a founding member of the San Diego Repertory Theater. Her friends gave her the nickname Whoopi Cushion, because, as she says, "I was very flatulent." She tried a fancier version, Whoopi

Couchant, for her stage name, before settling on Whoopi Goldberg, because she felt there were Goldbergs somewhere in her family tree. With her new name, she teamed up with comic Don Victor. They performed in the San Diego area, then got an important gig in San Francisco. On show night, Victor didn't show up. Goldberg was asked to go on alone. The audience loved her and Goldberg became a comedy star.

Other Birthdays
354   Saint Augustine
1906   Hermione Baddeley

November 14

1948   Buckingham Palace, London.

Charles Philip Arthur George Mountbatten-Windsor, Prince of Wales and heir to the British throne, was born to Queen Elizabeth II and Prince Philip. Unlike previous heirs to the throne, Charles was sent to boarding schools. At one, in Scotland, students were compelled to run outside, shirtless, to a cold morning shower every day, year round. Charles survived this to spend six months at Timbertop, an outdoorsy school in Australia. He received his advanced education at Trinity College, Cambridge, then was placed in the Royal Navy. He became a paratrooper, a jet pilot, and the skipper of a mine sweeper. In civilian life, Charles became a cellist, a scuba expert, a polo player, a skier, and, like many Englishmen, a proficient gardener. It has been reported that the prince talks to his plants.

In 1980, before his marriage to Diana, Charles remarked, "Falling madly in love is not necessarily the starting point to getting married."

Other Birthdays
1906   Louise Brooks
1912   Barbara Hutton
1919   Veronica Lake

November 15

1919   Los Angeles, California.

Joseph A. Wapner was born. His father, an attorney, provided Wapner with a middle-class boyhood, which was highlighted by a date with then-unknown Lana Turner. Wapner forgot his money and she had to pay for their dinner. He didn't get another date with her. During World War II, Wapner served in the U.S. Army in the South Pacific, where he was seriously wounded and won a Bronze star. After the war, he earned a law degree, went into practice with his father, then became active in California politics. In 1958, Governor Edmund G. Brown rewarded his support with an appointment to the Municipal Court, which handled small claims and traffic offenses. Wapner's work was well-respected and he moved on to the California Superior Court. He retired from the bench in 1979.

In 1980, Wapner was approached by the producers of the television program *The People's Court.* He accepted their offer to preside as judge on the show and became one of the best-known judges in America. In 1985, while visiting Washington, D.C., Supreme Court Justice Byron White asked to meet him. Wapner was delighted. Ironically, before going into the law, Wapner had considered an acting career.

Other Birthdays
1887   Georgia O'Keeffe
1932   Petula Clark
1940   Sam Waterston
1954   Beverly D'Angelo

November 16

1889   Pittsburgh, Pennsylvania.

Playwright George S. Kaufman was born, the third of four children of a middle-class Jewish family. Kaufman set out to become a lawyer but dropped out of law school after three months. He held a number of strange jobs, including hatband salesman, before discovering his talent for writing when a small piece he wrote for Franklin P. Adams's newspaper column was printed. Kaufman soon had his own column, going on to become the drama editor for the *New York Times*. He wrote over forty plays and the screenplays for several of his works, and helped write scripts for the Marx Brothers' films *The Cocoanuts* (1929), *Animal Crackers* (1930), and *A Night at the Opera* (1935).

Kaufman was tall but stooped, had poor eyesight, and shied away from any sexually related talk—he didn't even like to write love scenes. Despite this, he was extremely successful with women. A friend called him a "male nymphomaniac." When he was named as a correspondent in actress Mary Astor's divorce, and her diary, which was extremely complimentary to Kaufman, was made public, Kaufman became known as "Public Lover Number One."

In his role as theater critic, Kaufman once wrote, "I didn't like the play, but then I saw it under adverse conditions—the curtain was up." In his role as critic and sexual adventurer, he told Irving Berlin that the lyrics to his song "Always" were unrealistic. Kaufman said that instead of "I'll be loving you, always," Berlin should have written, "I'll be loving you, Thursday."

Other Birthdays
1964   Dwight Gooden
1966   Lisa Bonet

November 17

1925   Winnetka, Illinois.

Roy Harold Scherer Jr. was born. After finishing high school, Scherer enlisted in the U.S. Navy, shipping out to the Pacific in 1944 as an aircraft mechanic. As his night troopship sailed under San Francisco's Golden Gate Bridge, the bridge's lights suddenly went on and the ship's public address system began playing a favorite of the day, "Sentimental Journey," sung by Doris Day. Scherer later remarked that there wasn't a dry eye on the ship, including his own. Fifteen years later, after changing his name to Rock Hudson, the lonely soldier would costar with Day.

After the war, Hudson went to Los Angeles, where he worked as a vacuum cleaner salesman, a truck driver, and a mailman. One of the patrons on his mail route was Hollywood agent Henry Wilson. Wilson later recalled, "He had size, good looks, strength and a certain shyness that I thought would make him a star like Gable. He had the kind of personal charm that makes you think you'd enjoy sitting down and spending time with him." Wilson arranged a screen test in which Hudson did poorly, but Wilson persisted. He introduced Hudson to filmmaker Raoul Walsh, who cast Hudson in *Fighter Squadron* (1948). Hudson looked better in the film than he had in the test. He signed a contract with Walsh and Wilson that paid $125 a week—a little less than the post office had paid him. Still, it was a start. Universal bought the contract, and Hudson went on to a successful career.

In 1985, Hudson stunned fans by admitting that he was dying of AIDS following an unsuccessful trip to France to seek a cure. It became apparent that his 1955 to 1958 marriage to former secretary Phyllis Gates had been arranged by his studio to hide Hudson's homosexuality. The revelation added sad irony to a comment once made by Hudson about his life as an actor: "What do I see when I look in a mirror? A lie." Three months after his trip to France, Hudson died.

Of his first roles, Hudson said, "Most of them make me cringe. It's rather like having your old linen washed in public, but at least those lousy movies were good training. The only thing I can say in my defense is that I did the best I could. It was pretty rotten, I agree, but it was my best."

Other Birthdays
1942   Martin Scorsese

1943   Lauren Hutton
1944   Danny DeVito
1944   Tom Seaver

November 18

1901   Jefferson, Iowa.

Pollster George Gallup was born. His father was an eccentric schoolteacher who pursued studies in esoteric logic and built an eight-sided home on the theory that it would be safer in midwestern windstorms. He also turned over a small dairy farm to his 10-year-old son. Young George was soon earning enough money to buy uniforms for both his high school football and basketball teams.

George got into polling in 1922 as a college student through a summer job. The St. Louis *Post-Dispatch* hired him and fifty other students to poll every single one of their 55,000 subscriber households. George, after a sweaty day of ringing doorbells and getting exactly the same answers from more than one household, decided there must be a better way. Using well-developed mathematical techniques, Gallup demonstrated that polling a small sample was as accurate as polling an entire group. He used his work to earn a Ph.D. In 1930, he began doing newspaper polls. In 1935, Gallup did his first national poll. He asked 3,000 Americans: "Do you think expenditures by the government for relief and recovery are: Too Little? Too Great? About Right?" Sixty percent said "Too Great."

Gallup went on to plot the prospects of products and politicians, often proving correct. In 1948, however, he chose Dewey over Truman and Truman won. Gallup claimed he would have gotten it right if the poll had been conducted nearer to Election Day. The failure was a major embarrassment. For a time, people could address their letters to "Dr. Wrong, Princeton, New Jersey" and Gallup would receive them.

Gallup once defended polling by saying, "If government is

supposed to be based on the will of the people, then somebody ought to go out and find what that will is."

Other Birthdays
1923   Alan B. Shepard
1939   Brenda Vaccaro
1943   Linda Evans

November 19

1938   Cincinnati, Ohio.

Media mogul Ted Turner was born. Turner's wealthy father was a strict disciplinarian who augmented his browbeating with a wire coat hanger. Turner said, "One summer I made $50 a week, and my father charged me $25 a week rent. I asked him if that wasn't a little high. He said that if I could do better than that for food and lodging seven days a week I could move out."

Turner responded by doing what he was told and by becoming a loud, ego-driven good-ol'-boy, often getting into trouble. He was bounced from his fraternity at Brown University for setting fire to the homecoming float. After two suspensions, he left college for good. Turner was 24 when his father, despondent over his failing billboard business, killed himself. Turner's friends say that for years, suicide was a favorite topic for him. They also say that he still competes with his father's memory.

Turner inherited his father's business, which he parlayed into a media empire by buying "superstation" WTBS and broadcasting a solid fare of old movies. With the income from this, he set up the Cable News Network. Few thought it would amount to much, but its twenty-four-hour service became a worldwide reference. Turner's other acquisitions include the Atlanta Braves, MGM, and the 1977 America's Cup. Despite his successes, Turner is still driven. In 1989, he said, "I want to be the first trillionaire."

Other Birthdays
1933   Larry King
1936   Dick Cavett
1942   Calvin Klein
1962   Jodie Foster

November 20

1620   Aboard the Mayflower, Massachusetts Bay.
Peregrine White, the son of William and Susanna White, was born. He was the first child of English parents to be born in New England. He grew up to hold several government posts. This first native-born Puritan became a politician and bureaucrat.

1926   Cleveland.
Catherine Gloria Balotta was born. Her mother was an Italian immigrant, and Balotta grew up in an Italian neighborhood. As Kaye Ballard, she became a singing star and actress on Broadway and in Hollywood, but she remained a bit intimidated by her mother. When Ballard appeared in *The Ritz* (1976), her dialogue had a four-letter word in it. According to Liz Smith, Ballard said, "I told my sister to go to see the movie with my mother and when I say that word to cough real loud so my mother won't hear it!" Smith also quotes Ballard as saying that the reason all mothers have the same answers to childrens' questions is that "They all go to a school for mothers, and have to take a final. All those who fail become aunts."

Other Birthdays
1932   Richard Dawson
1956   Bo Derek
1956   Mark Gastineau
1959   Sean Young

November 21

1945   Washington, D.C.

Actress Goldie Hawn was born. She was raised in Takoma Park, Maryland, by her parents, Laura and Edward Rutledge. Her father was a descendant of a signer of the Declaration of Independence. He ran a watch repair shop during the day and performed as a professional musician in the evening. Edward indulged his children and had a wicked sense of humor. He once wrote an excuse note to Goldie's school claiming that she had to miss class for appointments with her parole officer and her psychiatrist.

Goldie started studying tap dance at three and eventually worked her way through American University by teaching dance. She majored in drama, but her first show business roles weren't quite the kind studied in colleges. She worked as a can-can dancer at the 1964 New York World's Fair, as a go-go dancer in a cage in a New Jersey bar, and as a show girl in Las Vegas. When she arrived in Hollywood, she was immediately signed for *The Andy Griffith Show.* This led to a flop series called *Good Morning, World.* Hawn got her big break in 1968 playing an updated version of Gracie Allen in the television comedy show *Rowan & Martin's Laugh-In.* She moved on to a series of profitable films.

Hawn's mother observed of her daughter's ditzy image: "She had to be pretty smart to be that dumb!"

Other Birthdays
1938   Marlo Thomas
1963   Nicollette Sheridan

November 22

1890   Lille, France.

Charles de Gaulle was born. He was the second of the five children of Jeanne Maillot-Delannoy de Gaulle and Henri de

Gaulle, who raised their children to be religious and patriotic. Dinner table conversations centered on current events, and the children were expected to contribute to the discussion. When de Gaulle chose the French Army for a career, his parents were proud. By the time of World War II, he had risen to a generalship. In 1940, France fell before the German Army. Jeanne de Gaulle, by then a widow, was living with her oldest son in Brittany when German soldiers began appearing. "Why does no one shoot?" she complained. "Are we going to let them take France like so many tourists?" Later in the day, the local priest appeared and told the family that a French general was on the radio from London, proclaiming that France would continue to resist. He was asked the name of the general. "General de Gaulle," he answered. "That is my son! That is *my* son!" Jeanne de Gaulle announced with pride.

Unfortunately, Jeanne de Gaulle died a month after the fall of France. The Germans thought her death might be used by the Resistance and tried to keep it secret. Nevertheless, word spread, and her simple grave became a patriotic shrine. A photograph of it was smuggled across the English Channel to de Gaulle by a Breton fisherman. It was four years before he could visit the grave, but then he went as part of the Allied Army liberating France. He would become the President of France's Fifth Republic.

Other Birthdays
1943   Billie Jean King
1958   Jamie Lee Curtis
1961   Mariel Hemingway
1967   Boris Becker

November 23

1804   Hillsboro, New Hampshire.
Franklin Pierce, the fourteenth president of the United States, was born to Anna Kendrick Pierce and Benjamin

Pierce, a veteran of the Revolutionary War. The couple had eight children, and Benjamin Pierce became governor of his state. Unfortunately, rumors about Anna tainted their happiness. It was whispered that she had a drinking problem. Worst of all, the rumors were true. A single sip of alcohol made her drunk, and she insisted on taking multiple sips at the tavern owned by her husband that adjoined the gubernatorial mansion. When drunk, Anna became frisky. She once attended church in a dress so short that her scandalized neighbors could see she was wearing red ribbons around her ankles. Nevertheless, she managed to raise her children to be responsible people.

Their son Franklin became a lawyer, then entered politics. He was a state legislator and then a U.S. senator. During the Mexican-American War, he was a brigadier general of volunteers. After the war, in 1852, he successfully ran for the presidency, despite the fact that he shared his mother's problem with alcohol.

Other Birthdays
1887   Boris Karloff
1888   Harpo Marx (see 3/22/1887)

November 24

1925   New York City.
Conservative author William F. Buckley Jr. was born to a Southern belle and a tycoon who made millions developing Mexican oilfields. He hired Mexican servants for his home, from whom young Buckley picked up Spanish. When World War II began, the U.S. government feared that German agents might stir up trouble in Mexico, as they had tried during World War I, or base sabotage activities there. Buckley, who had enlisted in the U.S. Army, was sent to Officer's Candidate School and given intensive instruction in Spanish so he could help conduct counterespionage activities in Mexico. The war

ended before he could put his training to military use. He did use it at Yale after the war, where he received a B.A. and taught Spanish.

Buckley objected to the way Yale faculty conducted the educational process. He compiled his opinions in *God and Man at Yale,* which thrust him forward as a conservative spokesman. Buckley spent a few months working for the CIA; then, in 1955, he founded the *National Review.* His magazine provided an arena for the development of modern conservativism. Buckley has also written several fiction and nonfiction best-sellers, and his column appears in newspapers nationwide.

Buckley is known for his dry wit. He once wryly observed, "If people would just take my advice, everything would go well." More seriously, Buckley once said, "Idealism is fine, but as it approaches reality, the cost becomes prohibitive."

Other Birthdays
1784   Zachary Taylor
1864   Henri de Toulouse-Lautrec
1868   Scott Joplin

November 25

1846   Garrard County, Kentucky.

Carry Moore was born. Her father was a slave-owner who dealt in livestock. Her mother was a more unusual person. She was absolutely convinced that she was Queen Victoria and forced her husband to provide her with a scepter and queenly coach. Carry's mother and her female relatives were unanimous in their negative opinion of men—they considered all of them unscrupulous seducers. Consequently, Carry's dating consisted of sitting in the parlor with her gentlemen callers discussing the Bible. Handholding and hayrides were prohibited.

In 1865, Dr. Charles Gloyd came to board in the Moore

household. Somehow, he managed to steal a kiss from the nearly six-foot-tall girl. Carry shrieked "I'm ruined!" It took Gloyd two years to win her hand. Unfortunately, he turned up for the wedding drunk. Carry found him to be an inattentive husband. Although pregnant, she left him, and he died in six months from drink.

Carry raised her daughter with the help of her mother-in-law. When she ran low on money, she married an ugly but rich widower nearly twenty years older than she. This marriage was also unhappy: He hated her religious fanaticism, and she found sex with him disgusting. Though they divorced, Carry kept her husband's name, and, as Carry Nation, she became a celebrity.

In 1890, saloon keepers in Kansas, then a dry state, got around the law through loopholes. With a small band of hymn-singing, female followers, an incensed Nation smashed up Kansas saloons with a hatchet. These "hatchetations," as she called them, helped Nation push through stricter dry laws not only in Kansas but also across the country. Prohibition was a direct legacy of her work.

Nation wasn't angry with just saloons: She also attacked tobacco, foreign foods, Teddy Roosevelt, Masons, nearly all men, buggy-riding couples, nude paintings, and sex in general. She published an uplifting newspaper that detailed all the reasons that these things were abominations. Her paper also carried a column for boys and girls which primarily attacked "self-abuse" in terms so explicit that it was a virtual how-to manual on the subject.

Nation described herself as "a bulldog running along at the feet of Jesus, barking at what He doesn't like." The image of Jesus setting a yapping bulldog on hapless sinners didn't seem at all odd to her.

Other Birthdays
1914   Joe DiMaggio
1920   Ricardo Montalban

1947   John Larroquette
1960   John F. Kennedy Jr.

November 26

1922   Minneapolis, Minnesota.

Charles Schulz was born. Like his creation Charlie Brown, Schulz was a less than stellar student. In the eighth grade he flunked every subject. Schulz, however, had a talent for drawing, and, at age 12, he published his first drawing, a picture of a dog in Robert Ripley's "Believe It or Not!" column. After high school, Schulz served in the U.S. Army in Europe during World War II. Following the war, he became a teacher at the Art Instruction Schools. According to Schulz, "One day I sat down and drew a boy and a girl sitting on a curb. He said to her, 'I know, Judy, I could learn to love you if your batting average was better.' Charlie Brown was born."

It took Schulz two years to place the cartoon strip with a syndicate. The strip debuted on October 2, 1950, in eight newspapers. Today, it appears in over 1,500 newspapers in several languages. Schulz disliked the name *Peanuts* and tried for years to get the strip's name changed to *Good Ol' Charlie Brown*.

Schulz once described an important event in his childhood. "When I was at Sanford Junior High in St. Paul, Minnesota, we were instructed to read a certain novel and, naturally, prepare a written report over Christmas vacation. Such assignments have always disturbed me, and I still do not understand a teacher destroying the Christmas holidays in this manner. At any rate, I failed to read this book and, naturally, had no report ready for when school began the Monday after the holidays. I went to school that morning with a terrible dread, but was taken quickly off the hook with the news that our teacher had slipped on the ice and broken her arm. This is one of my fondest memories of school days."

Other Birthdays
1938   Rich Little
1938   Tina Turner

November 27

1942   Seattle, Washington.

Short-lived rock guitarist Jimi Hendrix, best known for "Foxy Lady" and "Purple Haze" was the son of a black father born. He who was a gardener, and an American Indian mother, who abused alcohol. Hendrix lost his mother at a young age, and his father then married a Japanese woman. These varied influences may have produced Hendrix's complex and contrary character. He could, at times, be shy and polite, but at other times, aggressive and nasty. Hendrix played the guitar at an early age, but left home not to become a musician but an army paratrooper. When an injury forced him to leave the service, he used his guitar to earn a living, playing backup for such rockers as the Isley Brothers, B.B. King, Sam Cooke, Wilson Pickett, Ike and Tina Turner, James Brown, and Little Richard.

Hendrix demonstrated formidable guitar skills and, in 1966, a rock promoter spotted him. The promoter matched him with two Englishmen, forming the Jimi Hendrix Experience. After making a splash in England, the group went to America, where a clever bit of misrepresentation got them booked as the opening act for the mild, manufactured rock group, The Monkees. At their first performance, Hendrix and his fellow band members arrived on stage in front of teenaged Monkee chasers and their moms and launched into a raucous, racy performance. The Monkee-ites were outraged. The Jimi Hendrix Experience was dumped from the tour, but the resulting publicity made Hendrix an instant hit.

In 1970, Hendrix suffocated in his own vomit after taking too many sleeping pills. Despite this, he remains a mythic rock figure. He explained it himself before he died when he observed, "It's funny the way most people love the dead. Once you are dead, you are made for life."

Other Birthdays
1940   Bruce Lee
1976   Jaleel White

November 28

1949   Thunder Bay, Ontario, Canada.

Paul Shaffer was born. He was the only child of an attorney, who raised his son in Thunder Bay, a small, remote community on the shore of Lake Superior. Shaffer's link to the outside world was television and radio broadcasts out of Chicago. He loved listening to rock groups such as Darlene Love and the Ronnettes. He says, "Afternoons, I'd bash out their songs on the piano as loud as I could, exactly the way they played them, three, four hours at a stretch. There was nothing else to do. It was too cold to go out." Shaffer formed his own rock band, naming it the Fabulous Fugitives after his favorite television program, David Janssen's *The Fugitive*. The band played at such venues as hockey rinks. Despite this, Shaffer learned to love performing.

After studying law at the University of Toronto, Shaffer got a job working for a Toronto production of *Godspell*. This led to a TV pilot for a series called *A Year at the Top* about the adventures of a pair of ordinary guys who sell their souls to Satan to become rock stars for a year. The series wasn't bought by a network, but it led to Shaffer's job playing piano on *Saturday Night Live*. As music director of that show, Shaffer helped put together the successful Blues Brothers routine of John Belushi and Dan Aykroyd. That bit was followed by a Blues Brothers album, which featured the kind of music Shaffer had loved as a kid. Shaffer became a favorite music director for comics. David Letterman says that he never considered anyone other than Shaffer for the role of his musical sidekick on *Late Night With David Letterman*.

Shaffer once observed, "I started playing in a rock and roll band in high school, which gave me something to do on weekends. But, alas, I never learned how to dance, because I was always playing at the dances. That's why most musicians don't dance, have you noticed that? A little theory I have."

Other Birthdays
1931   Hope Lange

November 29

1832   Germantown, Pennsylvania.

Amos Bronson Alcott and Abigail Alcott had the second of their four daughters, Louisa May Alcott. Amos was a Transcendentalist writer and educator who believed in a strict, vegetarian diet that excluded dairy products, tea, spices, and even salt. He despised the use of wool, silk, leather, and any other product that caused distress to animals. Alcott would have had his children go barefoot rather than wear leather shoes, but for his wife's insistence that they would become ill in bad weather. Amos established a school to pass on his views to children. When it failed, he moved his family to Boston, where he opened another, similar school. Enrollment shrank to just five students, three of whom were his daughters. In 1840, this school also closed, and the Alcotts moved to Concord, Massachusetts.

In Concord, the Alcotts had two friendly neighbors: writers Ralph Waldo Emerson and Henry David Thoreau. With a few like-minded associates, Ames established a utopian community named Fruitlands. Abigail didn't enjoy the short experiment because she wound up doing most of the work. After the community's failure, the Alcotts bought a small house. Despite having little money, the family was happy. In the 1870s, Louisa May began publishing her writing, thereby ending their poverty.

Little Women made Louisa May Alcott a household name. It

was based on her own family life, although Louisa May said that the saintly mother in the story wasn't anywhere near as good as her real mother.

Other Birthdays
1927   Vin Scully
1940   Chuck Mangione

November 30

1835   Florida, Missouri.

John Marshall Clemens and Jane Lampton Clemens had the fifth of their six children, Samuel Langhorne Clemens.

In 1839, the Clemens family moved to Hannibal, Missouri, which had a population of 450. By the time Samuel left as a young man, it had grown to 3,000. Despite its boomtown atmosphere, Hannibal's citizens valued culture and started five newspapers, three bookstores, and a public library.

John Marshall Clemens was a merchant and lawyer. He and his son didn't get along despite their sharing several traits. Both were honest, Puritanical freethinkers. Samuel was too volatile and adventurous for his more sober father.

Jane Lampton Clemens and her son were closer. They shared a love for animals (cats in particular), an impulsive, assertive nature, a generous, gregarious character, a large measure of curiosity, and a love for the unconventional. Once, on a train, Jane Clemens overheard two men arguing about where Mark Twain was born. She told them where. When they expressed doubt, she said, "I'm his mother. I ought to know. I was there."

In 1847, John Marshall Clemens died, and Samuel went to work for his elder brother as an apprentice printer. He traveled on business to Washington, Philadelphia, and New York. In the 1850s, he decided to go to South America to make his fortune, but when he reached New Orleans, he changed his mind and became a riverboat pilot until the Civil War ended river traffic. For a short time, Samuel served as a Confederate guerilla in Missouri. This occupation soon lost its glamour and, when Samuel's brother Orion was appointed secretary of the Nevada territory by Abraham Lincoln, Samuel abandoned the Confederacy to go West. He mined silver, then became a staff writer for the Virginia City, Nevada, *Enterprise*. In 1865, under the name Mark Twain, Samuel sent "The Celebrated Jumping Frog of Calaveras County" to an eastern publisher. Soon, Samuel was the most famous humorist of his era.

Twain once said, "All you need in this life is ignorance and confidence, and then success is sure."

Other Birthdays
1929   Dick Clark
1955   Billy Idol
1962   Bo Jackson

December 1

1935 The Bronx, New York.

Allan Stewart Konigsberg was born to Martin and Nettie Cherry Konigsberg. His father's family had been wealthy, but lost their money in the crash of 1929. Martin wound up selling dairy goods and met Nettie in an egg-and-butter market. After marrying, they lived in Brooklyn, where Martin sold jewelry through the mail, worked in a pool hall, drove a cab, candled eggs, tended bar, waited tables, and even ran bets for gangsters. Nettie worked as a bookkeeper. Young Allan was left with a variety of nannies. Some were careless. Some brought their boyfriends over. Some stole. One threatened to smother Allan in his bed and throw his body in the garbage can. Even the good nannies soon left for better employment. The Konigsbergs couldn't pay very much. Their poverty, combined with Martin's free spending, caused continual family arguments. Flocks of assorted relatives, who lived nearby or with them, added to the color of the household.

A bright child, Allan could have entered a school for advanced children in Manhattan, but his mother didn't want him to make the long trip. Instead, Allan was placed in a school where he didn't fit in. Upset at the missed opportunity, Allan became fascinated with the glamorous existence he imagined Manhattanites enjoyed. He loved watching movies about life there and came to love movies in general. Bob Hope became a favorite. Allan decided to become a performer. He learned magic, tried playing jazz, but finally got his break writing gags for the newspaper. Allan figured he needed a funny name. He chose Allen for a last name and considered Max or Mel for a first name, but settled on Woody because, Allan said, it had "a slighty comic appropriateness and is not completely off the tracks." As Woody Allen, he went from writing to stand-up comedy to making his own movies.

Allen once observed, "Making a funny film provides all the enjoyment of getting your leg caught in the blades of a threshing machine. As a matter of fact, it's not even that pleasurable; with the threshing machine the end comes much quicker."

1940   Peoria, Illinois.

Richard Pryor was born. His mother named him Richard Franklin Lennox Thomas Pryor after four favorite pimps. She worked in a whorehouse-pool hall run by her parents, who raised Pryor.

Pryor was bounced out of Catholic school when his teachers found out about his background. He was kicked out of a second school for punching a teacher. He dropped out of high school and joined the army. Although his hitch was as problematic as his education, he did discover that he could make people laugh. After his discharge, Pryor went to New York City's Greenwich Village to perform as a comedian. His break came when Ed Sullivan put him on his show. Pryor went on to a long career complicated by problems with drugs, wives, heart disease, a fiery accident, and multiple sclerosis.

Pryor says of his childhood, "We were affluent—had the biggest whorehouse in the neighborhood."

Other Birthdays
1939   Lee Trevino
1944   Bette Midler

December 2

1925   Grosse Point, Michigan.

Julie Harris was born. Her father was a banker who sent her to finishing schools. Harris says, "I was very plain, all knobby knees." When boys failed to notice her, she escaped by going to the movies. "The movies became almost a sickness to me," she says. She studied acting at the Yale School of Drama and the Actors Studio. She became a Tony Award–winning Broadway star and inductee of the Theatre Hall of Fame but is probably best known for her film roles. She starred opposite James Dean in *East of Eden* (1955).

Harris is confident of her skills. Once, according to theatrical historian Peter Hay, as Harris was about to be presented to Queen Elizabeth II at the Kennedy Center in Washington, she critically watched the queen moving down the reception line and quietly observed to a fellow actor, "I could play her better than that."

Other Birthdays
1923   Maria Callas
1954   Stone Phillips
1973   Monica Seles

December 3

1928   Wall Lake, Iowa.

Andy Williams was born. He was the eldest son of a choir director who carefully trained his children's voices. He and his brothers went on to sing backup for nightclub performer Kay Thompson. Williams set out on a solo career and became a regular on Steve Allen's *Tonight Show,* which led to his own television show. Most often compared to Perry Como, Williams tallied fifteen gold records with tunes such as "Moon River," "Love Is Blue," and "Theme From Love Story."

As a boy, Williams's youthful alto was so clear and beautiful that, when moviemakers were looking for someone to dub Lauren Bacall's singing in *To Have and Have Not* (1944), they chose him. The4 film's makers ultimately decided to use Bacall's own voice.

Other Birthdays
1961   Daryl Hannah
1965   Katarina Witt

December 4

1861   Clinton, Iowa.

Helen Louise Leonard was born. Her father was a prosperous publisher of agnostic literature, and her mother was a suffragette. They thought their daughter showed a talent for singing and gave her voice lessons, hoping she would become an opera star. Leonard was too impatient, however. She got a job as a chorus girl in a production of Gilbert and Sullivan's *H.M.S. Pinafore* under the stage name Lillian Russell. It wasn't long before the blond, blue-eyed, hour-glass-figured Russell was spotted by an impresario who promoted her into a Broadway favorite of over thirty years.

Russell was also known for her scandalous life. It was rumored that she kept a circus strong man as her personal body servant and entertained her gentlemen friends on a tiger skin rug. "Diamond Jim" Brady once dumped a million dollars into her lap and invited her to marry him. She politely refused, returned the money, and told him that she thought marriage would spoil their friendship. In her fifties, Russell became a newspaper columnist and champion of women's suffrage.

In 1916, in her role as a columnist, Russell addressed the question "Is the Stage a Perilous Place for the Young Girl?" She wrote: "It has been argued that it is an offense to a woman to be gazed at by strangers from the audience. . . . However, any man can go into a department store and speak to any girl he wishes. He has only to pretend to wish to make a purchase. While a man who attempts to speak to an actress without an introduction does so at the hazard of being beaten by the stage doorkeeper. . . . There is more danger at a tango tea than in the theatre. The actor is less dangerous than the dancing master."

Other Birthdays
1921   Deanna Durbin
1934   Wink Martindale
1949   Jeff Bridges

December 5

1901   Chicago.

Walt Disney was born to Flora and Elias Disney. Elias was a sober farmer who typically showed little reaction to his playful son's jokes, then, a few days later, would say, "You know, Walt, I've been thinking. That joke you told me was funny. Very funny."

According to unofficial Disney biographer Marc Eliot, some mystery surrounds Disney's origins. Disney could find no legal record of his birth. Eliot says that it was rumored that Disney's real mother was a Spanish washerwoman who brought him to California as an infant and gave him to Elias, who was in California for one of its lesser gold rushes.

Whatever his origins, Disney showed a talent for commercial art at an early age—at 10, he was trading his drawings for haircuts. After attending the Chicago Academy of Fine Arts at night, Disney served as a Red Cross ambulance driver in World War I France. Following the war, Disney worked for an animator in Kansas City, but when his employer was resistant to producing more elaborate cartoons, Disney set up his own studio, which quickly went bankrupt. Disney and his brother Roy decided to set up a new one in Hollywood, California. Walt drew and Roy managed their finances. After a long period of financial hardship, they began producing unique, innovative cartoons. Their first series centered on *Alice in Wonderland.* They followed this with a series based on *Oswald the Rabbit.* In 1928, with a cartoon called *Steamboat Willie,* the Disney brothers made it into the big time. Mickey Mouse, originally named Mortimer Mouse, became their best employee.

In the 1950s, Disney opened the world's most successful amusement park, Disneyland. Jack Paar observed, "To restore a sense of reality, I think Walt Disney should have a Hardluckland."

Other Birthdays
1902   Strom Thurmond
1932   Little Richard
1934   Joan Didion
1935   Calvin Trillin
1947   Jim Messina

December 6

1924   Detroit, Michigan.

Wally Cox was born to advertising copywriter George Cox and mystery novelist Eleanor Cox (pen name, Eleanor Blake). When the couple divorced, Eleanor got custody of their son. Cox was a slight child, who, though raised in New York City, loved nature. He studied botany in college but left school to support his mother when she became partially paralyzed. Cox worked as a shoe weaver and puppeteer, then was drafted into the U.S. Army during World War II, but plagued with sunstroke, he was discharged in four months. Cox then became a silversmith, making cufflinks and shirt studs.

One day, Cox told his sister an amusing story about an officious fellow he had met in the U.S. Army. Cox's sister insisted he repeat it for their friends. One of these friends when a wanna-be actor named Marlon Brando. He brought Cox to theater parties to entertain. Brando and other theater celebrities encouraged Cox to try stand-up comedy. Nightclub appearances led to radio, Broadway, television, and films. Cox specialized in nerdish enthusiasts, such as deadly serious scoutmasters, who one reviewer acutely labeled "hilarious and curiously poignant."

Other Birthdays
1883   Kahlil Gibran
1886   Joyce Kilmer
1896   Ira Gershwin
1906   Agnes Moorehead

December 7

1876   Winchester, Virginia.

Willa Cather was born. Her parents moved the family to Nebraska during the great land rush that took half a million pioneers to that region from all over the world. In church, Cather listened to sermons given in Danish, Norwegian, French, and English. The level of education among the settlers was high. A neighbor taught Cather Latin and her grandmothers tutored her in the classics. She learned to love literature and decided to become a writer.

Cather worked as a journalist and teacher before joining the staff of the then-controversial publication *McClure's Magazine*. Her first success was the novel *O, Pioneers!*, which celebrated the Nebraskan settlers' generosity and industry and the beauties of Nebraska's landscape.

Cather wrote, "There are only two or three human stories, and they go on repeating themselves as fiercely as if they had never happened before."

Other Birthdays
1947   Greg Allman
1947   Johnny Bench
1956   Larry Bird

December 8

1925   Harlem.

Sammy Davis Jr. was born to Sam and Elvira (Sanchez) Davis, who were both dancers with Will Mastin's vaudeville act, "Holiday in Dixieland." At age four, the younger Davis joined his parents on stage. The act was reasonably successful, touring the nation and appearing in musical movies. While performing at a Michigan theater, the legendary Bill "Bojangles" Robinson spotted Davis and began coaching him. Davis quickly soaked up everything he was shown and gradually became the star of the act. In 1943, he was drafted into the U.S. Army. He served in an entertainment unit, putting on service shows and further honing his skills.

After the war, Davis, his father, and Mastin, who had become a surrogate uncle to Davis, formed a trio. This time Davis was the undoubted star. He could sing, dance, and do imitations of pop stars. Bookers, however, thought of them as the old "Holiday in Dixieland" group, and the act didn't get the bookings that would make them successful. Mastin overcame this problem by swinging an engagement as unknowns at Slapsie Maxie's Hollywood nightclub. The act won rave reviews and they were soon performing with such headliners as Jimmy Dorsey, Jack Benny, and Frank Sinatra. Eventually, Davis went solo when his father and Mastin retired.

In 1954, while performing in Las Vegas, Davis was involved in a serious car wreck. He was badly injured and lost an eye. He feared that his career was over. When he appeared at Ciro's a few weeks later in an eye patch and gave a spectacular performance, however, he got a ten-minute standing ovation. His pluck, talent, and the publicity following his accident turned him into a superstar. David didn't forget his old mentor Bill "Bojangles" Robinson. He recorded a song honoring the old-time dancer.

Other Birthdays
1933   Flip Wilson
1939   James Galway
1943   Jim Morrison
1953   Kim Basinger
1966   Sinéad O'Connor

December 9

1916   Amsterdam, New York.

Issur Danielovitch Demsky was born. Under the name Kirk Douglas, he became a matinee idol. Demsky's Russian immigrant father supported his seven children through a variety of lowly jobs, including that of a ragman. His son also labored at menial jobs. He dreamed of becoming an actor, but he was past 30 before he got his big break, when he was cast as a tough boxer in *Champion* (1949).

Douglas's intense performance got him more movie roles, including that of Vincent van Gogh in *Lust for Life* (1956), a Viking chieftan in *The Vikings* (1958), and a gladiator in *Spartacus* (1960). Douglas also produced four sons who joined him in show business. The most famous of these is Michael Douglas. Kirk Douglas has remarked, "All those years I was a young actor in Hollywood, I never dreamed my son would wind up owning it."

1922   St. Louis, Missouri.

John Elroy Sanford was born. He spent part of his youth in

Harlem, where he became friends with a small-time crook named Malcolm Little. Sanford achieved fame after going into show business and changing his name to Redd Foxx. Little also went on to fame after changing his name: He became Malcolm X.

Other Birthdays
1941 Beau Bridges
1953 John Malkovich
1957 Donny Osmond

December 10

1830 Amherst, Massachusetts.

Emily Dickinson was born. Her father, Edward Dickinson, was a lawyer and U.S. congressman. Her mother was a shy, sickly woman. Emily had a sister, Lavinia, and a brother, Austin. The family was so close that when Austin married, he lived right next door to his parents. Emily spent nearly her entire life tied to her family, leaving only to attend the Mount Holyoke Female Seminary. Upon her return, she became reclusive, seldom coming down from her room to meet guests. She wore only white and communicated mainly through letters and poems. She wrote some 1,800 poems, but only two were published during her lifetime.

Other Birthdays
1952 Susan Dey
1961 Nia Peeples
1985 Raven-Symoné

December 11

1949 Los Angeles, California.

Teri Garr was born to song-and-dance man Eddie Gonnaud and Phyllis Lind, a hosiery model and member of the original Rockettes. The couple met while performing on the *Jimmy*

Durante Show. Garr inherited her parents' talent. She started dancing at age six and hoped for a show business career. Her father wasn't encouraging. He told her, "Don't be in this business. It's the lowest. It's humiliating to people." Garr says, "He would sit in front of the TV extremely depressed, watching the shows, saying he'd missed the boat with TV. He drank. He died of a heart attack when I was 11."

Garr became determined to become a show business success. She says, "I absolutely went after it with blinders on. Was I compensating for my father? I don't know. A lot of kids do that—pick up the ball and keep running. I knew I was not going to let certain things stop me—whatever stopped him."

Garr's mother struggled to support Garr and her two brothers by working as a costume maker. She still managed to pay for dance classes for Garr. Just a few days before her high school graduation, Garr auditioned for a part in a production of *West Side Story.* She was rejected but changed her clothes and tried again. The auditioners didn't recognize her and this time she got the job. She went on to appear in many television shows, including *Star Trek, Shindig,* and *The Sonny and Cher Comedy Hour.* She also danced in films such as Elvis Presley's *Viva Las Vegas* (1964). Her first starring role was in Mel Brooks's *Young Frankenstein* (1974) as the doctor's buxom assistant.

Other Birthdays
1931   Rita Moreno
1943   Donna Mills
1946   Lynda Day George

December 12

1915   Hoboken, New Jersey.

Francis Albert Sinatra was born. His father was a fire captain who thought singers were "sissies." Sinatra set a lot of hearts afire after his debut as the lead singer for the Hoboken

Four on the radio show *Major Bowes' Amateur Hour* in 1937. The scrawny Sinatra was soon singing with bandleaders such as Harry James and Tommy Dorsey. His soulful love ballads made him an idol to millions of swooning bobby-soxers. He sang dozens of hit songs and had many starring roles in movies, including an Oscar-winning part in *From Here to Eternity* (1953).

Sinatra has led a turbulent life. His foibles have received maximum media attention, perhaps because of his often confrontational attitude, which he has demonstrated by smashing cameras and taunting reporters. He has said, "I detest bad manners. If people are polite, then I am; they shouldn't try to get away with not being polite to me." Marlon Brando observed, "He's the kind of guy that, when he dies, he's going up to heaven and give God a bad time for making him bald."

Other Birthdays
1923   Bob Barker
1941   Dionne Warwick
1962   Tray Austin

December 13

1925   West Plains, Missouri.

Dick Van Dyke was born. His parents were Hazel and L. W. "Cookie" Van Dyke, a traveling salesman for Sunshine Biscuits who loved jokes. They raised their family in Danville, Illinois. Dick Van Dyke says, "I guess you could say I had a Penrodian childhood; barefoot boy with cheek of tan and all." Dick's younger brother is Jerry Van Dyke (born 7/27/1931). Although Dick would become a comedy star, Jerry was the clown of the two. Jerry says of his brother, "Dick wore a suit and tie to school...he was popular, I was notorious."

Dick worked as a radio announcer before serving in the U.S. Army during World War II. The army stationed him in Oklahoma, where he continued working on the radio. After the war, he and a buddy concocted a pantomime lip-sync act. Dick toured with this and other small-time acts for years. He had so little success that he had to marry his wife on a radio show that staged weddings for poor couples. It wasn't until 1960 that he got his big break when he was cast in the Broadway hit *Bye Bye Birdie*. It led to his being cast as Rob Petrie in *The Dick Van Dyke Show.*

Dick didn't forget his brother, who had worked as a comic in the U.S. Air Force during the Korean War. In 1962, Dick put together two episodes of his show centered around Rob's sleepwalking brother, Stacey, played by Jerry, a character inspired by Jerry's own childhood sleepwalking. In real life, Jerry had once sleepwalked out into the street nude, carrying a set of golf clubs.

Other Birthdays
1887   Sergeant Alvin York
1929   Christopher Plummer
1949   Ted Nugent

December 14

1946   New York City.

Patty Duke was born. By the age of 12, she had appeared in fifty television shows. At 13, she was on Broadway in *The Miracle Worker.* At 16, she won an Academy Award for the film version of that play. At 17, she starred on television in *The Patty Duke Show.* She was the envy of millions of teenage girls, but the reality behind her success was dreadful.

Her father was an alcoholic cabdriver and her mother a restaurant cashier. They divorced when Duke was 8. Theatrical managers John and Ethel Ross recognized Duke's potential and persuaded her parents to turn Patty over to them. Duke charges that they introduced her to alcohol and drugs, and that John Ross molested her. Their "management" guided Duke straight into the 1950s quiz show scandal. One of her most prominent childhood public appearances was as a witness at the hearings that exposed how she, and other contestants, had been given answers to quiz show questions. It could have ruined her career, but her youth and talents allowed her to overcome the scandal.

Duke rebelled against the Rosses' bad management as she grew older. She resisted them and they became increasingly abusive. They demanded that she sign a lifetime contract. Certain that they were planning to force an adoption of her, Duke finally escaped when she was 18. A payment of $55,000 kept the Rosses away. Of the approximately $1 million Duke had earned as a child, she received just $84,000. It would be many years before she would repair the damage her greedy managers had done.

Other Birthdays
1911   Spike Jones
1935   Lee Remick
1946   Michael Ovitz

December 15

1949   Crane, Missouri.

Actor Don Johnson was born. The son of a farmer, Johnson got off to a shaky start in life. At the age of 12, he was arrested for car theft. That same year, he slept with his 17-year-old babysitter. By the time he was 16, he was living with a 26-year-old cocktail waitress. A lead role in a high school play got Johnson interested in acting, and he won a drama scholarship to the University of Kansas. He didn't stay there long, however. After a brief affair with a professor, Johnson left for Hollywood, where he married Melanie Griffith (see 8/9/1957). The marriage ended after a year.

Alcohol and drugs dominated Johnson's life, even as he was establishing himself as an actor. When his second wife became pregnant, both cleaned themselves up. Nevertheless, their marriage failed. Johnson did benefit from his new sobriety: He became a household name via his *Miami Vice* series, and remarried Melanie Griffith. They have since re-split, following more problems with drinking. Johnson has worked hard to surmount his alcoholism and is reported to be doing well.

Other Birthdays
1933   Tim Conway
1965   Helen Slater

December 16

1770   Bonn, Germany.
Ludwig van Beethoven was born to Maria van Beethoven, a former chambermaid, and Johann van Beethoven, the son of a choirmaster to Cologne's archbishop-elector. Johann earned a small salary singing tenor in his father's choir. Johann's father generously supplemented his son's earnings. When he died, this support disappeared. Johann took to drink, and his wife's health deteriorated. They had five more children, but only two lived past infancy. Ludwig had exhibited some precocious musical talent as a child, and Johann pushed him, hoping to turn him into a profitable child prodigy. Ludwig rebelled but, by the time he was a teenager, his skills fed the family.

Maria van Beethoven didn't live to enjoy her son's success. She died in 1787 when she was 40. Beethoven wrote, "She was such a good loving mother, my best friend; oh, who was happier than I when I could still say the dear name 'mother,' and it was heard."

Not everyone enjoys Beethoven's music. John Ruskin once said, "Beethoven always sounds to me like the upsetting of a bag of nails, with here and there an also dropped hammer."

Other Birthdays
1775   Jane Austen

1939   Liv Ullman
1941   Lesley Stahl
1943   Steven Bochco

December 17

1807   Haverhill, Massachusetts.

John Greenleaf Whittier was born. He was the second of four children in a poor Quaker farm family. Whittier had little education, but loved reading and began writing verse in his teens. In 1826, his sister sent a copy of his poem "The Exile's Departure" to abolitionist editor William Lloyd Garrison. Garrison printed it and the two became friends. Whittier published more poems and became the editor of an abolitionist publication. At 25, Whittier reviewed his life. Feeling that his poetry was less important, he devoted himself to the fight against slavery. He became a leader in that cause, helping Harriet Beecher Stowe publish *Uncle Tom's Cabin,* and aiding the movement that created the Republican Party. His poem "Barbara Frietchie" helped stir patriotic fervor during the Civil War. After the war, Whittier returned to poetry, becoming the most prominent New England poet of his day.

Whittier advised, "My lad, if thou wouldst win success, join thyself to some unpopular but noble cause."

Other Birthdays
1886   Ty Cobb
1894   Arthur Fiedler
1929   William Safire
1930   Bob Guccione

December 18

1947   Cincinnati, Ohio.

Film director Steven Spielberg was born. He was raised in New Jersey. His father, Arnold Spielberg, was an electrical engineer and his mother, Leah Spielberg was a pianist. They divorced when Spielberg was a teenager. Spielberg's mother encouraged her son's interest in moviemaking, buying him cameras and film, paying for its processing, chauffering him to locations, and even writing excuse notes so he could get out of school.

Spielberg produced his first film while in elementary school—a three-and-a-half-minute Western. When he missed a Boy Scout outing during which his fellow Scouts saw a UFO, Spielberg became fascinated with outer space themes. At 16, he wrote, directed, and edited a two-and-a-half-hour science fiction film he titled *Firelight*. His all-consuming interest in movies, however, caused him to get such poor grades that he couldn't get into any of the notable film schools. The best he could manage was California State College at Long Beach. It proved enough. While there, Spielberg shot a student film called *Amblin'*, which so impressed Universal Studios that he was signed to a seven-year contract at 21.

Universal put Spielberg to work directing television programs. His first effort was an episode of *Night Gallery* that starred Joan Crawford. He lent his skills to other television series, including *Marcus Welby, M.D.* and *Columbo*, before directing a television movie, *Duel* (1971), which related a battle between a motorist and a truck. *Duel* won an Emmy and Spielberg next directed the feature film *Sugarland Express* (1974). A critical success, he followed it with the commercial smash *Jaws* (1975). Spielberg went on to many other hits, including *Close Encounters of the Third Kind* (1977) and his *Indiana Jones* trilogy.

Spielberg's whiz kid reputation at Universal was sometimes hard for his associates to swallow. One episode of the *Columbo* mystery series lampooned Spielberg by giving a boy genius at a think tank the name Steven Spellberg.

Other Birthdays
1916   Betty Grable
1917   Ossie Davis
1943   Keith Richards

December 19

1915   Paris.

Anetta, a 16-year-old dope addict, and her lover, street acrobat Louis Alphonse Gassion, 33, had a baby girl, Edith. World War I was raging, and Louis, a soldier in the French Army, was at the front.

In 1917, Louis returned from the war and went back to street acrobatics. Anetta soon abandoned her husband and child. Louis's sister, Zaza, brought the starving Edith to live with Louis's mother in Bernay, Normandy. Grandmother Gassion was a cook at a bordello. The place was busy—Bernay was a military town—but the ladies of the establishment doted on Edith. The girl was happy until she was suddenly struck blind. The cause is unknown, but after she visited a shrine to St. Thérèse, she was miraculously cured. Although Edith remained grateful to St. Thérèse, she didn't adopt a religious life. She went on the road with her father.

Louis and Edith toured France and Belgium, entertaining wherever they could assemble an audience. Edith's voice soon became more of a draw than Louis's stale tricks. When he settled down with a young woman, Edith kept traveling, now in the company of another girl. Edith later said, "I was hungry, I was cold. But I was also free...free not to get up in the morning, not to go to bed at night, free to get drunk if I liked, to dream...to hope."

In 1934, this freedom passed when Edith had her own daughter. She took the infant with her everywhere. When the child died of meningitis, Edith paid for the funeral with what had become her part-time occupation, prostitution. Afterwards, Edith returned to her more usual work, singing on streetcorners. A nightclub owner heard her soulful, world-weary voice and signed her up. At just four foot ten, she reminded him of a "sparrow," so he gave her the last name "Piaf," which is French slang for sparrow. With such songs as "Non, Je ne Regrette Rien" and "La Vie en Rose," Edith Piaf, the street entertainer, became one of the most prominent singers of her generation.

Piaf, who enjoyed many men, observed, "You never know a guy until you've tried him in bed. You know more about a guy in one night in bed than you do in months of conversation."

Other Birthdays
1933 Cecily Tyson
1946 Robert Urich
1963 Jennifer Beals
1972 Alyssa Milano

December 20

1914 Atlanta, Georgia.

Bert Parks was born. He got his first job in radio at 16. WGST Atlanta paid him $7 a week to announce programs. His first big-time job was in 1933, as a singer on *The Eddie Cantor Show*. He next became a staff announcer for CBS. During World War II, he served in the China-Burma theater, winning the Bronze Star. When Parks returned to broadcasting, it was as quizmaster for the game shows *Break the Bank* and *Stop the Music*. The shows were hits, both on radio and on television. For a time, Parks had nine successful shows on the air at the same time.

In 1960, Parks won good reviews on Broadway while starring in *The Music Man*. Parks is best remembered, however, as the announcer for the Miss America pageant from 1955 to 1979. He was invited back in 1990 for the pageant's seventieth anniversary. Unfortunately, he became confused and the appearance was unintentionally humorous when he mixed up contestants' names. His rendition of "There She Is, Miss America," however, still got a big hand.

Other Birthdays
1889 Margaret Dumont
1898 Irene Dunne

December 21

1937   New York City.

Jane Fonda was born. Her parents were Frances Brokaw and actor Henry Fonda. Frances suffered from mental problems and killed herself while confined in a hospital. Jane's father told Jane, then 12, that her mother had died of a heart attack. It was years before she discovered the truth when reading a movie magazine. Soon afterwards, Fonda developed bulimia. She threw up as many as twenty times a day, but kept her vomiting secret from her first two husbands. She overcame the problem at 35.

After attending Vassar, Jane followed her father into show business. She appeared on Broadway in *There Was a Little Girl* and in a number of light comedy films. Dissatisfied with these roles, she left America to live in France, where she married French director Roger Vadim. She appeared in his science fiction comedy *Barbarella, Queen of the Galaxy* (1968) and adopted his fashionable, anti-American views. Soon, she surpassed him in her leftward spin and became the Betty Grable of the anti–Vietnam War movement. She traveled to North Vietnam, where she made propaganda broadcasts and was photographed clapping her hands in delight on an anti-aircraft gun that had shot down American pilots. Fonda also began getting better roles.

Fonda's marriage with Vadim fell apart as her career improved. Vadim later remarked, "She's a romantic pro-Leninist. Unfortunately she's lost her sense of humour. One day I called her Jane of Arc. She didn't laugh at all." After divorcing Vadim, Fonda married activist Tom Hayden. They were the model politically correct couple until their marriage broke up. Fonda has since given up her film career to marry millionaire Ted Turner. She didn't need his money, for, although she has often decried the excesses of capitalism, she has sold over 9 million copies of her exercise videos during the last decade.

Reportedly, Fonda became interested in exercising in 1978

when she was due to film a bikini scene in the movie *California Suite*. She wanted to appear her best and, instead of resorting to her previous bad eating habits, tried exercise.

Other Birthdays
1804   Benjamin Disraeli
1935   Phil Donahue
1940   Frank Zappa
1954   Chris Evert

December 22

1945   Glasgow, Kentucky.
Television journalist Diane Sawyer was born. She was raised in Louisville. Her father was a county judge. Sawyer says of her schoolteacher mother, "At a time when no one was worried about having it all, my mother was out there slogging to clean the house and cook dinner and work and take care of us and be with my father, so that it never occurred to me that it was a choice I had to make, or that I was going to break with Southern tradition. I never felt I wouldn't have a career. So, in that sense, my mother was completely supportive. When I go home, she still gets up in the middle of the night to see if the covers have come off."

Of her high school years, Sawyer says, "I was terribly extracurricular. I lived for overextension, and there are those who think I still do. I edited the yearbook, did a little basketball, was a junior varsity cheerleader, joined every club, all of which I took inordinately seriously." Sawyer won the 1963 American Junior Miss contest, a title which gave her some difficulties when she attended Wellesley College. She says some fellow students went out of their way to cut her down. Of her education, she says, "Bachelor of Arts.... That was it. Lots of poetry and identity crises."

After graduation in 1967, Sawyer was a weather girl on Louisville television. She left the weather map to become a press aide in the Nixon White House. She says, "The only thing I planned was to leave home. This sounds like Rebecca of Sunnybrook Farm, but I got to the airport in Washington, and called a friend of my father's, who said, why don't you talk to someone at the White House? So I went to the White House, and I thought, oh, this is more fun than Capitol Hill. That's why I worked there."

When Nixon resigned, she helped him assemble his memoirs. Her next television job was as a general assignment reporter for CBS. She was soon an anchor for the *CBS Morning News*. In 1984, Sawyer became the first woman correspondent on *60 Minutes*. She was later paired with acerbic Sam Donaldson for ABC's *PrimeTime Live*. Sawyer says, "Sam wants the Pope and Gorbachev to debate 'Is There a God?' and have the studio audience vote at the end."

Other Birthdays
1912   Lady Bird Johnson
1948   Steve Garvey

December 23

1926   Madison, Minnesota.

Robert Bly was born to Alice Bly, a courthouse worker, and Jacob Thomas Bly, a grain farmer. As a boy, Bly loved books so much that he would make himself sick in order to be able to stay in bed and read. After high school, Bly served in the U.S. Navy in Chicago. He later said, "As a navy recruit in World War II, I met for the first time a person who wrote poetry, a man named Marcus Eisenstein. . . . During a class on radar, he wrote a poem as I watched. I had never understood that poems were written by human beings, and I still remember that moment with delight."

Following his service, Bly earned a degree at Harvard, planning to become a poet. He holed up in a remote cabin for six months hoping for inspiration. This method had limited success, so he moved to New York City, where he worked as a typist, a clerk, and a house painter while surviving on three-day-old bread and haunting the New York Public Library. "I thought I would end up as a sort of bag lady," he says. Bly left New York to earn a master's degree at the University of Iowa. He settled on a farm given to him by his father, supporting himself through teaching and translating. He became a prominent poet and editor. However, his real fame came in 1990 when he published *Iron John: A Book About Men.*

Bly's *Iron John* became the bible of the men's movement, which advanced the notion that modern men are alienated from their true male role. Bly suggested reviving rites of passage. Participants dress in primitive outfits, go to the woods, form circles, sing, chant, tell stories, and, in a trademark of these encounters, pound drums.

Other Birthdays
1805   Joseph Smith
1948   Susan Lucci

December 24

1905   Houston, Texas.

Billionaire Howard Hughes was born. He was the spoiled only child of millionaire Howard Robard Hughes, who had made his money selling oil-drilling equipment. Hughes's mother, Allene Hughes, was a fretful parent who continually warned Hughes of germs and disease. Hughes had few friends, growing up mainly in seclusion. He did poorly in school and seemed destined to a life of indolence. When he was 16, his mother died suddenly. Two years later, his father also died. Hughes dropped the Jr. from his name and quickly showed that he was more than able to take care of himself.

Hughes persuaded a court to rule him a legal adult so that he could transact business, then bought out his relatives' shares in the Hughes Tool Company. After marrying, Hughes moved to Hollywood, buying a movie studio. While filming the classic film *Hell's Angels* (1930), he neglected his wife, and she left him. Hughes found solace in romancing starlets. The list of women he dated includes Jean Harlow, Katharine Hepburn, Ginger Rogers, Hedy Lamarr, Carole Lombard, Ida Lupino, Lana Turner, Gina Lollobrigida, and Ava Gardner.

Hughes's interests grew to include aviation. He founded Hughes Aircraft and bought TWA. He designed and test-piloted aircraft, setting a number of records but also crashing three times. Some think he sustained a brain injury in one of the crashes. Whatever the cause, Hughes became an eccentric. In 1944, he suffered a nervous breakdown. He was also placed under great stress when his project to develop a massive, troop-carrying seaplane fell far behind schedule and he was grilled by hostile congressmen. He proved the aircraft, nick-named the Spruce Goose, could fly, then stored it in a warehouse for decades.

Hughes went on to develop interests in Las Vegas and high-tech research. However, by the late 1960s, he had become a drug-addicted, paranoid hypochondriac. He seldom left his room, grew his hair and nails long, and, by the time he died at 70, weighed less than 100 pounds.

Other Birthdays
1809   Kit Carson
1922   Ava Gardner

December 25

1876   America.

Annie H. Ide was born. As a child, Annie despaired of the date of her birth because, as the date was also Jesus's birthday, she was considerably upstaged. In addition, there was the matter of presents. Poor Annie received combination gifts that were supposed to do the duty of both birthday and Christmas gifts. Annie's father mentioned this dilemma to writer Robert Louis Stevenson in 1891. Stevenson wrote to the then 14-year-old girl from his island home of Samoa, "officially" deeding over all his "rights and privileges" to his own November 13 birthday to the girl as of June 19, 1891. Stevenson declared that at his age—40—he "had no further use for a birthday of any description." Stevenson laid out as conditions for the deed that Annie use his birthday with "moderation and humanity," considering that it was not "so young as it once was," but that she also enjoy it. If these conditions were not observed, Stevenson directed, the deed would be revoked and all rights would be transferred from her to the president of the United States of America.

Annie Ide Cockran died at âge 68 in 1945 (Stevenson had died in 1894). Then–U.S. President Harry S Truman inquired of her family as to whether the terms of the deed had been correctly observed. They informed him that Annie had, indeed, satisfied all of Stevenson's conditions.

It should be noted that Mr. Stevenson might have had a reason in addition to sympathy for passing along his birthday: November 13, 1891, the next occasion upon which Stevenson would have had use of his birthday, was a Friday.

Other Birthdays
1893   Robert Ripley
1948   Barbara Mandrell
1949   Sissy Spacek
1954   Annie Lennox

December 26

1921   New York City.

Stephen Valentine Patrick Williams Allen was born to Carroll and Isabelle Allen, both vaudevillians. They appeared together as Billy Allen and Belle Montrose. Billy served as straight man to his comedienne wife. The Allens raised their son while touring America. He attended sixteen elementary schools, five high schools and two colleges. All the exposure to show business caused young Steve Allen to chose it for his own career. He set out to become a radio performer. His first job was with KOY radio in Phoenix in 1942. He announced, played piano, wrote commercials, and produced dramas. His first job ended when he was drafted into the U.S. Army in 1943. He served just five months because of an asthmatic condition, then became an announcer for KFAC radio in Los Angeles. After a stint as a comedian for the Mutual Broadcasting System, Allen got his first big break when CBS hired him as a disc jockey for their Hollywood radio station, KNX.

Allen's CBS program involved more than just record playing; he did interviews and comedy sketches. It was a demanding job—the hour-long program ran six nights a week at midnight. Allen still found time to write songs, narrate movies, write a newspaper column, and announce pro-wrestling matches on television. Allen soon became well-known as an amiable, talented announcer. In 1950, CBS moved Allen to New York City and put his radio show on television. Sponsored by Colgate-Palmolive, it featured guests such as Jack Benny, Groucho Marx, and Red Skelton. Allen also got a daily midday program and commonly substituted for such hosts as Arthur Godfrey. Allen's wholesome yet witty manner made him popular with audiences.

Allen's audience appeal made NBC network executives listen when he proposed a late night show that, like his Hollywood radio show, mixed music, comedy, and interviews. Allen called it *The Tonight Show* and hosted it for two years. Over the years, Allen's program idea proved to be the most profitable one anyone in television has ever had.

Other Birthdays
1914   Richard Widmark
1954   Ozzie Smith

December 27

1901 Schöneberg, Germany.

Marie Magdalene Dietrich was born to Lieutenant of Police Louis Erich Otto Dietrich, a mustachioed one-time major of the Uhlans, veteran of the Franco-Prussian War and winner of the Iron Cross, and Wilhelmina Elisabeth Josephine Felsing. They married in 1883 when Wilhelmina was 17. The beautiful Wilhelmina came from a wealthy watchmaking family. In 1900, the couple had a daughter whom they named Elisabeth. Elisabeth would become a schoolteacher and never caused the public eye to blink even once. The Dietrich's second daughter, born the next year, was quite different. Marie Magdalene Dietrich would, after changing her name to Marlene, become the very model of the *femme fatale* throughout the movie-going world.

Marlene showed talent early, becoming a skilled violinist in her teens. Perhaps she was compensating for her shyness (a school friend called her a "little gray mouse") or for her uncertainty following her father's death in 1911 and her stepfather's subsequent death in World War I. In 1917, she performed in a school recital dressed as a Mexican peasant boy, complete with sombrero and velvet pants—an ironic display, considering that her later film appearances in male dress were considered scandalous. After leaving school, Marlene went to Berlin, where she began singing in cabarets. She was soon a star.

1906 Pittsburgh, Pennsylvania.

Writer and musician Oscar Levant was born. He was a noted wit. When introduced to Greta Garbo he quipped, "Sorry, I didn't catch the name." On another occasion, after dinner at the White House, Levant turned to his wife and said, "Now I suppose we'll have to have the Trumans over to *our* house."

Levant's mother had wanted him to become a concert pianist and continually reminded him to practice, practice, practice.

Levant did become a fine pianist, and also a noted author. His mother, however, had some difficulty relinquishing her role as nag. One day, he called her to tell her that he had just asked his girl to marry him and that she had accepted. His mother replied, "Good, Oscar, I'm happy to hear it. But did you practice today?"

Other Birthdays
1943   Cokie Roberts
1948   Gérard Depardieu

December 28

1856   Staunton, Virginia.

Thomas Woodrow Wilson was born to Joseph Ruggles Wilson, an Episcopal theologian, and Jessie Woodrow Wilson, the daughter of a Scottish minister. Young Wilson was adored by his mother. One bad effect of her devotion was that Wilson didn't learn to read till he was nine—he preferred listening to his mother read to him. He was a delicate, shy boy and his parents kept him out of school for years. Wilson said, "I remember how I clung to her till I was a great big fellow: but love of the best in womanhood came to me and entered my heart through those apron strings."

Wilson stretched his apron strings when he went to Princeton. Upon graduation, he dropped his first name at his mother's urging. She thought Tommy was a boy's name. Wilson earned a law degree but grew bored with practicing law and entered academics. After graduate study at Johns Hopkins, he became a professor. In midlife, he decided to try politics. He became the governor of New Jersey, then, in 1912, he was elected president of the United States.

Wilson lost his first wife in 1914. In 1916, he married Edith Galt, a widow. During their courtship, Wilson often entertained her at White House parties. The *Washington Post* printed an account of one such party, but made a small printing error—misspelling *entertaining*. After describing the event and the guests, they reported: "...the President spent much of the evening entering Mrs. Galt."

Other Birthdays
1934   Maggie Smith
1954   Denzel Washington

December 29

1936   Brooklyn, New York.

Mary Tyler Moore was born. Her parents raised her in a strong Irish Roman Catholic home. The family moved to Los Angeles when Moore was nine. After graduating from Immaculate Heart High, Moore married Richard Meeker, a CBS sales representative. In 1957, they had a son, Richie. Moore was interested in television and put her good looks to use there. She played the three-inch sprite "Happy Hotpoint" in television ads. She also played a mysterious secretary on the detective series *Richard Diamond, Private Detective*. To maintain an aura of mystery, the series showed only her legs. It wasn't until 1961, when she won the role of Laura Petrie on *The Dick Van Dyke Show*, that Moore was able to show the country her comic skills. Unfortunately, the show coincided with her divorce. Her second husband was television executive Grant Tinker.

Moore next tried movies, with *Thoroughly Modern Millie* (1967), and then the stage, in a musical version of *Breakfast at Tiffany's*. Both endeavors were poorly received (Leonard Maltin said that *Millie* had "a fatal case of the cutes"). In 1970, Moore returned to television with the classic sitcom *The Mary Tyler Moore Show*. It rivaled *I Love Lucy* as a money-maker and spawned, via Moore's MTM Productions, a long list of hit television programs such as *The Bob Newhart Show, Rhoda, Lou Grant,* and *St. Elsewhere*. Moore's personal life wasn't as happy—she and Tinker divorced in 1980.

While Moore is strongly linked to her cheerful characters in the public's mind, she is actually a more reflective person. She once said, "Worrying is a necessary part of life."

Other Birthdays
1938   Jon Voight
1947   Ted Danson

December 30

1959   Hackbridge, England.

Comedienne Tracey Ullman was born. Her father was a Polish attorney who died when his daughter was six. Her stern grandfather took over her rearing. Ullman began attending theater school at 12. She says, "I was the ugly kid with the brown hair and the big nose that didn't get the Barbie commercials." In *Ms.* magazine, she said of theater school: "We don't burst into fabulous, unrehearsed choreographed dance routines in the hallways. It's more full of sad little blond children whose parents want them to be stars, and when they get to 13 and grow tits and get ugly, they're cast on the slag heap." Ullman was thrown out of the school at 16, then lost her dancing job when she inadvertently made an appearance onstage without her underwear.

Ullman's big break came at 21 when she became a member of the avant-garde Royal Court Theatre. Her characterization of a born-again Christian lounge singer in an improvisational play won her great reviews. She was even more successful when she came to the United States. After a few small roles, she got her own series, *The Tracey Ullman Show,* on the Fox Network. It won her two Emmys.

Ullman is frank when it comes to her opinion of other television shows. "...I find them all care-and-share mush. *The Cosby Show* gives me the creeps. At any one time they're all wearing $5,000 worth of designer clothes. It is funny, he is clever, but it's so unreal."

Other Birthdays
1928   Bo Diddley
1928   Jack Lord
1935   Sandy Koufax

December 31

1937   Port Talbot, South Wales.

Anthony Hopkins was born. His parents were Richard and Muriel Hopkins, who ran a bakery in their working-class town. Anthony Hopkins drew and played piano as a boy, but had few other talents. He describes his schoolboy self as "A moron. I was anti-social and didn't bother with the other kids. A really bad student. I didn't have any brains. I didn't know what I was doing there. That's why I became an actor." In part, he was inspired by a chance meeting with the Welsh actor Richard Burton, who encouraged his ambition. Hopkins signed up for a YMCA drama class, then won a scholarship to study acting. After a short diversion through the military and a steel foundry, Hopkins entered London's Royal Academy of Dramatic Art. He did well at the Academy, then auditioned before Sir Laurence Olivier for the National Theater.

The night before his audition, Hopkins attended a performance of *Othello* starring Olivier. Hopkins has described the experience as "like reading Shakespeare by lightning flashes." The next day, at the audition, Hopkins announced that he was going to do a piece from Shaw, a bit of Chekhov, and the closing speech from *Othello*. Olivier, who off-stage reminded Hopkins of a gray, spectacled bank manager, growled, "You've got a bloody nerve, haven't you?" Hopkins's performance so impressed Olivier, however, that Hopkins wound up as his understudy.

After starring on the English stage, Hopkins became a star in American films. His most memorable role was as the cannibalistic psychiatrist Hannibal Lecter in *Silence of the Lambs* (1991), for which he won the Best Actor Academy

Award. As a hobby, Hopkins likes to spend days driving America's interstates, going nowhere in particular.

Other Birthdays
1943   John Denver
1943   Ben Kingsley
1943   Sarah Miles
1948   Donna Summer
1959   Val Kilmer

Index of Entries